Representative Mom

Representative Mom

Balancing Budgets, Bill, and Baby in the U.S. Congress

Susan Molinari

with Elinor Burkett

DOUBLEDAY
New York London Toronto Sydney Auckland

PUBLISHED BY DOUBLEDAY
a division of Bantam Doubleday Dell Publishing Group, Inc.
1540 Broadway, New York, New York 10036

DOUBLEDAY and the portrayal of an anchor with a dolphin
are trademarks of Doubleday, a division of
Bantam Doubleday Dell Publishing Group, Inc.

Book design by Richard Oriolo

Library of Congress Cataloging-in-Publication Data
Molinari, Susan.
Representative mom : balancing budgets, Bill and baby in the U.S.
Congress / by Susan Molinari with Elinor Burkett. — 1st ed.
p.   cm.
1. Molinari, Susan.   2. Women legislators—United States—
Biography.   3. United States. Congress. House—Biography.
I. Burkett, Elinor.   II. Title.
E840.8.M65A3   1998
328.73′092—dc21   98-5015
[B]   CIP

Copyright © 1998 by Susan Molinari

ISBN 0-385-49220-0

All Rights Reserved
Printed in the United States of America
May 1998

First Edition
1 2 3 4 5 6 7 8 9 10

To Susan Ruby

I find it ironic how frequently women come up to ask me, "How can you go on television every week, I'd be so nervous," or, commenting on my keynote speech at the 1996 Republican National Convention, insist, "I could never have stood up in front of all those people, I'd be too scared." The women in question are almost always mothers, and motherhood—with the responsibility for the physical, emotional, spiritual, and social well-being of another human being—is the scariest job of all. My old friend Tracey DeBoissiere had a beautiful girl five years before I gave birth, and she tried to warn me. "It hurts your heart because you are never close enough, never sure enough that your child is safe enough, happy enough, healthy enough."

So, believe me: If you can deliver a child, you can deliver a speech. If you can raise a child, you can raise your company's profits or your network ratings. The best part of it all is that, for most of us, nothing in the world comes close to the sense of wonder and achievement one gets from motherhood. So it was easy to decide to dedicate my book to my baby.

To my daughter Susan,
    You have changed me. You have changed my world because I think of you twenty-four hours a day. I think of you when I'm not with you, and I feel guilty and lonesome. I think of you when you are asleep upstairs and wonder if I'm doing it right. I think of you learning and growing, and I feel proud that you are my daughter. I think of you and wonder what you think of me. I think of you, and I thank God (and my own mother).
    I think of you and decide to put down my pen and go inside to play with you instead.

Happy Birthday
Susan Molinari
May 1998

Contents

Representative Mom

It is not the critic who counts; nor the man who points out how the strong man stumbled. Or where the doer of deeds could have done better. The credit belongs to the man who is actually in the arena; whose face is marred by dust and sweat and blood; who strives valiantly; who errs and comes short again and again because there is no effort without error and shortcoming; who does actually strive to do the deeds, who knows the great enthusiasm, the great devotions, who spends himself in a worthy cause; who at best knows in the end the triumph of high achievement; and who at the worst, if he fails at least fails while daring greatly, so that his place shall never be with those cold and timid souls who know neither victory nor defeat.

—THEODORE ROOSEVELT

A copy of this quote was given to me by my father on the day I announced my intention to run for public office. He told me that I would need it. . . . He wasn't wrong.

Who Does She Think She Is Anyway?

In the eyes of my daughter, the floor of the U.S. House of Representatives probably looked like the world's biggest playpen, or at least the set of *Sesame Street*. She wasn't entirely wrong.

By the time she was fifteen months old, Susan Ruby knew the contours of that great hall—the eagle on the high ceiling, the flashing lights of the electronic voting board, the slope of the carpeted floor descending to the Speaker's platform—almost as well as she knew her grandparents' apartment. She'd slept through more debates about military spending and transportation than most viewers of C-Span. She'd cried to the hammer of the gavel ending scores of sessions and the booming baritone of Bob Livingston in the well.

Sometimes, during a lull in a debate, I'd watch her checking out the clutches of gesticulating members arguing down front. She'd giggle in delight, and I'd try to imagine who she saw as the Cookie Monster, and who was Oscar the Grouch—and whether her assessments were the same as mine.

Smart as she was, though, Susan Ruby never seemed to understand about the aisle, or aisles, really, since there are two of them in the House. If I turned my back, she'd waddle up the one that separated the Republicans from the no-man's-land that is the center section of that immense auditorium. But she lacked proper respect for the traditions of partisanship. If I didn't catch her, she'd veer off across the Berlin Wall of American politics to check out what the Democrats on the far side were up to.

In July 1997, two weeks before I left Congress to become a CBS anchor, I packed Susan Ruby into her stroller for one of the first House debates on a bill that would cut off much of the funding for the National Endowment for the Arts. The NEA had become a lightning rod for conservatives, a symbol both of the spendthrift ways of the federal government and the erosion of American values. For liberals, the NEA was equally symbolic—a bastion of tolerance, a force for "progressive" change. The battle had been joined. The debate promised to be both serious and acrimonious.

Susan Ruby, of course, did not care about the National Endowment for the Arts. All she cared about that afternoon was spending time with Nita Lowey, the grandmother of all grandmothers, a Democrat who was as firmly opposed to the change in funding for the NEA as I was in support of it.

Member after member took to the well, alternately, to denounce the "pornography" the NEA had promoted and to praise the vitality it stimulated in the American art world. Hollywood and the Christian Right had both mounted major lobbying efforts around the pending legislation, so no one expected an easy victory. Every few minutes Newt would pop out of his office to check on our progress. Our whips worked the room, counting votes. I moved from one group of Republicans to another across our side of the floor, working the members, doing my part as a member of the House Republican leadership. After one such huddle, I turned around, and Susan was gone.

I looked frantically across the floor and saw her blond head on the other side of the divide, headed for Nita and Nancy Pelosi, who were bent over in an intense discussion, probably pretty similar to the one I had just left. Nonetheless, they scooped Susan Ruby up off the floor, kissed her, and hugged her. Nita hadn't been home to see her grandchildren for weeks and played with Susan as her surrogate. I worried more about Nancy. She was always perfectly dressed, which is dangerous when you're holding a young child.

Then, even through the din of disagreement, I heard Susan start to fuss. Nita and Nancy turned my way. We all hesitated across the expanse of the room, the expanse of history and party infighting. Members rarely crossed into the territory of the other party when we were in session. But the matter was getting serious. Susan was wailing. As the debate thundered in the background, Nita ignored it and headed my way. We shared a hug, then looked at each other and laughed. The acrimony of the controversy dissolved. Ideology, even party loyalty, became irrelevant. The NEA fight was forgotten, at least for one moment. A really important and pressing matter was at hand: Susan Ruby needed her diaper changed.

◆

By 1996, the year Susan was born, the House wasn't exactly a playground, but it also was no longer the sea of gray suits and graying temples it had been even fifteen years earlier, when I'd first peered through the great doors and walked onto the floor with my father, whose seat I won in 1990. For me, the floor of the House was the place where my father had worked and the place where I learned to be a powerful woman, where my husband proposed to me, where my daughter became part of my work life.

Over those years, a new generation came to power in the House of Representatives, men and women struggling—just like their constituents—with the complications of two careers, limited day care options, and a profound desire to spend more time with their children. So Rick Lazio would bring his daughters to work and Bill Orton's son played tag with Rick's eldest in the back. Not everyone was pleased at their presence. No one ever came out and said it, but faint grimaces and frowns of disapproval at a baby's cry sent the message: This is a place of weighty matters and lofty considerations. I agreed. Which is precisely why I wanted my daughter at my side. Trade regulation and tax policy aren't the only weighty measures that concern Congress. The kids on the floor reminded us how much else needed our attention.

The disapprovers weren't confined to the House of Representatives. In fact, I remember their faces most clearly from a hearing that Pat Schroeder and I arranged just after the 1996 elections. We had run into each other in the bathroom at the *Glamour* magazine Women of the Year awards at the Sherry-Netherland Hotel in New York. I was being honored that year, while both she and Connie Morella, who was with her, were past honorees. The problem of sexual abuse among female recruits at the Aberdeen Proving

Ground had just hit the press, and I mentioned it in passing as we were combing our hair and adjusting our pantyhose.

"We should do something, Pat, at least hold a hearing," I suggested. Pat was one step ahead of me. Since her contacts in the Clinton administration were vastly superior to mine, she'd already been on the phone with officials of the Department of Defense. Since my power as a member of the leadership in the House was greater than hers, I offered to facilitate a congressional response. It was an almost perfect moment. There we were, female members of Congress at an event celebrating women, figuring out how to use our power to help women in trouble.

The following week, four generals arrived on Capitol Hill for our hearing, the beginning of our attempt to pressure the army into taking sexual abuse of female troops seriously. The members facing them were all female; Susan Ruby was in the stroller at my side. The generals fidgeted as we grilled them about sexual harassment policies, training of noncommissioned officers, and the treatment of female troops. One issued a mild *harrumph* when I reached down to stroke Susan Ruby's forehead. I could hear him thinking, "How can I take this seriously, a woman with a baby. What's the world coming to?"

◆

By then I'd had plenty of practice in dealing with people who didn't take me entirely seriously. When you're a short blond woman who looks like everyone's granddaughter, you don't have much choice. We seem to get pigeonholed as lightweights, pawns of powerful men, or, as in my case, both. That didn't change much even once I had a real record to stand on. There I'd be, in a war zone in Bosnia, and some reporter—usually female—would comment on how I was dressed, then turn to my male colleague for answers to questions of substance. I'd come back from a grueling day of arm-twisting and political hardball on the floor of the House to yet another press story in which the president of the National Organization for Women on Staten Island was denouncing me for being perky.

What was I supposed to do, eat myself into a stupor so I would seem more weighty? Dye my hair salt-and-pepper? Wear platform shoes? Imagine the controversy that would have created! And when did perky get a bad name? How did being lively and optimistic become a liability? Is dressing in black and weighing yourself down with public angst really morally superior? Why is it chic to smoke cigars and tacky to chew gum? Or okay to play golf but not lead cheers?

For years this all used to bother me the way women are almost always bothered when their hair, their figures, their mannerisms, and their lives are picked apart. But somewhere along the line I concluded that the best thing I could do when people criticized me unfairly was to get even by proving them wrong, which is pretty much the story of my life. I never started out to set the world on fire or be a member of Congress or a network anchor (although I did dream of the latter for years). I wound up there because someone, many ones, told me I couldn't. Every time someone told me I didn't have the right credentials, I set out to prove that you don't have to be Henry Kissinger to know that genocide is wrong, or a leading sociologist to understand that the nation's current welfare system has not served the poor well. Every time someone insisted I wasn't tough enough, I pulled back my shoulders and headed for the bargaining table to face down union leaders. Every time someone said, "Who the hell does she think she is anyway?" I silently turned the phrase back on the person who'd uttered it.

That strategy landed me in some pretty strange places—in Washington and Bosnia, on a very big stage in San Diego and on CBS on Saturday mornings. For a decade I inhabited a world that most Americans think of as lofty and powerful—making policy that would determine how the elderly would live, voting to send young men and women to war, and helping to control the national checking account when I can't even keep my own checkbook balanced. And I take it I was supposed to derive from those experiences some deep sense of gravity and self-importance. But frankly, most of the time I felt more like Alice in Wonderland, racing from a beheading (often my own) to a surreal tea party thrown by yet another group of boosters who often seemed mad as hatters, wondering what was behind the wide grin of the Cheshire cat in the White House who looked good-natured but had very long claws and a great many teeth, and watching the Lobster Quadrille that is American politics. For those ten years it got curiouser and curiouser.

Maybe that was inevitable since I entered politics as a Republican committed to fiscal conservatism and social moderation and wound up, probably also inevitably, getting hit from both sides—slammed for being, alternately, Newt's pom-pom girl and for being Bella Abzug without the hat. And things were bound to get curiouser since I entered Congress as a Republican when we seemed to be the perennial minority, lived through the era when we lost even the presidency, then woke up one morning to find myself at the center of the storm that was our retaking of the House and the launching of the legislative battle that would make our Contract with America reality.

During those years I met some of the great characters of the nation (in all senses of the word *characters*), and I saw, at times was even part of, some momentous events. I worked side by side with Newt Gingrich, alternately grateful for what many will find to be his surprising support for a dozen women's issues and chilled by the mercurial mien that made his House anything but a happy home. With awe and deep admiration I watched Colin Powell ascend the podium at the Republican National Convention.

I fought the abortion wars, and have the scars to prove it. I witnessed the slaughter in Bosnia, and went head to head with both Dan Quayle and Slobodan Milosevic, the president of Serbia, to try to stop it. Pretty heady stuff for a woman who began as a kid too nice to rebel against her parents, who grew into a cheerleader and still refuses to repent for that sin.

Throughout it all, I've been in some pretty wacky places, especially in the political arena. One Friday night I flew home to Staten Island from Washington, D.C., to make sure I wouldn't arrive late for a meeting of two hundred federal employees in Brooklyn who'd invited me to address them. I got up early and pulled up in plenty of time for the ten A.M. meeting, but I was the only one. When I walked into the building where the meeting was to be held, it was dark. The meeting room was empty. An elderly man out front informed me that the meeting would not begin until eleven. I went next door for a sandwich, and when I returned, there were still only a handful of people in the room, mostly over the age of eighty, and all unable to hear themselves think because a fan was clattering in the corner. When I rose to the podium, however, the sight of me ignited quite a stir, and for a moment I swelled with pride at my popularity in the district. Then I focused on the buzz in the room and realized that they believed I was Caroline Kennedy.

Sometimes the zaniness was actually generated by politicians, which must seem a contradiction, since we're hardly known as a fun group. But, trust me, it happens. Just after I moved into Congress, I went on a trip to Israel with eleven public officials from New York—district attorneys, city council members, and other city pols. We were earnest as we visited kibbutzim poised on the Syrian border, and thus on the brink of destruction. We were serious as we spoke with Soviet Jews still reeling from freedom. Matters of state, and matters of human conscience. But the Israelis ran us ragged, packing us in a school bus that criss-crossed the country from the Lebanese border to the Negev desert. By the fifth day, we were all so tired and punchy that giddiness was the only possible antidote. Finally, our guide, Shlomo, turned to Fred Cerullo, a member of the City Council, and urged him to lead us in a sing-along. We all assumed Fred would guffaw and remain seated, or appease Shlomo with a quick chorus of *"Hava Nagilah."* Instead, he stood up and began to belt out, "When you are lonely, life is taking you down, well, you can always go," then turned to our weary group and waved his arms to solicit an admittedly weak, "Down-town."

Fred had been my partner in all sorts of crimes, of politics and silliness, and we often didn't have very much choice. When you're from Staten Island, people expect you to get down and dirty, and when you're a politician, it's hard to say no. One night Fred and I were at a fund-raiser for navy families at Rab's Bowling Alley on Staten Island. The place was packed, and the karaoke machine in the bar working overtime. The owner decided that his city council-man and congresswoman should be the evening's entertainment. He handed us a microphone and insisted that we wow the crowd with a rendition of "Summer Lovin'." I'd never been told that playing Olivia Newton-John to someone else's John Travolta was part of my job description. But, what the hell. It's the kind of democracy in action Republicans usually only talk about.

But nothing could compete with the zaniness that entered my life when Susan Ruby was born. By the time she was one, she already knew how to play to a crowd better than any other Molinari, and she would stop crying on a dime if a camera appeared in view. Last year, Senator Alfonse D'Amato asked me to appear with him at a meeting of the Breast Cancer Coalition, and I took Susan Ruby with me. She was playing quietly on the floor in front of me when I turned my back for a minute. The next thing I knew, she was up front next to D'Amato, showing off her new dress. Then she started imitating the feisty senator, gesticulating as if she, too, were pontificating. The audience tittered, D'Amato continued. She upped the ante, parodying him sentence for sentence in perfectly timed gibberish. The audience laughed, D'Amato continued. Finally, Susan Ruby took a bow—an act she had never committed before, or since.

I left the meeting and called my dad immediately. "It has taken three generations of Molinaris, but we finally upstaged Al D'Amato!"

....

Chapter One

Family Business

Staten Island would be the thirty-fifth largest city in the United States—bigger than Miami or Pittsburgh—if it weren't irrevocably shackled to New York City. We Islanders like to think that if we were our own city, we'd spend summer weekends at pristine beaches, folks would gather in some of the finest Italian restaurants in the country, and a solid tax base of middle-class homeowners would keep our town clean, progressive, and well maintained.

But since my hometown is New York's last borough—or at least it was in any ranking of the city government's concern for its boroughs until Rudy Giuliani became mayor—when I was at the age when kids play beach volleyball and loll on the sand to show off their tans, the beaches of South Shore were littered with the hospital waste of the urban sprawl across the harbor. Manhattanites never thought of riding the ferry over for dinner, considering Staten Island too downscale for their tastes. And the borough's taxes poured into the coffers of the central city government, and were parceled out for parks in Manhattan, bridges in Brooklyn, and rotting housing in the Bronx.

What Staten Island got instead was what no one else in New York wanted: the garbage dump—the largest garbage dump in the world; prisons; and the sludge from New Jersey. Drive across the island with your windows down on a Friday night in the spring, and you'll smell what both New York and New Jersey have sent our way.

When people in Manhattan talk about "the island," they mean Long Island, which is widely considered to be a pretty good place to live. Most people never even think about the island directly across from Wall Street, and if they do, it is to make jokes about the blue-collar rubes or Edith and Archie Bunker–like white flighters who live there. In fact, when I was born, you couldn't even get to Staten Island from Manhattan without getting on a ferry.

Frankly, no one was all that unhappy about the psychic distance that created. While most New Yorkers were living in the mounting chaos of gridlock and crime, twenty minutes away by ferry, Staten Islanders were still driving down the road to farm stands. Parents didn't worry when their kids rode their bikes to the beach. And everyone knew everyone else. Really. You might not have known the new girl in your class, but your next-door neighbor's cousin went to elementary school with her. Or her mother worked with your aunt at the mall. It was the kind of place where people hugged and kissed each other instead of shaking hands, and everyone called everyone else "hon." Think Melanie Griffith's Tess in *Working Girl,* and you pretty much have the picture.

In other words, and at the risk of sounding like a Pollyanna, Staten Island was a pretty great place to grow up. I lived day to day in the easy warmth of what felt like a small town, where I could stop at the local gas station and tell the guy that I wanted to go out but didn't have enough money for gas, and he'd give me five dollars' worth because he knew I'd be back the next day to pay him. But it wasn't so isolated that I couldn't get on the ferry with my friends and go to Madison Square Garden to a Billy Joel concert, or so far removed from urban life that I was never forced to confront the kind of uglier realities that make childhood into something more than a fairy tale.

If I were Joan Crawford's daughter, I might actually have something titillating to offer about my childhood, which I would at least consider putting on these pages. Or I'd have something juicy with which to humiliate my parents, which would be fun if my mother had actually beaten me, or if I hated my father which, I admit, I don't. I know it is hopelessly out of fashion to admit it, but I actually like my parents, and always did.

In fact, mine was a pretty garden-variety television fantasy American family of my place, era, and social class. When I was growing up, my father was a real estate lawyer and my mom was a housewife who hated to cook. And nothing much happened to me that was neurosis-provoking, which I guess means that I'm pretty out of step with America these days. We called ourselves Italian, although that was biologically questionable since both my mother and father were both only half Italian. But you would never have known that from the climate of the household, so I can't claim any trauma over being lied to.

Journalists have combed through my childhood looking for "significant" incidents to explain either my interest in power or my membership in the Republican party. The only one any reporter seems to have dug up allegedly demonstrated my early aptitude for wooing public support. As a child, according to my mom, I hated to play outside. Exasperated by my refusal to conform to her image of a young child, she sought the advice of my pediatrician, who suggested that she simply bundle me up, push me out the front door, and lock it behind me. The first time she tried his technique, I turned the tables on her, sitting outside crying until some neighbors took pity on me. I defiantly informed them that my parents didn't want me anymore, which spurred them to action. They knocked on the door. When my mother responded, they planted both me, and their opinion of my mother, in the hallway.

I don't want to be disingenuous. If I look back far enough, I know that political roots were being ambitiously planted. My father trained me for politics even before I was out of feetie pajamas. At his insistence, every Sunday morning we'd sit around the breakfast table and elect a president for the day. I was expected to nominate myself and give a speech about why I wanted to be president. My mother and I would usually gang up on my dad and elect one of the two of us to that high office. It was my first encounter with a woman's caucus—but hardly my last.

But that's a no-brainer. The story that reporters seeking revealing details probably should have discovered concerns my childhood imaginary friend, a clown named Button Tang. Unlike James Stewart's Harvey, my imaginary friend was real, which is to say that he was an actual toy clown that I carted around with me incessantly when I was four or five years old. Some days I'd insist that he wanted to go to the office with my father, who would obediently stash the clown in his briefcase. Around two P.M. I'd invariably decide that my friend wanted to come home and demand that my father drop everything to accommodate that desire. When I reached the age of no longer needing an imaginary friend,

I drowned Button Tang, which I'm sure someone will use to explain my support for the death penalty.

◆

My father's father, Robert Molinari, was born in Calabria, Italy, came to New York when he was six years old, and died before I was born. His legend, however, loomed large, both in my household and on Staten Island. In his day, only Democrats had any chance of being elected from Staten Island, so before every election cycle, the Republicans would recruit a Democrat to run on their ticket. In 1942 my grandfather was the chosen Democrat, and he won a seat in the state assembly against the incumbent, making him the first Italian-born New Yorker to serve in the state assembly. But while he continued in politics all his life, his tenure in elective office didn't last long. In the next election he lost to the official Democrat by less than fifty votes.

Fighting Bob Molinari was a local character who worked three jobs, lost everything in the Depression, and spent his weekends and evenings playing his banjo to entertain patients in the local hospital. His wife, my stepgrandmother, was a quiet Old World sort of woman, which made her the exact opposite of my mother's mother, Susan, for whom I'm named.

Mama Sue was one of ten kids in an Italian family in Red Hook, Brooklyn, and her idea of a small crowd was anything less than two dozen people spilling out of her living room. Since my mother, Marguerite, has been ill since my birth, Mama Sue was my surrogate mother. My mom would go shopping with me and pick me up at cheerleading practice, but it was Mama Sue who was at home cooking supper.

She was extremely traditional in her own way. She did the food shopping and the laundry. She came to our house to clean. She cooked, made sandwiches, shoved snacks in me, along with loving advice. She never would have sat me down to talk about Life with a capital L, or to tell me, "Here's what you should do with your life" or "You should have a job instead of getting married." But imbedded in her traditionalism was a rock-solid sense of self that left no room for insult. Mama Sue's lesson No. 1 was: Never take shit from anybody. She wore tight jeans, off-the-shoulder blouses, and high, open-backed pumps—and didn't care if you liked it or not. She made the worst Bloody Marys this side of a roadside dive, played the horses, and, even well into her seventies, kept her hair platinum and never missed an opportunity to flirt with some young guy.

Mama Sue was one hundred percent unconditional love. It didn't make any difference whether I was showing her my report card with all A's or just walking down the block. She was proud of me. There was no need to perform. She was my role model and my best friend, even if she disapproved of the fact that I preferred sneakers to heels and T-shirts to sexy tops.

Mama Sue loomed large in my life because my mother developed serious peritonitis shortly after I was born and was sick for a long time. Then she suffered a severe whiplash fracture in a car accident and spent years in pain while doctors passed off her complaints as neurotic woman stuff. While the bone in her neck slowly deteriorated, she went from doctor to doctor, then to acupuncturists and chiropractors, psychologists and psychiatrists. By the time anyone took her seriously enough to diagnose what had happened and offer to operate, her neck was so severely injured that they insisted she sign a waiver releasing both the doctor and the hospital from liability if she were left paralyzed. She took the risk because she simply couldn't live with the pain any longer. She and my grandmother taught me about how easily women get dismissed, about strength, courage, and how important family really is.

But I've jumped ahead of my own life. I was born on March 27, 1958, which suggests a great deal about the world I was raised in. James Agee won the Pulitzer Prize in fiction for *A Death in the Family*, but the year's news was dominated by Elvis's shipping out to Germany with the army. *West Side Story* was the toast of Broadway and the airwaves were awash with Little Anthony crooning "Tears on My Pillow" and Connie Francis wailing "Who's Sorry Now?" Television was still black and white, which probably didn't make much difference since the hits of the season were *Love That Bob* and *Peter Gunn*.

My mother, of course, was not June Cleaver. She'd suffered too much to live in that kind of fantasy world. And as I grew up, she imbued me with a firm sense of self that matured into feminism. She didn't use that language, at least not while I was a kid. But, like Mama Sue, she taught me to stand up for myself, to be proud of who I was no matter what anyone else thought—which is pretty much a protofeminist upbringing.

Nonetheless, she was intent on making me a real girl. She painted my room pink and white, bought a four-poster, and covered it with a spread I never dared sit on. I didn't exactly hate it, but I didn't spend much time there either. My real room, the room where I hung out, was a small third bedroom in the ranch home my parents bought when I was in second grade. The walls were papered with sheets and Cat Stevens posters. It was absolutely, gloriously messy.

Despite my antipathy to order, I still fell into the girl mode my mother and my era had mapped out for me. My friends and I all kept those little books that girls keep, and I dreamed of being a ballerina or something else very feminine. What else could I have dreamed? I grew up watching *Bewitched*, where Samantha gives up all her powers to marry an ugly guy named Darrin Stephens. Then I saw Jeannie, who lived in her bottle. Those were the TV role models for women of my generation—women with extraordinary powers who gave them up because men asked them to. The message was pretty clear: You can't have both your power and the man you love because the man you love doesn't want you to have any power.

Marlo Thomas might be a great feminist now, but *That Girl* wasn't much better. In those days she was just a kid who'd left home and was still having a constant nervous breakdown, which suggested that things hadn't improved much after June Cleaver moved off the air. The only role model I found interesting was Peggy Lipton on *The Mod Squad.* She was an excitingly tough risk-taker, which I found totally thrilling. But her hair was gorgeous and mine was terrible, so, with the logic of a kid, I decided I could not aspire to her feats of derring-do.

The high points of my youth were family weekends either in the city or in New Hope, Pennsylvania. Every month or so, we'd pack our bags and take off for two days, just the three of us. Sometimes my dad would book a room at the Plaza and make dinner reservations at the Persian Room. Other times he'd get tickets for a rock concert, and we'd eat dinner at my favorite place, a restaurant filled with old cars that served both as table and chairs. Even a quarter of a century later I cherish the memory of the night my parents took me to a Noel Harrison concert because the male star of *The Girl from U.N.C.L.E.*—who happened to be Rex Harrison's son—was my idol. No one else seemed to think the young Brit with his dirty-blond mod haircut hair should be popular music's new sensation. But that didn't make any difference. I was desperate to go to the concert, and my father, as usual, facilitated my fantasy.

My parents indulged me shamelessly, but I don't want to leave the impression that I was raised to be a brat. I was taught at an early age that whatever I did would reflect on my father, and, nonrebel that I was, I took the admonition seriously. Actually, the Daughters of Divine Charity didn't leave me much alternative. They ran St. Joseph Hill Academy, where I spent kindergarten through twelfth grade, with an iron fist. Virtually everything was prohibited: bleached hair, hair that touched your collar, jewelry, chewing gum. Our skirts had to be hemmed so that they would touch the floor if we knelt down, which we were expected to do regularly, in and out of Mass.

I admit that I was never properly reverent, even in that thoroughly Catholic environment, which foreshadowed the problems I'd later have with the archbishop of New York. My mother still kids me about the day she walked me through a church to tell me about God. I ignored the lecture and began blowing out every candle in sight. I didn't understand her dismay, she says. I saw candles, thought birthday, and acted accordingly.

In retrospect, what annoyed me most about my Catholic education was the incessant preoccupation with sin. There I was in second grade, and I was sent home to memorize a list of sins so that I could confess them. And if I didn't have any, no one believed me, so I wound up making up sins—talking back to my parents or arguing with them—which meant that I sinned in order to avoid being accused of hiding sins. I've had problems with confession ever since.

Then the nuns upped the ante and demanded that I learn the difference between mortal and venial sins. Whoever decided that kids in second grade needed to know the difference between mortal and venial sins? I was a dumb, suburban eight-year-old worried about whether I'd get a new bike for my birthday, which is what I was supposed to be worried about at that age, and the nuns wanted me to forget about all those worldly concerns and concentrate on the state of my immortal soul. Please.

Neither of my parents ever seemed particularly disconcerted by my lack of respect for the Church, and as I grew up, my mother shared her own disappointment with me. When it was time for my first communion, she had asked her parish priest for confession so that she could participate in the ritual. He refused, as did every other priest she approached. Her sin? She was on birth control because her doctors had warned her that another pregnancy would be dangerous to her health. It was not until I reached my mid-thirties that I was able to put my early experiences with the Church far enough behind me that I could reclaim my religion and my relationship with God.

While I chafed at the restrictions and the obsession with sin, I was incredibly proud of being a student at St. Joseph Hill, the finest school on Staten Island. I loved wearing the uniform—a sky-blue pleated skirt and matching jacket with a white shirt, white stockings, and oxfords or saddle shoes, and, in retrospect, I realize how important those uniforms were to dulling the differences between those of us from families with money and those from families of more modest means. Only as an adult, furthermore, as I listened to female friends talk about being interrupted by the boys in their classes, or belittled by their teachers, did I come to understand how lucky I'd been to have gone to an all-girl high school.

I was lucky, too, that my parents had high expectations for me. I was privileged—I never needed an after-school job, my family was intact, and I was at least reasonably intelligent—and they expected me to perform accordingly. If I had missed it earlier, that message was drummed home the day I discovered that my classmates were receiving money from their parents when they got good report cards. Mine had always been terrific, and I had never seen a dime, so I protested to the authorities when I handed over yet another semester's worth of A's and was offered nothing more than a celebration dinner. They refused to part with a penny. "You should get good marks for yourself, not for me," my dad said. "I like you and love you and will do whatever you need me to do whether you get A's or fail. So you better get A's for yourself."

I knew they must be serious because, like most parents, they weren't beyond offering me the occasional bribe. My favorite offer, my folks say, occurred in my pediatrician's office, the first time he asked me to give him a urine sample. My mother led me into the bathroom, handed me a cup, and told me to pee in it. I refused. She patiently explained that the doctor really needed to examine my urine. I did not become reasonable. In desperation, she promised me that the doctor would give me a dollar if I would fill the cup with urine, which threw me into absolute hysterics. She looked at me frantically, trying to assess what was wrong. How could I tell her that I was just beside myself at the thought of all that valuable urine I'd been flushing down the toilet.

Even without any financial incentive, I was always a pretty good student, except in Sister Christopher's math class. But that didn't stop me from making myself into a neurotic wreck over every exam I ever took. I was a perpetual Prophet of Doom. I'd spend days poring over my schoolbooks, obsessing. My parents would interrupt me. "It's a beautiful day, put your homework away and go outside." I just couldn't.

I'd come home from every test and announce that I had failed. "How do you know?" my father would ask. "I just know," I'd answer. "You don't know," he'd insist. "You couldn't have failed. You studied for three weeks." His words made no impact. I was not only convinced that I'd failed, but that I'd gotten the lowest grade in the class. My pessimism became a recurring joke in my family that haunted me for years. When I entered politics and started complaining about a bad speech I'd given, or worrying that I'd never get the votes to get a given bill passed, my father would always say, "You failed the test, right?"

The highlight of my high school career was making the cheerleading squad, which I have since learned is supposed to be an acute source of embarrassment to me. In certain circles, in fact, my refusal to disavow my passion for cheerleading has been as controversial as my support for abortion or my support for welfare reform. I can never remember wanting anything as much as I wanted to become a cheerleader, and I failed the first time around, which was in sixth grade. I was sure my life was over. My cousin Tommy came to pick me up from the tryout, and I was sobbing and sobbing inconsolably. I started working on my cheers every day. My friends came over to teach me how to do the jumps and make my voice deeper until I finally won a place on the team.

I should note that my father used all of his persuasive powers, which were considerable, to squash my cheerleading obsession. I'd been offered a place on the debate them, and that was the kind of after-school activity he approved of. I didn't care. I was fourteen years old, and there was no way I was going to give up my squad for some dry debate. It was my greatest act of teenage rebellion.

In those days in New York, at least, cheerleaders didn't spend much of their time twirling around with pom-poms at football games. It was extremely serious business, more like a precision drill team with the emphasis on competition. Before important meets we glued our socks to our legs with Elmer's to make sure they didn't fall down and embarrass us. We practiced for hours every day with the same energy and dedication guys put into basketball and football.

We certainly didn't do any of this for the approval of our teachers. The nuns hated cheerleading and pegged us as some kind of fast group, which is almost laughable. None of us would have dared smoke a cigarette while in uniform, even if we had been in China. The worst things we did were to chew gum and bleach our hair.

I had the occasional brush with trouble, of course. One night I almost got arrested at a party when some of the boys got rowdy, picked up some guy's Spider, and hauled it around the block. The owner was not amused and called the cops, who arrived on the scene to find dozens of rowdy and raucous high school kids on the front lawn. I was saved from arrest by the fortuitous arrival of some friends of my parents, who talked the cops into letting me go. It was no big deal in the scheme of things, but I paid for that evening. As a punishment, and a precaution, I was barred from going to parties alone. My father had to drive me to make sure adults were on the premises.

All in all, then, I was a pretty ordinary kid. I wasn't the smartest student in the class. I certainly wasn't the prettiest. I had braces and pimples and hated my hair every day of my life.

Our world changed dramatically in 1974, when my father gave up his law practice and threw himself into politics. He'd been a politics junkie for years—not the kind of junkie obsessed with policy, but a person who gloried in the rough-and-tumble of political in-fighting. He had been active in the Republican party for years but had declined every invitation to run for office. The child of a politician himself, he refused to let me suffer for his fascination with the intrigue of government.

By the time I was in high school, however, he knew he could make his play, and an irresistible opportunity landed in his lap. My father had long disliked our state assemblyman, who had been in Albany for sixteen years, because he hadn't done much of anything that my father could see. There was also a personal element to his antipathy. The assemblyman had once made a nasty crack about my grandfather and, loyalty maniacs that the Molinaris are, my dad couldn't let the insult go unpunished. So in 1973, when he came up for reelection, my dad informed the county Republican chair that he was going to challenge him. The chairman did his best to deter my dad, arguing that the incumbent was unbeatable. That only spurred him on. He spent six months walking from one end of Staten Island to the other, ringing doorbells, and won both the primary and the general election.

My dad's victory wasn't all that sweet since Republicans were in the minority, which meant that he didn't have much clout. But he had enough friends on the Democratic side of the aisle to sneak a bill into the hopper occasionally and thrived on the strategizing and deal making and campaigning. He was in heaven.

My mother was not. She blanched at each and every attack

launched against him, even though she knew that they were just part of the game. She could never get comfortable with the intrigue, the backstabbing, and humiliation, and it only got worse later, when both her husband and her daughter were getting beaten up. My father's leap into politics also caused a dramatic change in our living circumstances. He'd been an extremely successful attorney and we'd been driving around in Lincoln Continentals, taking five vacations a year, and shopping at Saks. Suddenly he was earning the salary of an elected official. There were no more cars, five vacations became one, and Saks became Macy's. The nosedive in our standard of living was hard on my mom since she wasn't trading away her vacations for other kinds of fulfillment. My dad, however, had never been so happy. That was my first major lesson in how much weight to give wealth over satisfaction in planning my life.

Since we no longer had our weekends in the city, my father took me along on his new outings—Republican dinners and meetings and conventions—and I was pulled into a vortex of middle-aged men in suits arguing about tax policy and garbage collection and the stupidity of Democrats. One day, in the middle of a party convention, he turned to me and announced that I had been chosen to second his nomination. I knew full well who had made that selection, and I was not thrilled. In fact, I thought I would die. When the time came, however, I obediently opened my mouth. I didn't die. I didn't even throw up or get booed off the floor. Doing the impossibly uncomfortable suddenly became uncomfortably possible. At the time, I was hardly grateful for that lesson, but it has saved me on dozens of occasions.

Those mini-forays into politics had no impact on my dreams for the future. I did not daydream about becoming the president of the United States, or a member of Congress. Like most of the high school girls I knew, my dreams were pretty much confined to finding a great guy to take me to the high school prom and getting into college. I was too sheltered and protected to imagine myself operating as a powerful person in the world. I desperately needed to get out on my own, sink or swim.

Going away to college was my ticket to that reality, and by the time I graduated from high school, there was no question that I would take it. In the world around me, the only children from upper-middle-class families who didn't go to college were druggies, hippies, or losers. I had none of those excuses. No one ever came out and told me: "You *will* go to college and you *will* leave home to do so." The assumption was woven into the fabric of our lives, along with the assumption that we'd get married, have children, become professionals, and not commit any major criminal acts.

I was still too young, and too much a daddy's girl, to fly far from the nest, so I enrolled at the State University of New York at Albany. It was only 150 miles from home, the education was excellent, and my dad's office was right across town. Nonetheless, it was an extraordinary culture shock. I'd never come up against the "princess" mentality before. At Hill, everyone wore the same blue uniform, and no one paid much attention to who had money and who didn't. SUNYA was rife with students with attitude—attitude about money and privilege and status. I was entirely unprepared for the competitiveness, for students who cut pages out of books and stole research materials from the library to get ahead.

I was a good student, but an altogether typical one who could swill beer with the best of them and never participated in a single college activity. The closest I came to organized activity was a brief involvement in a losing crusade to stop the building of a mall. I wasn't ready to do anything significant, and neither were most of my classmates. SUNYA in the late 1970s was not a cauldron of ferment, either political or intellectual. Which left me plenty of time to party with my friends.

I went from major to major trying to find my niche. From journalism, I tried political science for a while, but the Federalist papers, comparative governments of Europe, and the writing of the Constitution weren't exactly what I had in mind. So I wound up majoring in communications, which offered the advantage of a class schedule that began late in the morning. What did I expect to do with such a degree? I had no idea. My dream was to work in television news. But that world was so remote from my life, my experience, it seemed more a fantasy than the kind of dream I could turn into reality. I told people I wanted to work in public relations, but I didn't have any concept of what that meant in practical terms.

The most important part of my academic career was women's studies, which was an active and vibrant program at SUNYA. Feminism 101 hadn't been part of the curriculum at St. Joseph Hill. I'd read plenty of literature, but I'd never considered how women were portrayed in the Great Books. I'd studied years of history, but I'd never even thought about the power of the patriarchy. I'd never asked why my old girlfriends were working their way through state universities while their brothers, who frequently weren't very good students, were being financed by their families at private colleges. Women's studies provoked a revolution in my thinking by forcing me to reevaluate everything I'd ever passed off as normal, everything that had seemed normal to me for eighteen years.

The women's studies program created a community among female students, and I was drawn into it, although at the margins. My best friend, Patti, another Hill alum who is now a lieutenant colonel in the army, and I both enrolled in the classes, attended the lectures, and, occasionally, dropped by their parties and pot luck suppers. That was the first time I moved in circles that included significant numbers of open lesbians, although it took me years to realize that fact. I was so clueless about those matters that I didn't realize until I'd left Albany that many of the core members of the women's studies program had assumed that Patti and I were a couple.

The summer after my freshman year, the summer of 1977, was a turning point in my life. Instead of going home to Staten Island or taking an internship in Albany, I got a job as a cocktail waitress at Lake George. That might sound like pretty mild stuff to other people, but it was a huge, defiant moment for me. I didn't discuss my plans with my parents, or ask their permission. I just went up to Lake George with my friend Maria, whose family had a big house there, and talked my way into a job as a cocktail waitress at the Sky Harbor Cocktail Lounge.

My father flipped. Several days after I told him about my plan, he called to inform me that he'd had the place checked out, and that it was a nest of drug dealers. I was totally bummed because there was no way I could spend the summer at Lake George without a job. But something started nagging at a corner of my brain. I called my mother and asked her to repeat to me the name of the place where I'd found a job at the lake. She replied Harbor House, which is the name of a restaurant on Staten Island. I realized my father had cooked up a lie to manipulate me into staying home for the summer. I called and confronted him. "Well," he said, "if you couldn't figure out that I was lying, that I would do that, then you don't deserve to be a waitress."

That wasn't quite the end of that. He still tried to convince me to intern for a state senator or work at the university. You know, to do something that would build a résumé. It was probably the only bad piece of advice he has ever given me. He didn't realize that I needed to be on my own, to work in a job that did not entail dealing with him, or with people who knew him. And that's what I did. I lived with Maria's enormous, sprawling family, worked as a cocktail waitress and then a bartender, and nobody cared what my last name was or what my dad did for a living.

When I graduated from college in 1980, I had no plans at all, so I did what most aimless college grads do: I stayed in school. My department at SUNYA offered me a teaching assistantship, so I didn't have to take Graduate Record Exams or pay tuition, which soothed my conscience. I comforted myself with the thought that I'd get some teaching experience and that I could even try out the wider world by asking for an internship.

Then my father was elected to the House of Representatives, and I was forced into that wider world unexpectedly. He had made elaborate plans for his swearing-in—busloads of supporters would travel to Washington and join him at a luncheon where Jack Kemp had promised to speak. But the night before the great event, he was rushed to Walter Reed Hospital with what doctors believed was a flare-up of the malaria he'd contracted during the Korean War. Although it turned out to be just a nasty virus, he was laid up for a while, so we were stuck with all these people we had to make feel important. Suddenly the burden of representing the Molinari family shifted onto my shoulders. I played the political hostess with all the aplomb I could muster. And at the luncheon I rose to introduce Jack Kemp in my father's stead. I guess that everyone expected me to stutter or stumble or make a complete fool of myself, so when I didn't, they were all impressed. Years later I learned that that afternoon political operatives on Staten Island began talking about me as a potential candidate, as the next Molinari in the party. Good thing they didn't mention it to me at the time. I would have laughed in their faces.

When I finished my graduate program, I moved back to Staten Island and tried to find a job in public relations. I say tried because I had no idea how to look for a job. That wasn't part of the curriculum at SUNYA. I knew somebody at AT&T, who got me an interview that led nowhere. My father arranged a few more meetings. But nothing panned out. As always, my parents urged me to relax. "You've worked hard," they said. "You haven't taken any time off. Why don't you just hang back?"

As always, I couldn't. It just wasn't in my makeup. I moved to

Washington and volunteered at my dad's office while I tried desperately to get a job at BizNet, the Chamber of Commerce television station. Again, no luck. Everywhere I heard the same story: We have no openings, you have no experience, come back in six months. I actually scheduled an interview with the CIA, and was saved only by a call from the Republican Governors' Association offering me a job.

My title was finance assistant, but what I really did was lick stamps, send out Christmas cards, and arrange hotel rooms for contributors coming to town. That was enough, because Capitol Hill is a fabulous place to be if you're not ready to get married and start your career. Congress, the think tanks, and lobbying firms are packed with the under-thirty crowd, young people who make no money but who are always ready to have fun. Instead of scrounging the cash for dinner, you crash big receptions. You mingle with the famous and powerful. Your job at a party convention might be trivial in the grand scheme of things, but you feel part of the action, and that's enough.

The Republican Governors' Association was a small operation with Byzantine politics and, after two years, even with all the other distractions, I was fed up. I moved over to the Republican National Committee, where I ran outreach programs to Eastern Europeans and Asians. Asians immigrants, especially Vietnamese, had been streaming into the country, and we believed that they were natural constituents for the Republican party even though we hadn't been much better at reaching them than we had been at reaching women.

The job was pretty straightforward, and there was nothing innovative about my approach. I wrote brochures telling Asians why they should join the Republican party and had them translated into various languages. Did I know what buzz words to use, how to make the cultural connections between the Republican party and those groups? Of course not. I winged it, which is par for the course for a young person. The high point of the experience was the Republican convention in Dallas. Since there was a huge Vietnamese population in the area, I was more than a young gofer, which gave me some modest status. But I didn't really care. I loved being part of the team. It was the adult version of what I felt when I was cheerleading. Okay, I know it sounds ridiculous to those of you who haven't had the experience. But that's my point of reference, and I'm not about to change it to football metaphors after all these years.

It was while I was working at the RNC that I first met my husband, Bill, although nothing in that first encounter suggested the eventual outcome. I was teaching a training course at a political seminar at the Hyatt Hotel in Alexandria, Virginia, and Bill, who was in the New York State Assembly, came down for the event. He insists that he was interested in me immediately but was too shy to ask me out on a date. I'm not so sure. We wound up going out only because I asked him to have dinner so we could talk about being young and running for office in New York.

Of course, that wasn't really the reason. I'd begun to fantasize about running for office someday. But that day had not yet arrived. The truth is that I was mad at my boyfriend and had decided that it would be fun to torture him with the details of my evening out with a cute young assemblyman who was in town from Albany. If I hadn't felt so vindictive, I would never have had the courage to ask a guy out. But Bill didn't know that at the time. He didn't even know what he had gotten himself into when he said yes to my invitation. In his world, going out to dinner meant going out to dinner, but that's because he's compulsive. I'm completely disorganized half the time, so before dinner I made him go apartment-hunting with me.

I like to think that I made it up to him afterward with dinner and scintillating conversation at the American Cafe. But that was as far as things went. There were no shooting stars, clanging bells, or romantic melodies. At that point I was still into dating men who were bad for me. Bill Paxon did not fall into that category. At the end of the evening we shook hands, said good night, and I promptly forgot him.

Chapter Two

A Minority of One

By 1986, Washington was getting old. Fun wears thin after a while if you're treading water, and I was marooned along the Potomac without a plan. There wasn't much of a future at the RNC for a kid with no outside political experience. I still fantasized about finding my way into television news, but I was clueless how to make a connection. I was in politics for better or worse. When all the partying was done, what Hill Rats, which is what the young people who work on Capitol Hill are affectionately called, talk about is politics. I knew all my dad's buddies—Al D'Amato, who'd been his roommate when he first went to college, Gerry Solomon, his handball partner. What did my dad and I talk about when we got together? Politics.

Two years earlier, some prominent Staten Island Republican leaders had asked me to think about running for the state assembly, but I'd declined. I wasn't even twenty-five years old. I couldn't imagine myself walking the streets of Staten Island, selling myself to total strangers. Anyway, the RNC had put a lot of time and money into training me, and at that point I thought it would be unfair to leave before the 1984 election.

So I kept working as an ethnic liaison, hoping to pump up voter registration as we moved toward the election. I flew out to Portland, Oregon, for an absentee ballot drive, worked the convention, and celebrated the second inauguration of Ronald Reagan. When the campaign was over, however, the letdown set in. Staffers hung around the office collecting their paychecks without doing much work. I wasn't raring to set the world on fire, but I was too young and restless to skate.

For a while I seized on the Peace Corps as my road out of the RNC, and I was waiting to hear from them in 1985, when a group of Staten Island political leaders asked me if I would consider running for the New York City Council. That time I agreed to consider it, or perhaps bowed to the inevitable. Although I was aching from lack of self-confidence, or perhaps because I knew it was time to get over it, I was intrigued by the thought of becoming the wiseass Republican kid in that sea of Democrats. The last Republican to serve on the thirty-four-member council had been defeated two years earlier. Forcing the powers that were—and, in New York, they were some powers—to hear a Republican voice was a tantalizing possibility.

By then I was enough my dad's daughter to also be ticked off at the way the Democratic machine kept control over Staten Island. For years they had played a game we called Rotategate with the borough presidency and City Council seats. Shortly before the borough president's term was up, just after the point when a resignation would trigger a special election, the borough president would resign and appoint his deputy as acting borough president, which gave him the advantage of incumbency in the next election. Then the City Council member would become the deputy, and the party would appoint someone else to the council seat. Denting that stranglehold was a delicious fantasy.

I talked the idea over with John Zagame, who had been a member of the New York State Assembly and was working at the RNC at the time. He knew precisely how to convince me to give the seat a shot. "Hey, why not?" he said. "You'll test yourself, you'll get the New York market to know you, and even if you don't win, who knows? Maybe you'll get that job in television you always wanted."

Although most New York political types assumed that my running was my father's idea, he was, in fact, horrified when I mentioned the possibility of trying for the seat. It was not that he didn't want me in politics. Despite his protestations to the contrary, he had always pointed me in that direction, although I suspect that he wouldn't have done so if I'd had a male heir to his mantle. But he believed that a run for council would be a lose-lose situation. How could a young Republican conservative with no experience win in a liberal Democratic city, and how much fun, and impact, would a Republican have on that august body even if she won? It didn't help that I was thinking about running in the Republican primary against a friend of his, an older Italian-American man— although he was in no position to argue. In our community, that borders on disrespect. I won't bore you with the full script of our conversations, but they pretty much boiled down to "Do you really understand what you are getting into?"

Once he realized that I was committed to running, however, my dad started planning with a vengeance. I might not have expected to win, but the honor of the Molinari family was at stake. Guy Molinari had never lost an election, and I knew even then that defeat would not be a pretty sight. So I was a basket case when I arrived at the Montebianco catering hall on Staten Island on Lincoln's birthday, 1985, for the press conference where I would make my announcement. It was pouring that morning, and the wind was so strong that billboards had fallen over, closing major roads. Nonetheless, close to three hundred people had jammed into Montebianco for the event, and for every supporter in the crowd, there were at least three skeptics. Fortunately, I didn't understand the depth of the skepticism at the time. I hadn't yet learned that half of the well-wishers slapping me on the back while declaring "We're here for you" were really thinking, as politicians so often do, "We're here for you unless we decide it serves our interests to stab you in the back."

I probably couldn't have handled that knowledge at that point in my career. I had enough to cope with confronting my own skepticism. "Who am I kidding?" I wondered. "What do I know about garbage and sewage and fire districts, the kinds of things council members have to be interested in if they are going to serve their constituents." I was serious about wanting to work for my neighbors. I believed everything I was about to say about the importance of breaking the Democratic stranglehold on New York. But I was still terrified. I wasn't sure I could disguise my wobbly knees and shortness of breath.

But I was saved by the absurdity of the situation. When I walked to the podium to deliver my speech, I couldn't see over it to the audience. It had been set up for the average male politician, some guy five ten or six feet tall. I am barely five feet two. There I was, trying desperately to present myself as a serious and mature young woman, and I wound up looking like some kid aping her father. Someone ran out and found three milk crates that he stacked up for me to stand on. That made me look impressive, but I wound up so tall that I couldn't see my own speech.

My campaign handlers were almost apoplectic with concern that voters and the press might refuse to take me seriously because I was so young and small. So they decided to remake me into their image of a viable female candidate, which was somewhere between Jeane Kirkpatrick and Christie Todd Whitman. First they discarded my entire wardrobe, banishing the jean skirts and granny boots I wore in public and the jeans and tennis shoes I donned in private.

Then they arranged for a makeover at a beauty salon on Staten Island, where the staff was instructed to do whatever was necessary to turn me into a more mature and serious-looking woman. The beautician grimaced as she frosted my hair and pulled it back into a severe do. She never said a word, but she was clearly as convinced as I was that the desired effect would make me look like a kid dressed up to look like a adult.

They didn't stop there. They put me in a car and took me to the loft studio of a professional photographer in Manhattan, who dressed me up in a white man-tailored shirt with a bow tie. It was awful. My hair was pulled back in some kind of severe style, I was wearing button earrings, and had dark eye shadow smeared across my eyelids. We tried several different poses, and everyone agreed it just wasn't working. I let them readjust my bow tie, fool with my makeup, and restyle my hair. It made no difference. Finally I went into the bathroom and changed into a green silk blouse, took off half my makeup, and let down my hair. Within five minutes they were oohing and aahing at how much better it was working. But they still didn't get the point.

To be fair, they were trying to copy how many women in business and government were projecting themselves at that time. But that wasn't me. Let other women parade around in the female version of corporate drag, I thought. I can't pull that off. No, I wasn't willing to try. I didn't think I needed to become the female version of a male politician. I would follow my dad's credo and go to the voters as myself.

No matter how I dressed, no one took my candidacy very seriously—at first anyway. It was a constant barrage of "Who the hell does she think she is anyway?" I hadn't paid my dues in the local party, so I had no "equity" to trade on. I was too young. I wasn't a lawyer. And I'd been away from Staten Island since I was eighteen years old.

Frank Fosella was the incumbent, and a Democrat in a district with a heavy Democratic registration. I was a nobody wannabe who everyone assumed was trading on the fact that she was Guy Molinari's daughter. That alone would have been enough to make me work like crazy. Do people refuse to take Joe Kennedy seriously because he's just his father's kid? Do they accuse Kathleen Kennedy Townsend of capitalizing on the family name?

In fact, being Guy Molinari's daughter was a mixed blessing. On the one hand, I inherited a terrific group of experienced campaign handlers and could count on the support of dozens of political movers and shakers who owed my dad favors. On the other hand, people saw me only as Guy's daughter—Guy's Doll is what the local newspaper called me—and treated me accordingly. The antiabortion crowd, for example, went after me with a vengeance because I, as Guy's daughter, should have known better than to be pro-choice. My father's enemies reveled in attacking me, the ultimate payback to a protective and loving dad. Just before the primary, for example, Judge Rose O'Brien removed my name from the ballot on what she considered to be a technicality, although the Court of Appeals disagreed. Her action was hardly surprising. My father had defeated her brother in the congressional race in 1980.

In the end, however, the assumption that I was nothing more

than Guy's Doll played to my advantage because my opponents assumed that my race wasn't serious, that it was simply my father's way of giving me a trial run for the future. We did nothing to discourage that belief, so they dismissed me as a small nuisance, a piece of fluff who couldn't compete and barely mounted a campaign. What a boon! By the time they realized that I was a threat, the damage had been done.

In fact, they should have woken up to that threat the night of my debate with Fosella, the first debate of my political career. Almost two hundred people packed into a senior citizens' center that night to watch the new kid on the block take on the incumbent. Fosella wasn't sure how to handle an opponent who looked suspiciously like everyone's granddaughter, so he opted for nice, almost condescendingly so. Gently, he challenged my inexperience, expecting me to respond in kind.

I refused to play his game. I needed to assert myself as a serious person, and for every declaration of experience he offered, I responded by asking how life on Staten Island had improved as a result. Unwilling to be obscured by yet another podium, I moved out from behind the one assigned me, approached the audience, and looked back at my opponent. "If you've spent so much time in office, why is Staten Island a garbage dump?" I asked pointedly. "Why do we live without working sewers? Why are the tolls on the bridges so high?" Fosella was stunned into silence. The little girl could actually debate.

While he and the Democrats wallowed in overconfidence, I traipsed across Staten Island—street by street, supermarket by supermarket, train station by train station. Until my father ran for office, no one had ever campaigned that way on the Island, and no one did again until I followed in his footsteps. He had taught me that when you knock on doors and meet people face-to-face, they pay attention and, all other things being equal, give you their votes.

So I woke up before dawn every morning and went down to

the ferry terminal or a train station by six-thirty A.M. to meet voters
and force palm cards into the hands of poor, unsuspecting folks
who wanted their hands back so that they could drink their coffee
or put on their makeup. I'd catch a quick nap before lunchtime,
then hit the supermarkets to meet—they might say annoy—shop-
pers. By rush hour I was back at the train stations talking to com-
muters before spending my evenings ringing doorbells.

Once I started the campaign, people began to stop and talk to
me about whatever was bothering them—the toll on the Verrazano-Narrows Bridge, which connects the Island to Manhattan;
the smell coming from the Fresh Kills landfill; schools, police, sewers. Sewers were, in fact, a huge issue since they were so inadequate
that people's property was being flooded with overflows. Men and
women who had saved for years to buy nice homes suddenly
couldn't let their kids play on the front lawns they had spent a
lifetime imagining. What did I know about sewers? At first, nothing. I wasn't pulled into politics because I was a policy wonk or an
ideologue. I was pulled in by the game. But I wound up caring
deeply about them. Sewers might not be glamorous, but they are,
after all, immensely important to people's lives.

When people asked why I wanted to run, I talked about the
dangers of New York's long history of one-party rule, especially
since that party was so comfortable in power that it had ignored its
constituents. That wasn't the whole thing, of course. I had personal
reasons. But the more I got into the campaign, the more committed
I became to new solutions to the problems of homelessness, sewers,
bridge tolls, and fire stations, and the angrier I became at the incumbents.

For seven months I survived a grueling schedule of ferries
and train stations, supermarkets, community board meetings, and
the constant scrutiny of the press. I had to debate the city budget,
community planning board problems, homelessness, crime, the
problems of senior citizens, and the plight of youth. I put myself

through a short course in government, which didn't leave much time for sleep.

Despite all my work, when I walked back into my campaign headquarters where voters were polled nightly, I was treated like a little girl. The men who ran my campaign refused to let me see the poll results lest I get the vapors and pass out. Most of those men never had the *cojones* (to use Secretary of State Albright's phrase) to run for office themselves, and the one who did lost. But my chutzpah didn't dent their overprotectiveness.

I knew they were trying to keep me upbeat and excited, but it pissed me off to walk into the office where they were discussing negative results and watch them shut up. I went to my campaign manager, Michael Petrides, who always gave me more credit than anybody else, and told him that the secrecy was outrageous, that it was ruining my ability to do my job. He wouldn't budge. "You can't look at one night's polling and know anything," he said. "Wait and look at the results every third day, after we analyze them."

The problem was that most of my campaign handlers, like most all campaign handlers, then and now, had no experience working with female candidates. So, on the one hand, they tried to make me into a feminized man, and, on the other, they treated me like a dainty flower. It's true that as a woman candidate you are forced into a constant battle to convince voters that even though you weigh less than one hundred pounds you're still tough enough to do the job. But you can't make a woman butch just to win votes and then, when times get tough, treat her like some 1950s idea of a woman.

And times did get tough. When I first announced, it looked like I would have four opponents for the Republican nomination, so I had an uphill battle on my hands before I could even get to the real battle, which was against the Democratic incumbent. Fortunately, by the time of the party convention, two of my Republican opponents had bowed out of the race and thrown their support to me. But Anthony Ruggiero, a lawyer and a fixture on the Republican scene, wasn't about to give up. I laid awake at night worrying about the scene he'd make at the party convention.

That lost sleep was for naught, because Ruggiero opted to get his name on the ballot by petition rather than launching a floor fight at the convention for the party's endorsement. But that didn't make the convention any easier. I was blindsided by a problem I had not taken seriously: abortion. Abortion is hardly an issue that the City Council of New York has much power over, but the fact that my father was active in the antiabortion movement made my pro-choice position especially controversial. I'd been warned that some people within the party might make my abortion stand an issue, but I wasn't prepared for those people to be members of my extended family. I knew all too well that some of the politically active members of my family would refuse to support me because I was pro-choice. But I thought we would simply fight it out in private. I was dreaming. During the convention, with the whole crowd waiting and watching me, they harangued me. It was hardly the way to begin my political career. But it was a harbinger of things to come.

While I'd been naive about the abortion controversy, I was impossibly naive about the press. I knew that reporters would dog and question me, but I never considered that any of them would find me important enough to hate. So I was surprised when pieces began appearing in the papers that suggested I had gotten under a writer's skin. I tormented myself: I've never met this person, never talked to her, or him, and she doesn't even explain what it is about my politics that has enraged her. Why? What's going on here? Now I can sort of laugh about it because I understand both the politics and the game behind it. But it's hard to live with so much venom directed toward you, especially if you're a woman. We seem constitutionally more eager to make people like us, which makes politics a tough road to travel.

I got through the worst of it because my dad never let me lose focus. He was always there reminding me, "You're bigger than this, you're better than this, we're going to get through this, these people are just trying to bring you down. Keep it in perspective. There are bad people out there. They're going to try and come after good people making a difference and we're going to get them. Just think toward election day. They're trying to get you off focus. Don't let them." Those speeches kept me grounded, especially because I was still trying so hard to prove to my dad that I could stand on my own. "See, Dad, how am I doing? I'm doing okay, aren't I, Dad?"

Gradually, I began to have fun. So much of elections is posturing—throwing the other guy off balance, faking him out, feeding him misinformation. And, like my father, I relished a good win. During the primary fight, for example, we decided to demand copies of the petitions Tony Ruggiero had used to get on the ballot. We had no reason to believe we would find anything untoward. But we gave it a shot. That's the kind of legal game candidates play with one another. The problem was that we had to serve Ruggiero in person, and we knew he would do his best to avoid accepting the summons. The night he had to be served, I was at my headquarters with two advisers, racking my brain for a strategy, when Rosalie Flanagan entered decked out in the sexiest outfit we'd ever seen. Rosalie, who worked for my father, had been at a March of Dimes event and was wearing a flaming red dress with matching red shoes and stockings.

The minute we saw her, we knew our problem was solved. We tucked the summons into her waistband and sent Rosalie over to Ruggiero's house. She knocked on the door and, striking the least decorous pose she could muster, confronted Ruggiero's wife. "I have to see Tony right away," she said. "Tell him it's Rosalie from the Wayside, he'll know." Wayside was a bar. Ruggiero's wife smelled trouble, although she was way off base as to what kind. Tony finally came down in his skivvies, clearly nervous about the strange woman at the door. Before he could gather his wits about him, Rosalie yanked out the papers and served him. Our own lady of the night became the heroine of the campaign.

I won the primary handily and in the final weeks before the general election we were cooking like a well-oiled machine. Dozens of volunteers crowded my headquarters on Amboy Road. In the morning, old men would lick stamps while their wives served crumb buns. Mothers wheeling baby carriages stopped by to stuff envelopes. In the afternoon teenagers wearing our red T-shirts with black letters reading A NEW GENERATION OF LEADERSHIP would drop by after school. In the evening volunteers who had day jobs would work half the night, leaving with the plea, "Some of us do have jobs, after all." In the background, Cory Hart's "Never Surrender" played nonstop.

People raced around handing out boxes of sponges and ice scrapers with my name printed on them. The phones rang constantly with new poll numbers, demands from reporters for quotes, and new suggestions for strategy. In the midst of the chaos, Mama Sue would always show up to make sure I was okay, that I had eaten, that I had clean underwear.

By the time the election came, I was exhausted. I woke up the morning of the vote, thinking, whichever way it goes, at least it's over. All I wanted to do was to get through the day, win or lose, and get on a plane for Paris, which was exactly the plan. My friend Suzanne had a zillion frequent flier miles and had invited me to go to Europe with her for ten days. The plane couldn't leave soon enough. I spent the afternoon and evening huddled over in a corner on the floor, waiting. But as the polls closed and the counting began, the race got closer and closer. By the time the board of elections stopped counting, we were 101 votes apart, with eight hundred absentee ballots still outstanding. They locked the machines and scheduled a recount. I was numb.

We took off for the VFW hall where we'd scheduled the

victory celebration, which felt more like a wake. I was too battered to enjoy myself. The uncertainty was driving me crazy. I thought I should cancel my trip, but I knew no one would let me sit in on the recount, so what for? I took off for Europe vowing to forget about Staten Island, the City Council, and politics. I didn't, of course. I couldn't. I didn't know whether I would return to New York as a member of the City Council or as yet another unemployed twentysomething. I called in every night, praying for news.

Finally, I wound up staying at the flat of a friend in Paris, a tiny apartment without a shred of privacy. Since I had to call home in the middle of the French night, I'd taken the phone into the bathroom to avoid waking everyone else up. The night I received the news that I had won—by 161 votes out of forty thousand cast—I was hunched over in that bathroom, staring at an old cracked toilet.

My father had warned me that the press might show up at Kennedy Airport the night of my return, but I didn't even think about them when I climbed into my jeans, sweatshirt, and sneakers for the long flight home. Fortunately, what greeted me instead was three busloads of friends and supporters waiting to sweep me away for the celebration of the underdog. It was a far cry from the party at the VFW less than two weeks earlier. Five hundred people showed up at Montebianco, scores of whom were virtual strangers. A Dixieland band kept the tempo upbeat. But our core group needed a private moment, so we found an empty room, hauled in a boom box, and danced the night away to "Never Surrender."

◆

The celebration didn't last long. When I arrived at City Hall, I didn't even know where to go. I still thought the president of the City Council—a position that no longer exists—was elected by the council members, like the Speaker of the House, when, in fact, he or she was elected by the public. I'd met Mayor Koch a few times, but I didn't know who the other members were or what they looked like. And I couldn't even begin to decipher the tome that was the city's $30 billion budget.

All the while, no one was entirely sure how to treat me, since I was the only Republican in a group that had been entirely Democrat for three years. Theoretically, as the de facto minority leader I had the right to the minority leader's suite of offices. But that suite had been handed over to the Sergeant at Arms when the last Republican had been ousted, and there was a real question as to whether he would give it up for me. After the election results became official, the press asked the council spokesman, Joe Fitzpatrick, who was your classic old cigar-smoker, whether that office would become mine. "Give her that office?" he said. "Come on, she doesn't even know where the little girls' room is yet."

That was my welcome to City Hall.

I arrived in the City Council in the midst of one of those classic exercises in political jockeying that are endemic in America's big cities. Two of the powerhouses of Democratic politics were facing off in a contest for council majority leader, and each had pulled in the support an almost equal number of the party's bosses. Peter Vallone, a Queens politician, was backed by Donald Mannis, one of the old party clubhouse types, who later committed suicide. Sam Horowitz of Brooklyn was supported by Stanley Friedman, who wound up in jail for corruption. The Democrats were deadlocked, 17–17.

The race came down to a single vote, mine. The fact that I would swing the election was enough to make council members resent me all the more. The city's powerbrokers couldn't afford to indulge that distaste, however, so I was courted with respect by the famous and infamous of the city. Vallone probably would have been my natural choice because he was more conservative than Horowitz. But voting for him was particularly sweet because Horowitz's people hadn't known how to handle me. Shortly before the election, which was my first vote in the City Council, Meade Esposito, a quintessential old-style party boss from Brooklyn, called my dad's office to lobby him for my vote. I happened to be there. My father offered to put me on the phone. Esposito objected. "You talk to her, Guy. I can't talk to a young girl. Tell her what to do." When the election was held on January 8, 1986, his candidate lost by one vote.

If my first vote was an exercise in power, my second was an exercise in absurdity. After the election for the majority leader, I raised my hand and nominated myself as minority leader. There were, of course, no other nominations. Then I seconded my nomination. The chairman called for all Republicans to vote. I elected myself, then graciously accepted the position, thanking the Republican minority for their unanimous vote of confidence. "I can confidently predict one hundred percent attendance at all Republican caucuses," I declared. Then, unable to resist a slight jab at my colleagues, I pledged that while the Democrats might bicker, "the minority will always be united."

Although I had won that election fair and square, the Democrats still didn't take to the idea of giving a twenty-seven-year-old novice politician from Staten Island the traditional perks that belonged to the minority leader. They'd been running the City Council for what seemed like 150 years and working in the closets they called council offices in a building across the street from City Hall. Suddenly some kid from the smallest borough who ran around in tennis shoes was demanding a suite of offices overlooking the main marble staircase in City Hall itself, diagonally across from council chambers. Not just that, I was also demanding the extra salary ($20,000), extra staff money ($26,000), extra power (membership on every major council committee), the executive secretary, and car and driver that came with that job.

Carol Greitzer, who represented Greenwich Village and Chelsea, dismissed the idea out of hand. "Ms. Molinari seems like a pleasant enough young woman, but I can't see that she's made a major contribution to the council," she told the press. "So why is she entitled to an office in City Hall and her own car and driver?" Stanley Michels declared, "It's unnecessary. She should have to prove she needs it." And Ruth Messinger added, "I think it is not the best investment of the council's resources."

I couldn't blame Carol and the other members for resenting me. But Vallone owed me a favor, and I had learned enough from my father to know how to collect. I wound up with the office, the chauffeur, an ex-officio position on all council committees, and a vote on the Finance Committee, the Rules, Privileges and Elections Committee, and the Committee on Standards and Ethics. Not bad for me, and not bad for Staten Island, which had never had a council member in a position of that much power.

Once the immediate crises were over, I needed to get down to business fast, and I was lucky to have a competent staff to help me do so. Few people understand how critical the role of staff is to elected officials. They're the people voters talk to about their problems and complaints, so they can make or break you when you run for reelection. They schmooze with the staffs of other members and keep you up on the critical gossip. They do the background research on your bills, write your legislation, and help you find the votes. If you're new in office, you count on them to guide you through the Byzantine bureaucracies that inevitably tangle the unwary in knots.

Barbara Palumbo, who'd been working with my father for years, deserted him and came to work running my district office. My campaign manager, Michael, had promised to help me find a great legal counsel, and one Saturday morning he set up an appointment for me to meet a young guy from Staten Island who was just finishing law school. Fred Cerullo walked into my dad's district congressional office looking very Tom Selleck, very Magnum PI, with a mustache and a deep tan. Wearing a beige plaid wool suit, he was an unlikely counterpoint to me, in my jeans, sneakers, and jacket. I, at the age of twenty-seven, actually felt like the adult. Fred was just twenty-three. But we were an immediate team. Together we launched a Republican assault on New York City that landed me in Congress, and Fred in my council seat, and later in Mayor Rudy Giuliani's inner circle.

Then, of course, neither of us had a clue. We didn't know the names of the people on the council, so we'd sit in meetings and try to decide if that woman with the salt and pepper hair was Carol Greitzer or Carolyn Maloney. It was like casting a movie, trying to link people to what we thought they should look like. We'd sit around City Hall, trying to figure out how New York's government worked, which was really tough because most of the other council members didn't have all that much understanding of what was going on either.

When we began dealing with the city budget, we were utterly lost. There I was, about to start negotiating on all these fiscal issues, and I didn't know what B-100 meant. The formula said that in order to figure out what percentage of a given item was going to Staten Island, I should multiply and divide by numbers I couldn't even find. I went from member to member, begging for guidance. No one had a clue. Then I knocked on Ruth Messinger's door. Ruth, who lost to Giuliani in the 1997 mayoral election, was famous for being prepared. She was the type of politician who carried sheaves of paper with her and always seemed to be poring through yet another tome of regulations. The most liberal gadfly in a group of gadflies, she knew her stuff cold, and used her knowledge to trump the mayor on a daily basis. Ruth became my budget mentor, sitting next to me in meetings and coaching me through the process. It was a generous gesture, since she knew I wasn't going to use my knowledge to advance her agenda.

The City Council was a pretty wacky place. One bald council member from the Bronx would stagger into meetings with his arms overflowing with books and mail and brochures. He'd waddle over to a desk, plop himself down, and be covered with paper. At first I didn't understand why he was always so overloaded. Then I discovered that he came to City Hall only for council meetings, which were held once a month. That's what he gave his constituents for his $47,000 salary, and their votes.

No kidding. Another time, during a hearing on education, we were discussing a program that cost $10 million. One council member—Jay O'Donovan, my colleague from Staten Island—started ranting and hollering that only $6 million had been allocated, and where were we going to get the other $3 million. Fred and I sat there, looking at each other, trying not to break down laughing. The man simply couldn't add.

I thought the budget process was particularly bizarre, at least until I discovered that it wasn't all that different from the budget process in other legislative bodies. Everyone waits until the eleventh hour to hammer out a budget, both for the drama and in order to wear the other guys down. It always become a do-or-die situation, and those with the most stamina produced the most for their districts.

In New York City, the negotiating team consisted of representatives from each borough, the head of the Finance Committee, and the speaker, as well as the borough presidents. For the first three or four days of negotiations, the days are long and hard, but not ridiculous as the group pared the budget down to within sight of the revenues due to come in. Then, with millions more to cut and no more time to waste, everyone got serious, which meant that you were lucky if you found time to shower. Since the strategy was to wear the other members down until they collapsed, negotiations went on around the clock. You couldn't leave the room even if your bladder was in danger of bursting, because the second you did, someone would propose axing your favorite program. By the time you got back from the bathroom, it would be gone.

In the midst of the frenzy there were interminable waits while the mayor looked over our proposals, while the budget guys crunched the numbers, or the printers churned out copies of what we'd done. Only then could I catch a nap in my office chair or stretch out on the floor. One year, we were waiting for the printer about three A.M., and council members, staff assistants, and reporters gathered on the steps of City Hall, punchy and slaphappy. Someone had the bright idea that we should play touch football on the sidewalk in front of City Hall. I was crazed from lack of sleep, but not that crazy. Fred Cerullo, my legal counsel, was, however, and he managed to crack open his head during the game. No one was willing to take him to the hospital in the middle of budget negotiations, so the borough president of Staten Island, who didn't know squat about medicine but had patched up his sons frequently enough to know something about what he was doing, did a butterfly stitch on him in the majority leader's office.

Many of the wackiest moments were gifts from constituents. The first time I realized that the people who elected me could be as odd as the politicians I was working with was the day a woman called my district office and started screaming at Kathy Schweitzer about my absence from a City Council meeting. Kathy took a deep breath and explained that I had, in fact, been at that meeting. "Don't tell me that," the woman screeched. "I know she wasn't there. She was probably at one of her father's fund-raisers." Kathy tried again to explain that I had not missed the meeting, but the woman was too outraged to listen. Finally, Barbara got on the phone and asked the woman how she knew I hadn't been there. The woman replied haughtily that she'd been in the audience. Barbara proceeded to explain precisely where I'd been sitting. "Oh, you mean that little blond girl up there was Susan Molinari?" She harrumphed and hung up.

But my favorite constituents were those who wound up in my office because the door pronounced me to be minority leader. I'd never considered the implications until the phone rang one after-noon and a man demanded to talk to me about minority set-aside contracts. I was puzzled, almost confused. Then the second call came, from a teacher reporting an incident of racism. I still didn't get it. Finally, a man walked into the office and asked to file a discrimination complaint. One of my staff members politely asked him to explain the circumstances, and he launched into a long story about how he was living in a box. "Where is the box located?" my staffer continued, taking notes so that she could deal with the case. "In the Bronx," he responded. She explained that I represented Staten Island, not the Bronx, and referred him to the councilman who represented that district.

The man was not deterred. "I don't want to talk to my coun-cil member," he insisted. "This is a discrimination problem. I want to talk to the minority leader."

Aside from the weird and offbeat, what surprised me most about the City Council was the extraordinary collegiality extended to me by that gaggle of Democrats. Members who'd decried my extra perks wound up drinking coffee in my office, comparing notes, and working out cosponsorship of bills. Those who'd accused me of being anointed, not elected, were generous in recanting their skepticism. After I'd been on the council one year, Herb Berman of Brooklyn told the press, "I expected a female version of primogeni-ture, the right of the father to pass down the mantle of power. I thought she was here on her father's name. I thought I was sitting next to another political brat. But she is substantive. She's way ahead of the normal progress of a council member." Peter Vallone compared me to a young Geraldine Ferraro, adding, "She's ahead of where Geraldine was at her age."

Berman and Vallone couldn't have known how much those statements meant to me. Even though I'd resented the skepticism, and the hypocrisy of leveling it at me but not at the Kennedy offspring, for example, it had driven me to work harder and think deeper, to prove to everyone that I was more than my dad's daughter. When they started treating me like an adult, I knew I was succeeding.

I even managed to get along with Mayor Ed Koch, a New York original. He and my dad had a stormy history, both in public and private. But I liked Koch. He was respectful, always giving me credit for the work I had done, inviting me to the signing of bills I had cosponsored. I understood his shtick and was impressed that he seemed to be able to take it as well as dish it out. When he tried to place a large prison on Staten Island, we fought each other tooth and nail in the press, demeaning each other's motives, anticipating and blocking each other's strategies. Down and dirty, but never below the belt—and Ed Koch held no grudges.

I can't say the same for David Dinkins, who replaced Koch as the mayor in 1990. It's not just that Dinkins was too understated for me, as for most New Yorkers, or that he was too liberal for my tastes. He was incredibly confrontational, aloof to the point of dismissal, and strangely fastidious. When he rode in his car to a public event, he'd change into a baseball jacket to avoid getting wrinkled. He changed clothes completely, in his office or van, several times a day.

One day I just couldn't take the aloofness, the arrogance, anymore. We'd been locked away for two days, trying to hammer our the city budget. Dinkins, who was then borough president of Manhattan, had missed the entire first day. On the second, he sauntered in and started ranting because Peter Vallone was missing. Vallone, who'd worked the previous day, had left for a quick meeting, but that made no impact on Dinkins. Finally, I exploded. "We've been sitting here all day debating and negotiating this, and you walk in here late every time and expect us to start over again." Unlike Koch, Dinkins did hold grudges.

In between the meetings and hearings and public events, I tried to have a life. I lived in a small apartment near the New Dorp train station on the ground floor of a small complex that also housed a chiropodist. Reporters made fun of my place because it looked like a dorm room—a lumpy sofa, a faded reproduction of Monet's "Water Lilies," and photographs of me with Ronald Reagan and Al Pacino, two of my favorites. I simply don't care enough about my living space. I'd rather be out with friends than picking out new curtains.

I did, however, care about having a social life, and I wanted a boyfriend, which was not an easy accomplishment. I was too obsessed with garbage to be a very good date. Some guy would ask me out to dinner, and I'd spend three hours talking about primary, secondary, and tertiary sewage treatment, or the importance of a rising fecal count in our waters. I'd spot an open garbage truck while we were driving to the movies and insist that my date chase it so I could write down the license plate number. How many men understand when you say "Sorry, honey, I can't go out tonight because I have to wade out to the floating garbage barge from Islip, Long Island, to serve an injunction on the captain"?

Then I met John Lucchesi, who was a staple on the Republican scene in Staten Island, and thus at least moderately interested in my goings-on. We ran into each other at dozens of party functions and finally wound up going out for a drink or dinner, in groups or alone. Three years younger than me, he ran a limousine company with an office next door to my district headquarters. Gradually, he started popping in during the day, or coming by to kidnap me for lunch or coffee.

John made me laugh—and laughter wasn't all that common in the ponderous circles I was traveling in. He was totally irreverent, especially about the bloated egos who tend to be attracted to politics. At the Republican Christmas party he'd make scores of middle-aged men and women dance in a conga line. One night at a county Republican party, he passed around a salad bowl and roped everyone into wearing it as a hat. He'd sneak into my office when no one was around and disconnect all the phone lines or string all the paper clips together. Today it sounds silly, but in the midst of all that serious business, his refusal to take anything too seriously was a welcome antidote.

That levity became even more important when Mama Sue was diagnosed with breast cancer. My beautiful, strong grandmother, my best friend, was dying during my first years in the City Council, and John was there to help me through the hard times. During those final weeks, when her suffering became unbearable, her hospital room was my office. Even as she lay in a coma, I couldn't bring myself to leave her although the nurses warned me that patients often refuse to die if the people they love are in the room. But I simply couldn't let her die alone.

Then, one cold February night, I was about to leave the room to get some supper, when I heard her gasp. I couldn't stand to hear her suffer anymore. I leaned over her bed and gently gave her permission to give up. I've never been sure whether acts like that are for the living or the dying, but I needed to tell her, or perhaps myself, that I would be all right. I needed to promise her that someday I would have a little girl, that her name would be Susan, and that I would raise her to be just as beautiful and tough and loving as her namesake. She came out of her coma for a minute, opened her eyes, and looked at me. Then she was dead. When the nurses rushed in to try to revive her, I stopped them. It was time to let her go. I went home and fell apart. The best of me was her, and now I was all I had left.

I knew that I was shaky from her death when a few weeks later Barbara Palumbo and I drove past the corner of North Avenue and Railroad and I spotted an old woman just sitting there in the sun who reminded me of Mama Sue. I had to stop. "Buy me a beer?" she asked. I demurred, offering her water or a soda instead. "What about a jelly doughnut?" she countered. That was more my style, and I invited the woman, whose name was Theresa, to my office for lunch and doughnuts. We were sitting there eating and talking, when Theresa abruptly stopped mid-sentence and sat staring into space. I screamed. Barbara raced in and called 911. Theresa had had a stroke.

John stepped into the breach during this rough time, and it was inevitable that we would decide to get married. At the time, I convinced myself that he was my ideal man, but I think that I knew subconsciously from the start that we'd wind up apart. The day before our wedding on July 16, 1988, Barbara found me crying on the porch behind my office. She took me for a ride and reminded me that I could call off the wedding, that we could drive away into the sunset in a sort of pre–*Thelma & Louise* fantasy. But the next day I donned my white gown and walked down the aisle of the chapel at Fort Wadsworth on my father's arm. As we approached the altar, he paused for a moment, but it was not to take a last look at his baby. Bob and Elizabeth Dole were seated on the aisle, and he couldn't resist being Guy Molinari for the one moment it took to greet them.

Everyone expected me to have a "real" wedding—white gown, big reception, waiters lined up wearing white gloves. That's hardly my style, so I opted—predictably—for a compromise. The wedding was a formal Mass, followed by a formal cocktail reception where everyone could feel elegant. But I'd told the guests to bring comfortable clothes for the party afterward. I changed into a white denim dress and hightops a florist friend had gussied up with lace, and we spent the afternoon playing volleyball and softball and dancing to a rock-a-billy band. My kind of wedding!

Even as I was getting my personal life in order, or at least trying to, I threw myself into my job, intent on establishing my reputation as hardworking, innovative, and serious. During my first year or so on the council, I concentrated on the issues I knew were most important to my constituents, most of which were environmental. People have always been surprised that a Republican

57

would be "environmentally sensitive," as if only Democrats could possibly care about the quality of the air. Anyway, when you represent a district that is New York City's garbage dump, you wise up fast. My first piece of legislation was an asbestos control law designed to stop midnight dumping of hazardous materials by mandating a careful tracking system. It didn't set the world on fire, but it was the kind of policy that would protect ordinary people.

I was barely past my asbestos phase when the garbage barge began its journey from Islip, Long Island, looking for somewhere to dump 3,100 tons of trash. Six states and three countries denied it entry, and I was certain that someone would come up with the bright idea of dumping it in Fresh Kills, our already overburdened landfill. As the barge wended its way back into New York waters, I launched a preemptive strike by asking a judge for a restraining order to block the dumping of the trash on Staten Island. At two A.M. I went out to the off-loading area at the dump and handed the order to the night-shift workers.

Keeping the barge trash out of Fresh Kills felt like a victory, but I had a much bigger goal: the closing of the dump. I forced the council's Environmental Protection Committee to come out for a one-day tour so members could get at least one whiff of what they were doing to our community. I asked my constituents to keep track of health problems that might be related to the dump and laid the information on the desks of the powers that were. When none of that worked, I devised a new approach to convincing city officials of the seriousness of the problem. I set up a special program in my district office for taxpayers who wanted to protest their house assessments by claiming their property values were decreased by their proximity to Fresh Kills. I hoped that the specter of losing tax dollars might motivate Koch and the council to take the complaints of Staten Islanders seriously. It did not.

The environmental issues never stopped. I fought a two-year battle for a medical waste bill that would increase the penalties for illegal dumping and require all generators and transporters of hospital waste to track the refuse. The other council members were skeptical at first, refusing to believe that hospital waste wasn't being disposed of properly. They clearly had never been to South Beach, where needles were constantly washing up on the sand. The morning of my wedding, during a jog on the beach with my father, I decided to start collecting samples. Then I sent out two of my staffers with gloves and plastic bags, so I could wave them before my skeptical colleagues.

In 1989 I helped kill a proposal for a new toxic waste incinerator in Perth Amboy, New Jersey, just across Arthur Kill from Staten Island, and a city plan to dump future incinerator ash— which contains lead, cadmium, and volatile organic compounds— in Fresh Kills. We'd barely fought off those disasters, when a company began negotiating for a hazardous waste incinerator in Linden, New Jersey, which would burn 150 tons of hazardous waste daily just one-fifth of a mile, and upwind, of our borough. Then, on January 2, 1990, a half million gallons of oil spilled into Arthur Kill; our own Exxon oil spill.

I wasn't focused exclusively on Staten Island's environment. One of my proudest accomplishments was my cosponsorship of the city's recycling law, which required the city to recycle twenty-five percent of its trash within five years. It's hard to believe now that recycling has become common practice, but in those days the opposition was fierce. Too expensive, unnecessary, opponents insisted. So with Sheldon Leffler of Queens and Ruth Messinger of the Upper West Side of Manhattan, I organized a recycling demonstration for September 19, 1988. One of my constituents showed up chained to a trash can to make the point that Staten Island was a prisoner of the city's dump. My staffer Kathy arrived dressed in garbage—a shirt and pants decorated with half-eaten sandwiches, orange peels, and used bags. I wore the matching hat.

I wasn't a one-note council member and spent as much time

on transportation as I did on the environment. For years Staten Islanders had been subsidizing the subway system that links all the other boroughs by paying high tolls for the bridges that were our primary link with the outside world. Lower tolls, one-way tolls, and consultation with the public before toll increases seemed to be entirely reasonable demands, but the Triborough Bridge and Tunnel Authority did not agree. When lobbying and pleading didn't work, we decided to find a statute that would become our leverage.

My dad, who was still in Congress, managed to attach a rider to an appropriations bill mandating the one-way toll. But that didn't stop the TBTA from raising it from $4 to $5. We went back into court, arguing that the increase, which was designed to subsidize mass transit in other boroughs, was highway robbery that violated the Federal Interstate Highway Act and Port Authority governing restrictions.

It wasn't just the TBTA. The Port Authority, which controlled the bridges between Staten Island and New Jersey, was no more responsive. Their Christmas present to Islanders was a $1 increase in bridge tolls. We staved off that hike, but I knew the fight wasn't over. Buried in the Port Authority's capital improvement plan I found a notation showing a projected increase of $2 by 1993 to pay for improvements at the city's airports, which, of course, are not even on Staten Island.

Does this make the job sound boring and tedious? It's not. Sewers and tolls are precisely what people need their politicians to worry about. If yours don't, vote 'em out.

During my first months and years on the council, the growing problem of the homeless was a priority in New York City, and in order to bone up on the crisis, I volunteered at Project Hospitality, a private shelter on Staten Island, working and sleeping there to find out what the homeless wanted and needed. I quickly concluded that what they did not need, and what Mayor Ed Koch was giving them, was to be warehoused at armories and welfare hotels.

I believed that a better solution would be to house people in small shelters scattered around the city. The homeless would have housing that actually resembled a home, and no single neighborhood would be overtaxed.

That position was one of dozens that led to the accusation that I was "flaunting" my conservative politics, although I never understood why finding a better solution for dealing with the homeless meant that I was conservative. It is true, nonetheless, that I dissented regularly from knee-jerk liberal posturing or easy solutions to complicated problems. For example, the City Council was inordinately fond of passing meaningless resolutions about world affairs, and I thought it had enough work at home. So whether it was honoring Daniel Ortega of Nicaragua, or congratulating Cory Aquino on her election to the presidency of the Philippines, I dissented, usually alone, and was branded a heartless Fascist.

I fought every tax increase I could, convinced that they were making life impossible for the kind of middle-class New Yorkers I represented. Koch and I went head to head when he proposed coping with the budget shortfall by increasing taxes on one- and two-family homes, a classic "soak the rich" scheme. On Staten Island, most private-home owners aren't the kind of fat cats who have brownstones on the East Side of Manhattan—the kind of people most voters are all too happy too soak. They are blue-collar workers and plumbers and auto mechanics, hardly rich people, and they would have borne the burden of the tax shift.

Sometimes people didn't know what to make of the stands I took, since they didn't fall into the easy liberal-conservative categories everyone seemed to crave. During my first year on the council, the members voted on a piece of legislation prohibiting discrimination against people with children when they are trying to rent or buy. I opposed it because I thought, and think, that senior citizens should have the right to live in buildings of their own. The liberals treated me like an antikid monster, but they seemed equally indifferent to the needs of retirees who wanted the quiet and comfort that's possible only without teenagers around.

For every allegedly right-wing stance I took, I worked with liberal council members on a dozen bills. Herb Berman and I cosponsored legislation to protect homeowners from unscrupulous builders—a phrase that seemed redundant in New York in that era. One major area of corruption was builders' habit of doing just enough work to get a temporary certificate of occupancy, then disappearing, leaving homeowners with half-finished houses. Our bill mandated that no temporary CO be issued until the builder showed proof that he had posted a bond guaranteeing completion of the work.

In 1989 I started working with Carolyn Maloney on child care. Although we were ideologically about as far apart as two human beings can be, we agreed that the city desperately needed to encourage the development of more high-quality facilities for the young children of working parents. So we cosponsored legislation giving building owners tax exemptions if they set aside space for child care facilities, giving business tax credits to employers who reimbursed workers for child care expenses, and making available space in city-owned buildings for day care centers that served a population that included at least fifty percent city employees. In my mind, those were classic Republican solutions to the problem. Carolyn and I broke ranks on only one of her proposals, a variation of a measure adopted in San Francisco that required developers to set aside a certain percentage of their commercial space for day care centers.

There was one issue I shied away from during my tenure in City Hall, and it taught me a valuable lesson. Shortly after I took office, we began arranging the city's school board election. There were a dozen things I objected to about the antiquated electoral system the city used, but one seemingly tiny matter stuck in my craw. The ballot instructions about write-ins repeatedly referred to the potential candidate as "he." Now, I'm not one of those women who worries a lot about every misplaced he or chairman or congressman. But so much of voting is subliminal that a "he" or "him" might, in fact, influence voters' thinking.

I was surprised that none of the prominent liberal women on the council noticed the language, and I wanted to complain to the Board of Elections and send out a press release. But when I mentioned the idea to my handlers, they pitched a fit. I'll never forget it. We were having lunch in a Chinese restaurant, and they went ballistic. "Susan, Susan, don't let the first issue out of the box you deal with be a women's issue. Don't let yourself get identified that way. Don't become the woman candidate." I admit—with shame—that I folded, and I've been kicking myself ever since. I spent more than a year shying away from women's issues because of that advice, and dozens of other women in politics have done, and continue to do, the exact same thing. Somehow you let yourself be convinced that you shouldn't work on the very issues that voters most need women in politics to care about because the men won't touch them. It's not just language. It's child care and abortion and violence-against-women programs and child abuse. And too many women, myself included, get scared away from them by handlers who don't have a clue.

Budgets and bridge battles and toxic waste dumps, Emergency Medical Services funding, library hours, street repair, senior citizens' programs and bus depots sound like grinding work, and it is. But we found ways to make it fun. One time the Environmental Protection Committee was holding hearings about an idea lofted by local fisherman for "blowing up" Staten Island waters to harvest our clams and transplant them into the cleaner waters off Long Island. Fishermen on Staten Island objected because they were sure all the fish would be blown out of the water in the process. To drive home the point about the dangers to our fish, I sent Barbara to Fulton Fish Market to buy a dead fish to use as a prop during the session. The problem was that Fulton Street was a wholesale market, so Barbara didn't have much luck when she walked in trying to buy a single fish and couldn't even tell them what kind. Barbara, however, doesn't take no for an answer. She wheedled and insisted until someone took pity on her and handed her a fish, which she brought back to City Hall, where it became the centerpiece of my testimony. By the time we were done, of course, the council chamber was reeking as badly as the fish—which didn't prevent a homeless man from asking if he could have it.

I admit that I was annoyed, though, that my successes somehow were overshadowed by the continuing preoccupation, obsession, really, with my clothes and my demeanor. The press printed dozens of stories about how I'd show up in the office in jeans, about my gum chewing and boots. Confusing form with content, they insisted this was a sign of lack of seriousness of purpose. Women were supposed to be as dour as Ruth Messinger, whose idea of fun seems to be reading the city budget, or as dry as Carol Greitzer, who once put me to sleep during a discussion of noise abatement.

Some of my constituents were equally outraged by my "look." Women would come up to me on the street and suggest that I could use a touch more makeup. Old men would opine that I should wear heels more often. It got exceedingly tiresome. It was New York, and I was twenty-seven years old. I was never informal in committee meetings, when I was voting, or when I went out to make presentations. I figured that what I wore the rest of the time was nobody's business. If the voters didn't like it, or didn't take me seriously, they'd vote me out of office. If the press didn't like it, well, the press doesn't vote.

Mostly, I had no reason to complain, either about my constituents or the press. When I was done fighting with a dozen bureaucrats, the mayor and three or four newspapers, I would go into a senior citizens' center, or a shopping center, or a restaurant, and people would stop to thank me. Especially when you're still in your twenties, the notion you are doing something that directly helps your neighbors is a heady feeling. When you protect senior citizen meals or get a new school open or help a neighborhood stay safe because you keep a jail out, you can go to bed feeling that you've made some contribution to the quality of life in your community. It doesn't get much better than that.

And I learned that the reporters were just doing their jobs, and a twenty-seven-year-old councilwoman, the youngest in that body's history, was news. Just after I took my seat, the *Daily News* ran a picture of me hunkering on my desk in a long dress and boots on the cover of their Sunday magazine. The story that followed began with the reporter entering my suite of offices and finding a petite young woman wearing pink Cyndi Lauper eye shadow behind the receptionist's desk. He figured she was the secretary. Of course, that secretary was me. That was perfectly fair. It was true, and in a universe of politicians who are graying and serious, it might actually have been news.

Even when I probably should have been steamed by press stories, I often found it hard to work up the appropriate anger. One time a local magazine reported that a member of my staff had called Bob Gigante "a piece of shit," which was hardly a big piece of news because he and I were engaged in a pretty tough race for Congress. The reporter had been a little unfair in recording the comment since it was made in an informal conversation, while he was sitting in my office waiting for an interview with me. Maybe I should have complained. But the comment was so funny, such an accurate reflection of our private conversations, I couldn't find room for anything more than hysterical laughter.

◆

In the end, what I learned on the council was that I didn't have to become someone else's idea of a politician in order to succeed. I had inherited from Mama Sue an allergy to pretense, a sort of "to-hell-with-them-if-they-can't-take-a-joke" attitude. And feminism had taught me not to let anyone, male or female, push me around. That's the antithesis of what politicians, and most women, are supposed to do, at least according to conventional wisdom. But I don't find all that much wisdom in convention, and I discovered that I could triumph politically while breaking the rules.

In fact, many of the memories I most cherish of my life in politics have to do with moments when I flaunted the fact that I was young and unwilling to play the game. I still chuckle at the shock my colleagues expressed the day my driver was sick, and my temporary driver got a flat tire on the Brooklyn-Queens Expressway. The man started to call for help, and I just couldn't believe that he'd waste our time that way. I got out of the car, opened the trunk, and proceeded to teach him how to change the tire on the car. Why should this be shocking behavior? This is not the nineteenth century, after all. And I was a young woman in a hurry.

Chapter Three

Taking the Torch

Thanksgiving 1989, and I was inching toward adulthood. That's a common problem with my generation, the first to include a sizable number of people who never had to work as children, who were financed by their parents in a prolonged adolescence. By the time we came along, the mile markers that had moored our parents to a carefully constructed road to adulthood had become overgrown and invisible. Only a few milestones—marriage, first professional job, childbirth—were left. I had finally reached at least the first two of them, and I was ready to give thanks. I loved my job, had been reelected with seventy-four percent of the vote, and John and I were comfortably settled into our home. I actually seemed to be getting it together to be an adult. Then my father threw a monkey wrench into it all by announcing that he was considering giving up the congressional seat he'd held for almost a decade.

I knew he was restless in Congress. He'd lost his place on a key subcommittee in a fight with Newt Gingrich and was disillusioned with the scene in Washington. Fine, I said. Quit Congress, come home, and relax. Fat chance. Not only did he not intend to relax—which was hardly surprising since his notion of relaxation is to map out the next century of Staten Island politics—he intended to run for borough president of Staten Island.

Borough president? Who'd want such a thankless job? With the Democrats who ran City Hall convinced that the Island was an enclave of unrepentant Archie Bunkers they could well ignore, that job would be nothing but a nightmare, especially for a Republican. But my dad reinvented, or at least reclaimed, the borough presidency. His grand plan was that Rudy Giuliani, who was then the leading federal prosecutor in New York, would become the Republican mayor of New York, and that we would become borough president. With a friendly Republican in Manhattan, he believed that job could actually be fun.

The only good thing about that plan was that he never announced it publicly. His sanity would have been seriously questioned had he done so. The scheme made no sense unless Rudy could capture the mayoralty, and no Republican had been mayor of New York—a city where voters are registered five to one in favor of the Democrats—for a generation. Even worse, he planned to leave Congress and capture the borough presidency before that mayoral election, before we even knew whether Rudy would be elected. How could he give up his seat in the United States Congress for some pie-in-the-sky dream? One member of his staff was so incensed that he refused to help my dad write the announcement that he was going to run.

Nevertheless, he called a press conference, and when all the relevant parties showed up at the boardwalk on South Beach, he delivered the news. I'm not sure how many people believed that he was serious about the run, since it seemed so ridiculous. Ed Koch was quoted as saying "Guy Molinari doesn't have the guts to run for borough president." Once that came out, there was no possibility that my father would back down.

Most observers assumed he was giving up his seat to make way for me and just didn't want to make that admission. Those observers obviously didn't know my father. He loves and encourages me, but he is way too competitive, and way too respectful of my abilities, to do something like that.

(Before I continue with me, I should jump ahead and note that he won the borough presidency, which threw him into political exile while David Dinkins was mayor. But just as he envisioned, Rudy beat Dinkins in 1993, Staten Island suddenly had the chance to get on the city's map—and my dad was there, in his grand old office across from the ferry terminal, to make it happen. It was a classic sign of my father's political astuteness.)

Since I'm my dad's daughter and grew up in politics the way some showbiz kids grew up in vaudeville, it was inevitable that I would make a run for his seat in the special election called for March 1990. If you're raised in that world, you know that you can't stand still. The New York City Council might sound important to New Yorkers, but to politicians it is the ground floor of a skyscraper, and I was just thirty-one years old.

No one was surprised at my decision, of course, but everyone was nonetheless absurdly nervous when I made my formal announcement, a road show scheduled to begin on Staten Island, where Rudy Giuliani would stand at my side, continue on to the steps of City Hall, where the party's luminaries would meet me, and end in Brooklyn, the other part of my congressional district. Charlie Degliomini, who was a friend of my husband's, walked into the room, where I was getting ready to meet the press, and freaked out at my outfit. I had on a multicolored suit with a black turtleneck. It might not have been the perfect outfit, but was certainly sufficient, and at that point, my wardrobe was hardly varied.

"I can't believe you wore black!" Charlie screamed at me. I tried to calm him down. "Please, I'm announcing for Congress, who's gonna care what I'm wearing as long as I'm clean?" But when tensions get high—whether it's a convention speech or an announcement or the night before your big parade—your handlers and the other people around you feed off drama. They moan when there's even a tiny mistake in the campaign and blow it out of proportion instead of trying to buck up the candidate. They want to mourn and go out and pound down Scotches. Charlie was so caught up in that melodrama, in the notion that black would show up terrible on television and ruin all my press shots, there was no stopping him.

I should probably digress to acknowledge that I know that image is not irrelevant. That's why men now worry about their makeup, about their shirts and ties and the way their jackets hang. When people first meet you, all other things being equal, they look for emotional symbols to direct them, and clothes are powerful emotional symbols. That doesn't mean that if Bill Clinton showed up tomorrow with dirty shoes that it would make much impact. People already know what they feel about him. But if the first-time voters had seen him wearing dirty shoes, they might well have dismissed him as a yahoo they couldn't trust. So it's a question of getting to the point where you are past such judgments.

The congressional race was my first campaign that demanded serious money, which was enough to make my stomach turn. My father had never raised money aggressively—he never had to—and

in my 1989 race for reelection to the City Council, I spent just over
$70,000 that my handlers collected almost without any involvement
on my part. Suddenly, I needed money, real money, and I knew I
was incapable of asking for it. That's when Julie Wadler saved my
life.

Julie was even more of a kid than I was, but my father had
met her when they worked together on the Bush campaign in New
York and had brought her to Staten Island to raise money for his
race for the borough presidency. He didn't just bring her to Staten
Island, in fact, but to my house, since Julie needed a place to stay.
She showed up on my doorstep one afternoon just as John and I
were about to leave for Chincoteague on vacation. I handed her the
keys to the house, the title to my old broken-down station wagon,
and the leash for my dog. That was typical in a household that had
become a sort of home for wayward political operatives.

Julie was my ideal alter ego. As a politician, I had to watch
every word I uttered; Julie let loose with whatever was on her, and
usually my, mind. She always seemed tough and secure, which kept
me balanced, since I always felt terrified. She thought of me in
precisely the same way, which, I guess, is what female friendships
are about.

Julie's job wasn't all that difficult. By the time I ran for Congress, I had a cadre of firm supporters, which included my old
acquaintance Bill Paxon, who helped organize a Washington fund-
raiser for me. I attracted some outside money from groups eager to
see my dad's seat stay in Republican hands. We pulled in money
from people willing to give a boost to Guy Molinari's daughter and,
ironically, from others who were thrilled to see him depart. He was
no friend of the pro-choice movement, for example, and they were
all too happy to help out the new, pro-choice Molinari.

I opened my campaign headquarters in January 1990, a little
more than two months before the election, and immediately was hit
by court challenges. While the Staten Island party had endorsed my

candidacy at a special convention, the Brooklyn party chair had opted to give me the nomination without that formality. Robert DiCarlo, the head of a Brooklyn Republican club, was angry at that decision, and filed suit. The suit he filed was a power play. He knew that the law didn't demand a convention. But he couldn't resist the kind of antics that adult male politicians play to replace hide-and-seek.

Robert Gigante, my Democratic opponent, turned DiCarlo's action into a squeeze play when he filed a complaint with the Board of Elections, and then with the state Supreme Court, asserting that I should be erased from the ballot because the state Republican bylaws governing the selection of party candidates in special elections had not been attached to my application. He knew damned well that the bylaws were on file in Albany, and he could get a copy with a single phone call. He also knew that the Court of Appeals would throw his case out. But he was playing a time-honored game: trying to distract me and throw me off balance.

With the legal problems and just two months to the election, the activity was frantic. Some of my old volunteers reappeared and started ordering T-shirts and lapel pins, hats and ice scrapers (which was lucky, since it snowed like crazy the week before the election). My father's supporters and my friends from my council work joined them for mailings and brainstorming. High school and college kids showed up, volunteering to do anything because I was young. And people just seemed to wander in off the street. It was a real collection of characters that became an instant and riotous team. Our house became into a dormitory where half the campaign staff lived at any given moment. White cartons with Chinese food—and empty white cartons that had been filled with Chinese food three days earlier—were scattered all over the living room. Rental movies were stacked on the VCR. The telephone was constantly ringing. Someone always seemed to be awake.

Everyone knew that the stakes were high—for me, for my

father, and for both political parties. Washington political types had declared the race a test of Republican strength, and Gigante, a young attorney, was a strong opponent because the district voter registration was two to one in favor of the Democrats. Furthermore, Gigante told the press he expected to spend $400,000, and we assumed he'd bring in Governor Mario Cuomo and a host of Democratic luminaries to buttress his efforts. So angst was the glue that held us together, angst and a determination to grind him into the dust.

We matched him dollar for dollar, luminary for luminary. The race was the most expensive campaign in the history of the district, $708,170, and just over half of that amount was mine. Gigante lined up money and support from labor unions and liberal PACs. I pulled in the help of the Women's Campaign Fund and endorsements from six law enforcement groups. Cuomo did appear on Gigante's behalf, but President George Bush came to town on mine, the first time a president had visited Staten Island since a jaunt by LBJ in 1966.

I knew the Bushes because my father had been a member of Bush's core group of supporters in the House and spent months working on his presidential campaign. When I was thinking about running for Congress, I'd paid him a courtesy call in the White House and received the full encouragement I'd hoped for. That meeting was my first glimpse of Bush's persona as a dog fanatic, a trait I shared with him. As I entered the Oval Office, I almost tripped over a tennis ball belonging to his dog, Ranger—who's gotten much less publicity than Barbara's dog, Millie. I had to move a rawhide bone out of the way to sit on the couch. He was my kind of guy.

The day of the campaign luncheon the president was due to attend, he flew into a small airport in New Jersey, and I drove out to meet him. When he, Lee Atwater, and I boarded the presidential helicopter for the quick flight to Staten Island, I knew I had moved up in the world. It was enormous, the size of an airplane, fitted to a level of comfort I'd never seen before. Bush was wildly popular on Staten Island at that moment, and children lined the streets between the landing field and the Shalimar, where the luncheon was to be held, cheering and shouting for the president. At the event, the president delivered a short speech about me. "I know Susan Molinari's smart," he said. "I know she'll be effective. And I can promise one more thing: She'll have a friend in the White House." It was quite a moment.

As the race proceeded, Gigante harped on a single theme in his campaign that drove me to distraction. Over and over again, at public meetings, on television, in the middle of parades, he dwelled on the fact that he was a "family man" and I had no kids. All I had was my membership in the dynasty, he said, making it sound as if being a Molinari was akin to being part of Joan Collins's menagerie. For weeks I threatened to respond. I longed to snap back, "At least we're not the Brady bunch," which seemed right on target since he never went anywhere without dragging along his wife and children. My campaign advisers begged me to bite my tongue. But one night my teeth gave out. When Gigante repeated his tired old line yet again, that response just slipped out. The audience laughed. He never mentioned my lack of children, or my dynasty, again.

Staten Island hadn't had a hyped-up, all-out congressional election for years, and we almost drowned in our own adrenaline. By the end of the campaign I was too giddy to be responsible for my own actions. I knew things were serious when I began having a dream about jumping off the Verrazano-Narrows Bridge. I wasn't trying to kill myself. In my fantasy, when I hit the water, I found blessed peace and quiet.

After weeks without sleep, caught up in the self-induced hysteria that is a campaign, I reached my nadir just twenty-four hours before my debate with Gigante. Julie and I were scheduled to take a quick trip to Washington for a fund-raising breakfast sponsored by the Chamber of Commerce, and organized by Vin Weber, who'd worked with my father on the 1988 Bush campaign. Frankly, the last thing I wanted to do the day before the debate was to drag my ass to Washington. But that's what I'd signed up for when I'd announced my candidacy.

The weather was miserable. It had been raining all day, and by the time we were ready to leave for the airport, it was closed. Julie, who's rarely the perky partner in our friendship, booked us on the Metroliner, and tried to cheer me up by chattering on about how great Amtrak was, as if we'd never been on a train before. I was not amused. I became even less so when the woman in front of us sprayed her seat with Lysol, which left us gasping. Then two guys we'd bumped into in the parking lot appeared in our car, clearly on the make. "So, what do you two do for a living?" they asked in a tone that suggested that they believed they'd invented a clever, original line. "Garbage," Julie responded flatly. "Public relations," I answered simultaneously. We looked at each other quizzically. "We do PR for garbage." Julie then launched into what became a two-hour discussion of garbage export, and there was no way I could resist the game.

By the time we arrived in D.C. at one A.M., my mood was considerably better, but I was reeling from exhaustion and a long line of people were lined up waiting for cabs. We wound up sharing a taxi with a gay couple who were fighting like cats and dogs, screaming and smacking each other over the backseat of the car. Since they insisted on being dropped off first, what should have been a thirty-minute drive took close to an hour. By the time we got to Julie's, it wasn't far from dawn. She had no blinds, so we couldn't sleep. All I could do was stagger around hoping that I wouldn't make a fool of myself at the breakfast, and that I would get back to New York with enough sanity left to debate my opponent.

For the most part, that campaign was remarkably clean and

civilized, although a group of Catholic priests did buy an antiabortion ad in the local paper that was effectively an endorsement of my Right to Life party challenger. But by then, antiabortion activists hardly gave me pause. The only dirtiness I confronted was the work of a single reporter, the kind who gives the rest of the press a bad name. She should never have accepted the assignment to cover my campaign since she was living with a man who worked as a paid communications consultant for Gigante. But that didn't stop her or her editors (no bias in journalism there!). Maybe it even egged her on. She followed me everywhere. She rifled through my car phone messages looking for dirt on me. When the police endorsed me, she showed up and grilled them about why they were supporting someone who had voted against the City Council assault weapons ban resolution.

She lambasted me for voting against the perennial nonbinding resolutions council members loved that urged African countries to stop torturing people, or Congress to ban nuclear weapons. I felt we had big enough problems in the city that we shouldn't spend our time telling Congress or the government of some other nation what to do. And I wasn't about to support resolutions that always seemed to include some phrase like "whereas Ronald Reagan is the worst president in the world." But that made those votes sound like I was a reincarnation of Attila the Hun.

Toward the end of the campaign she wrote a story that suggested that my husband, John, had used my father's position to secure contracts for a security firm where he was operations director from 1986 to 1989. There was no truth to the accusation, but it was juicy enough to occupy two full pages of the paper two days before my election. It was also illustrated with our wedding picture.

The piece ran on St. Patrick's Day, and when I arrived at campaign headquarters to get ready for the local parade, gloom and doom pervaded the place like a thick fog. I had just rolled out of bed and hadn't seen the paper yet, so I had no idea why everyone was acting as if we were getting ready for a wake. When I saw the article, I fell apart. There we were, two days before the election, and the parade was an enormous event. I went into one of the offices and lost it. I can handle attacks on myself; but attacks on the people I love are something else. Finally, my dad came in. "You will not do this," he said firmly. "You will walk in that parade. You will smile and give interviews. You are Susan Molinari and have nothing to be ashamed of." I dried my tears and went to the parade as if nothing had happened. Never let the suckers know that they have hurt you. That mantra has gotten me through even the worst of times.

◆

Election night was a glorious moment of revenge against the naysayers. I crushed Gigante almost two to one, sixty percent to thirty-four percent, in a district that had twice as many registered Democrats as Republicans. By ten P.M. the results seemed firm. I had received a congratulatory telegram from President Bush and was ready to celebrate. We left campaign headquarters and headed over to the Shalimar, a huge banquet facility we'd reserved for the evening. At that point we were all being very mature, very serious, because the press was following us. I went in with my father, my husband, and scores of friends and volunteers, made my victory speech, and offered the obligatory interviews to the media.

Then we waited impatiently for the outsiders to depart. Once the coast was clear, and only the core group remained, we cranked up "Love Shack," our campaign theme song, and danced on the tables. Every once in a while one of the policemen who was outside would peek in. The expression on their faces said it all: "What the hell is going on? The new congresswoman is dancing on a table." Ah, victory is sweet!

One week later, my father and I walked onto the floor of the House for the passing of the torch. Congress. Dozens of friends and supporters had come down for the occasion, and they packed the House gallery for my swearing-in. As we entered the chamber, dozens of old friends of my father's, members of the New York delegation, and women from both sides of the aisle celebrating the arrival of yet another female member surrounded us. John led the cheering section in the gallery, as Tom Foley, the Speaker of the House, moved me to the front of the room and swore me in. I looked at my dad, who stood next to me, both of us shivering with pride.

I'd been hanging around the House of Representatives for the ten years that my father had served in Washington. I knew the members, the back halls, the traps and traditions that governed that body. I thought that I was beyond awe. But when I took the well to thank Foley—which, in Housespeak, means moving into position to make a speech—I was dumbstruck. My father's friends, men who had patted me on the head and indulged me as a teenager, were suddenly my peers. The business of the House, the business of the nation, was suddenly my responsibility.

After my first mini-speech, I raced off to my first congressional press conference, although my dad managed to siphon off most of the media. Competition for media attention was already a tradition between us, and he got plenty that day complaining about my crazy sneakers, unconventional coats, and "superior jogging prowess." Then it was off to work as a member of Congress. While I was on the floor voting, my friends and supporters jammed into my new office, carted chairs out onto the terrace, and brought in pizzas and beer. When I came back, they were ready to party. Members flooded in from all over Capitol Hill to join us, including Bill Paxon, whom I'd seen only once since our first meeting. The next thing I knew, Dad and Bill were chatting in a corner while the junior member of the House was dancing with her friend Julie and the rest of our friends were spilling out onto the corridor on the seventh floor of the Longworth House Office Building.

We had no choice, really, since my new suite of offices wasn't big enough to hold the crowd. That's not a testament to the number of friends but to the size of my office. Congressional offices are assigned by a rigid system of seniority, and there are few issues about which members are more serious than where they hold court. Every two years a lottery is held for open offices, and woe be the member who tries to jump rank.

The pinnacle of achievement is a suite in the Rayburn Building, a sprawling marble monstrosity where some offices have private kitchens and showers. The Rayburn not only offers luxury, but convenience, since it is the only House office building with a working subway system, good elevators, and air-conditioning that doesn't cut out regularly during Washington's notoriously torrid summers. Since it's also where most of the major committee hearings are held, members with offices there don't have to spend their days sprinting across Independence Avenue, praying that they'll make committee meetings, and even floor votes, on time.

Junior members wind up in the older Longworth or Cannon Office Buildings, usually in airless cubbyholes in the basement or the unreachable attics. The top floor of Longworth was where I landed after my dad's office went up for grabs and everyone else played musical chairs with more livable space. I was lucky that by then I'd become a regular jogger, because the elevators in Longworth are so finicky that members whose physiques demand mechanical assistance often don't arrive on the House floor in time to vote. I'm not much concerned with status or luxury, but the office suite assigned to me was so tiny that two of the five members of my staff had work out of closets in other parts of the building, which was hardly an efficient way to run a congressional district. The only up side was that we had a view of the Potomac River and the Washington Monument—even if it took a little neck-craning to enjoy it.

The euphoria of my victory couldn't last, of course. I had just won an election, but the next one was only eight months off. I hadn't been in office one week before Ron Brown, the chairman of the Democratic National Committee, declared me beatable because I had no experience. I was steamed. No experience? I had four years on the City Council, which was four years more than his party's candidate in the special election had served in elected office. The declaration brought me back down to earth. Not only did I have a job to do; I had an election campaign to launch.

Then, two weeks later, I was ready to deliver my first floor speech, a speech about the navy's Staten Island home port, which I believed was critical for the local economy. I donned a pair of black silk pants, threw on a black and white silk jacket, and rose to deliver my remarks. Not bad, I thought as I left the floor and returned to my office. When I walked through the door, everyone was in an uproar. The *Daily News* had called. The *New York Post*. The Associated Press, *People* magazine, even Regis and Kathie Lee. Wow, I thought, that speech must have been something. That was a fantasy. Nobody cared what I had said about the home port. They were calling because I had become the first woman to wear pants on the floor of the House of Representatives.

My outfit that day was not a political statement. I knew that I was breaking with tradition, but I wasn't acting on principle. I just hate pantyhose. They're itchy and sticky and uncomfortable, as women readers know, and men should. But my intentions were irrelevant. My pants became big news.

Everyone was up in arms because I had allegedly violated the congressional dress code. Don't scoff. There is, remarkable as it may seem, such a code, which requires men to sport ties and refrain from wearing hats. It says nothing, however, about pants, since it always seemed highly unlikely that even the most rabid congressman would appear on the floor flaunting his bare legs. The framers of the rules never considered the possibility that women would break into the male club that was Congress, however, so while House officials have had to rule on whether Dan Hamburg's bolero or Neil Abercrombie's lei qualified as ties, they could find no regulation governing my attire. Theoretically I could have shown up in hot pants and a halter top.

Ironically, my pants, not my work, were what gave me my first national television exposure, which is pretty typical of what happens to women in positions in power. That first shot was on *Regis & Kathie Lee,* and I was in a complete state of frantic nervousness at the prospect. I shopped carefully for the perfect outfit— a blue power suit—so that I could turn the light topic of the "first woman in the House to wear pants" into a showcase for myself. Typically, moreover, because absurd situations seem to be the norm in my life, I never got to wear the suit. When we flew up for the broadcast, my chief of staff, Dan Leonard, left my suit bag on the plane, so I wound up wearing whatever I could scrounge out of my closet in Staten Island.

My first months in Congress were a blur of activity as I tried to master the ropes and establish myself as a productive and potentially powerful member. That wasn't easy because I had to waste an inordinate amount of time just proving that I was a member at all. When I tried to walk into the members' dining room, or onto the floor, guards stopped me, assuming that I was a staff assistant or secretary. When I tried to park my car in the members' lot, or get on an elevator reserved for members rushing to vote, people would look at me askance. "Who does she think she is pushing in among elected representatives?"

I had feared that my father's old friends would have trouble making the transition to treating me as an equal rather than as my dad's little girl. Much to my delight, they managed to make me feel like a peer from the first. But dozens of silly things kept me from hitting my stride. When I first arrived in the House, for example, the only bathrooms available to female members were the public ones, the nearest of which was downstairs from the House floor, or the private one belonging to the Speaker, which was through his office and required a special key. That doesn't sound like a big deal, but when you're waiting to make a speech and have to go to the bathroom, you constantly had to worry whether you could get there and back in time. Meanwhile, the men could rush to their bathroom right outside the chamber.

As I learned the ropes, I threw myself into the issues I believed my constituents cared about, which weren't so different from those I'd fought for when I was on the City Council: transportation, economic development, and the environment. There was always another ferry fare increase or bridge toll hike to worry about, and my job was to find ways to use my position in Congress to muscle New York City. Once my dad was firmly planted in the office of the borough president, that became infinitely easier.

Our biggest ongoing battle was to close the Fresh Kills dump, of course, a fight I'd already been waging for five years. Being in the federal government, however, opened up dozens of new possibilities for attack. When the city persisted in its plan to dump incinerator ash there, for example, I fought to have incinerator ash declared hazardous waste, which would effectively block their action. I pushed the Environmental Protection Agency to undertake an impact study of the dump itself, hoping that it would provide me and my father with ammunition to demand its closure.

As I looked into the impact of dumps on other communities across the country, I realized that while they might have to deal with the stench, at least they benefited from host fees. We, however, had the stench without the cash, since the city considered Fresh Kills our "municipal" facility. So I began a crusade to force the city to pay us host fees for Fresh Kills because most of the trash dumped there wasn't ours. My line was simple: You stole the property from us, so at least pay us rent, build us some parks, or decrease our electrical rates in return.

Fresh Kills ran me smack up against Mayor David Dinkins, but that was hardly a disaster. We were already barely speaking because of his opposition to the Staten Island home port. When my father was in Congress, he had convinced the navy to establish a home port on Staten Island, believing that it would bring jobs and money into the area. That was a political coup because members are constantly jockeying for new military installations in their districts. Liberals moaned and complained, of course, since what he saw as an economic boon they saw as the militarization of New York. But Molinaris have always worried more about delivering jobs than delivering rhetoric.

When my father retired from Congress, however, the opponents of the Staten Island home port figured out that it was the perfect time to attack it. So I landed in Washington to find a dozen members trying to close the home port before it even opened. David Dinkins was the least of my opponents. Pat Schroeder, a member of the House Armed Services Committee, wanted to close the base as part of her attempt to cut military spending across the board, and Charles Bennett, who chaired the subcommittee that would decide the fate of the facility, was targeting it in order to protect the bases in his own district. The two ganged up on me less than a month after my arrival in Congress by introducing a bill to close the Staten Island home port—not to close all five of the home ports, or to close ours along with a dozen other bases. They singled out Staten Island.

Members on both sides of the aisle lined up behind them, and my mission was to stop the momentum. I grabbed a little book that told me who was on which subcommittee and went out to lobby to save the facility. The problem was that I had no idea what the members I needed to lobby looked like, so I wound up hanging around in the hallways grabbing random men in hallways and asking, "Excuse me, are you on the Armed Services Committee?"

One afternoon I was on the elevator, returning to my office, when Bennett entered with a member of his staff. Without even looking at me, he called out his floor number, assuming I was the kind of low-level clerk he could boss around. I pushed the button but did not correct him, because I was too intent on his conversation. "We just need to get past the vote to close the Staten Island home port, which will be easy," he said to his aide. I listened intently as he laid out his plan, his strategy. When the elevator stopped at my floor, I walked through the doors, then turned back and held them open. "Representative Bennett," I said politely. "I'm Susan Molinari from Staten Island, and I promise it won't be as easy as you think."

That statement was bravado, of course. As the new kid on the block, I had no chits to call in, no favors to offer to trade in my quest for votes. To make matters worse, the mayor of New York was opposing my efforts. Although the facility was ninety percent complete, ready to receive ships, and the source of hundreds of jobs, Dinkins, along with the majority of the City Council, threw his weight behind the movement to shut it down, warning that the navy's refusal to guarantee that nuclear weapons would never be placed on ships docking there meant that it might turn New York into Chernobyl 2. I'd been around politics long enough by then to have heard some stupid arguments, but Dinkins's staged concern was over the edge. He knew damned well that the navy never issued such guarantees. That would be dangerously irresponsible.

He pushed himself even further into rhetorical nonsense by insisting that his election constituted a mandate to stop the opening of the facility. Mandate, I thought. What mandate? I reminded every member who would listen that the mayor had been elected by a one percent margin, which was more than ten percentage points less than my margin, and that the home port was supported by both Molinaris, Governor Mario Cuomo, and the majority of the state legislature, all of whom had their own mandates as well.

But House members trying to divert ships and personnel from the home port to bases in their own districts ignored all those supporters. "Look, it's obvious we should cancel the home port; even the mayor of New York doesn't want it," they'd insist. I knew that Dinkins's position was just a excuse, but it provided opponents of our home port with powerful ammunition.

All I had was an argument that I thought should sway even members mired in politics: The base closure commission had not yet issued its recommendations, and I insisted that the House should not, could not, undercut the commission's work by deciding the fate of the military facilities it had been created to chart. I knew that a good argument wasn't enough, so I mounted a campaign on every front I could imagine. I called Governor Mario Cuomo and asked him to send letters to the appropriate members of Congress. He hesitated at first. It seems that his aide in Washington was telling him that the home port was a losing issue. Ultimately, however, he called in some chits which moved a few votes my way.

Gerry Solomon, one of my dad's best friends in Congress, lobbied on my behalf, and my father was able to twist a few arms on his own. I appealed to members of the New York State delegation by calling for state solidarity. I turned to the other northeastern members, emphasizing regional solidarity. I reached out to the members who represented the districts where the other home ports were located with a kind of "one-for-all" theme. Then my staff and I threw the net wider with a campaign to remind members from all over the country that what was taken away from Staten Island one day could well be taken away from their districts the next. We went over the list of members almost daily, devising individual strategies for each one.

It was like a self-taught course in lobbying—and the stakes were enormous. One of the Brooklyn newspapers ran a front page headline asking, "Can Sue Save the Home Port?" I could not begin my tenure in Congress by delivering a public no. Too many jobs were at stake, including mine.

The day of the vote, I spoke at the Republican conference meeting and pleaded for support. "This is extremely important to me," I said. "I'm in this position because the Democratic mayor and the Democratic City Council of New York are opposing me. Don't hand them a victory." As members filtered onto the floor for the vote, my staffers handed out information sheets reminding them, for the final time, "Your base could be next."

As the votes were cast, I stood watching the tally board. I thought I had enough support to stop Schroeder and Bennett, but I knew even then that a promise does not count until it's registered on that board. Bill Paxon appeared at my side. "Holy shit, you're gonna win," he said, as surprised as everyone else at what I had pulled off. I've often kidded that that must have been the moment he decided he was attracted to me. Just a few weeks in Congress and I'd rolled over Pat Schroeder and Charles Bennett. Just Bill Paxon's kind of woman!

I couldn't spend all my time in Congress working on local issues, of course, and I never tried. The learning curve for new members is extraordinarily steep, since one day you're voting on the federal budget, the next on transportation, before moving on to public housing, clean air regulation, the funding of a new weapons program, and a project to divert the Missouri River. Debating the overarching social issues of the United States after spending my time worrying about sewers and street signs was disconcerting, to say the least.

Even more so was finding myself on a team that expected me to play by rules developed by other people. As the sole Republican on the City Council, I'd made my own rules and carved out my own positions without having to worry if the party caucus would agree, or if I was stepping on powerful toes. Suddenly I became accountable to a wider group, a group with which I did not, or could not, always agree. Although I broke with the position taken both by the party caucus and the president twice within my first month in Congress, I came to understand the impact of such dissent only when the Family Medical Leave Act came up for debate.

That legislation, which required large employers to give employees unpaid leave during family emergencies, was sponsored by the Democrats. Both Bush and the Republican conference opposed it as unnecessarily intrusive into corporate policies. I disagreed. While I, too, felt that companies should offer their employees such leave without a government mandate, I knew that many did not, and that too many women wound up fried and frazzled trying to handle both their jobs and sick children or parents. Republicans are supposed to care about families, and I could think of no more dramatic way to demonstrate that kind of caring than to support the Family Medical Leave Act.

It's one thing to take a position—to analyze a piece of legislation, take a stand, and send out a press release—and another to take the well and defend it forcefully against your own side. On the day of the debate I sat nervously on the floor, waiting my turn to do just that. The speaker before me was Fred Grandy, who had achieved national fame as Gopher on *The Love Boat*. Fred, in fact, was one of the brightest members of the House and one of the very few really good public speakers. He reiterated the standard Republican arguments against the legislation, then ended his presentation by reminding members that it was Small Business Week. The point was tellingly effective, as we all understood that small businesses were most forcefully opposed to the legislation we were debating.

I hesitated when I rose and moved toward the well. I had never before stood at the Republican microphone to argue like a Democrat. I couldn't very well cross the aisle, but I felt a peculiar sense of vulnerability as I began delivering my dissent. When I concluded my remarks, I leaned back into the microphone for one moment to remind members what else that week stood for in the popular imagination. "When it comes time to vote," I added, "don't forget that this isn't just Small Business Week. Sunday is Mother's Day."

The Democrats applauded. The Republican side of the floor was silent. Fred Grandy didn't speak to me for an entire year.

◆

Between organizing my office, launching my campaign, and doing my job—which included dozens of meetings, having my photograph taken with Boy Scout delegations, sitting in long-winded briefings on upcoming bills, explaining myself to reporters, and trying to be polite to lobbyists—I didn't have much time for a life during my first year in Congress. I rented an apartment in Old Town, Alexandria, a wonderfully funky historic neighborhood filled with restaurants and shops and young people. But the fridge rarely had more than some pasta and a jar of sauce in it, and I had little time to enjoy the sights. I arrived in the office before eight A.M., worked through the day until ten or eleven P.M., running miles between meetings, committee hearings, and the House floor—usually in heels. On weekends I flew back to my district to meet with constituents and campaign for reelection by going to parades, cutting ribbons at restaurants and shopping centers, and speaking to every possible civic group.

Thankfully, none of this left much time for the endless round of social activity designed to entertain members of Congress. Every night a different group would organize its own lobbying event in one of the House cafeterias—a Texas shindig or a Taste of Buffalo. Local Chambers of Commerce, medical societies, teachers' associations, and trade groups offered to wine and dine members who are so inclined, which I was not.

The one invitation I actually accepted within minutes of its arrival catapulted me to the pinnacle of the Washington social calendar, a White House invitation. I'd been in the White House several times for dinners or Christmas parties, although always with my father. The first time was just four days after President Bush's inauguration. He'd invited my father and a few of his other closest supporters in the House to dinner to thank them for their efforts on his behalf. While Bush was still vice president, they'd met at his residence weekly, planning strategy, advising him on issues, helping prepare him for his debates.

I was still on the City Council, and my father asked me to go with him as his "date." About forty of us gathered for dinner— Gerry Solomon of New York and his wife, Don Fundquist from Tennessee, Judd Gregg, from New Hampshire. After an elegant dinner, George Bush asked if we wanted to see the private quarters. Even members who'd been in the White House regularly when Ronald Reagan was president were excited. No one had ever been in the residence before.

We toured the living quarters, which aren't exactly the Élysée Palace. More like a nice hotel, really. We all chuckled at Bush's enormous stereo and stacks of country and western tapes. He'd talked about being a country and western fan, but we'd never seen the proof before. When we got to the Lincoln Bedroom, the president showed us in and offered to take photographs of the couples on Lincoln's bed. He actually pulled out a Polaroid camera and, two by two, we paired off for our special photographic session.

Everyone was wandering around, giggling and excited, looking around corners and peering into bathrooms—even the one that had a slip on the floor, along with glasses and dirty towels—the normal jumble we all live with. Suddenly Barbara Bush appeared in a fluster. "George, you can't take people in there, it's a mess in there," she said, sounding like any other American woman whose husband had allowed outsiders to see the detritus of their lives.

George Bush was too exuberant to be deterred. "Come on, Barbara, these are our friends," he responded, laughing. Barbara Bush paused, then walked across the room and opened a tall set of doors. "In that case, they might as well see your dressing room," she said with a twinkle of revenge in her eye. "Look," she continued, pointing us toward a small room with the expected pile of crumpled, dirty clothes. "This is where George keeps his things."

That was fun, but the invitation I received after my election was special. It was the first I'd earned on my own merits. The occasion was a lobster bake for representatives, senators, and members of the Cabinet. There was only one problem: The invitation permitted me to bring a single guest, and both of my roommates, Julie and Joanne, wanted to go.

We plotted for weeks until we devised a strategy for keeping our threesome together. I listed Julie as my official "date," then we made a deal with a friend who worked in the White House. The day of the party, Joanne camped out in his office for hours. Then, just as the party crowd began to flood in, she opened his window and emerged on the White House lawn to mingle with the rest of the guests.

But little of my life was about events that grand. Mostly I worked, and the work was all the more taxing because that year Bush reneged on his pledge not to raise taxes, launching a nightmare budget marathon that kept us in session throughout the summer and into the fall. Rather than being at home campaigning, we were all forced to stay in Washington while the budget negotiators holed up at Andrews Air Force Base to hammer out a compromise.

That long session, added to the stress of the daily work, took a toll on my young marriage. When John and I became engaged, I'd been more worried about how he would react if I decided not to stay in public office than how we would handle the strain if I decided to move up by running for Congress. He was a hard-core politics junkie and seemed to relish my life in the rough-and-tumble. But I was naive, as are many other junior members whose spouses work back home in their districts. Even though I was on Staten Island almost every weekend, being apart during the week took its toll. Then Fox offered me a weekly Sunday morning news analysis program, on which I was pitted against Democratic pundit Bob Beckel. Taping was on Friday evening, which meant that I had even less time at home. The new people, especially the new men, in my life made John feel insecure, and I wasn't around enough to keep him, and us, grounded. And while he wasn't trying to hold me back, he also wasn't comfortable with being Mr. Molinari. Perhaps in the end it was simply that as I grew more self-confident, the distance between us widened. We hit a brick wall and couldn't find any way to grow and change together. John stopped coming to Washington, and I moved out of our house and into a room behind a garage in Staten Island.

I licked my wounds either by working or hanging out in a crowd of young members of Congress and other Republican activists. My friend Maria was a member of the group, so it was inevitable that I'd been thrown together with Bill Paxon. Maria was his chief of staff. Paxon and I were natural friends—two young, single, conservative members from New York. Although he was far more conservative than I was, particularly on social issues, he was also from a political family—his father was a judge in Buffalo, his mother a serious party activist, and his grandmother, who died in 1994 at the age of 107, had been a Republican suffragist.

We'd go out with the crowd and gradually fell into having dinner alone once or twice a week. Over the years, after John and I divorced, our friends whispered in corners, waiting for the romance to flower. I made them wait a very long time. Bill was just what I needed in a man; he was solid, serious, at ease with strong women, and incredibly nice. But there was no way I was ready to make that admission.

◆

The real challenge and satisfaction of Congress, however, isn't deciding how to cast your vote on someone else's bills, but crafting your own legislation. The greatest privilege in serving in the House was the ability to propose solutions to the problems I cared about. And with the memory of how I wimped out on the first women's issue that came my way in the City Council, I was determined never to be quiet about women's concerns again. There was certainly no lack of pressing issues, and one of the joys of my first years in Congress was the easy cooperation between Democratic and Republican women active in the Women's Caucus.

We had plenty in common since plenty of men on both sides of the aisle still hadn't moved into the twentieth century. They had a nasty habit of calling me names like "little missy," and of confusing the female members, suggesting that they really thought all women looked alike. My closest friends in Congress were Deborah Pryce of Ohio and Ileana Ros-Lehtinen of Florida, who are also short and blond, although we use different packages to achieve that effect. Members would come up to me to try out their Spanish, which is Ileana's native language. Or they'd ask Ileana or Deb how their dad was doing as borough president of Staten Island. Times change, but not that quickly.

We all bore the scars of attempts by our handlers, and our parties, to remake us, and no matter how successful we became, that didn't stop. I remember one appearance I made on GOP-TV, the party cable and satellite television operation, years after I'd been elected to Congress. The makeup woman was a southern belle who just couldn't imagine a woman who wasn't "adorned." She looked at me with horror and ran out to borrow a scarf and big round earrings so that I would look "appropriate" on the program.

Even while we wrangled like fully partisan beings on dozens of other issues, we couldn't help but feel a sense of sisterhood since there were dozens of issues on which the men simply were clueless. That was certainly the case when the flight attendants union lobbyist began complaining that Delta Airlines—the same company that for years advertised itself with the slogan "I'm Cheryl, fly me"—would not remove the weight standards it maintained for women. No one thought that a woman so overweight that she couldn't get down the aisle of an airplane, or so heavy that she would have insufficient stamina for the work should be hired as a stewardess. But the airline maintained no such arbitrary standards for stewards, simply requiring that they be capable of performing the necessary work. Refusing to judge women in the same way reeked of discrimination.

In my mind that was a perfect opportunity for Republicans to demonstrate their commitment to ending discrimination, at the very moment we were beginning to talk about abolishing quota-intensive affirmative action programs. But the men couldn't get it. They just didn't understand how offensive Delta's regulations seemed to women. So I joined forces with Nancy Pelosi to collect signatures on a Dear Colleague letter written to muscle Delta into the late twentieth century.

We found dozens of opportunities to cross party lines with proposals to promote women that ran neither side into trouble with their caucus. Olympia Snowe and I joined with Pat Schroeder, the senior Democratic woman in the House, to devise legislation to reduce inequities in women's health care. Nita Lowey and I worked together on the funding for the Violence Against Women Act. We all pulled together for the Women's Educational Equity Act, to increase funding for breast cancer research, and to save a woman's right to choose from constant attack.

Sometimes, however, we couldn't find common ground because we had fundamentally different approaches to how women's advancement might be achieved. For example, most of my Democratic female colleagues hated the antirape bill I authored because it included a provision for the death penalty in sex-murder cases. Obviously they weren't opposed to strengthening measures to prevent and punish rape, but they rejected capital punishment entirely. Similarly, they fought against my proposal for mandatory HIV testing for accused sex offenders because they agreed with the American Civil Liberties Union that it violated the civil rights of accused rapists. In those cases, I rarely had trouble finding supporters among my male Republican colleagues—in particularly, Bob Dole, who sponsored several of my pieces of women's legislation in the Senate.

Similarly, there was no way we could find consensus in the Women's Caucus around the Kennedy-Hawkins bill, the Civil Rights Act of 1991. That legislation mandated that an employer, large or small, could be convicted of discrimination if the workforce in his company was predominantly of one race or gender. I couldn't support that. In fact, I couldn't support any legislation that didn't require proof of an actual act of discrimination. I agreed that we needed to move more vigorously against discrimination. But I also believed that the approach they'd devised was wrongheaded.

Because I was a member of the Education and Labor Committee, I became a key negotiator around that legislation, along with Henry Hyde, Gary Franks, and Steve Gunderson—an interesting group: the House's leading antiabortion activist, a pro-choice woman, a black man, and a gay man. We worried that Republican opposition to the bill would be misinterpreted as indifference to discrimination, so in our meetings with White House staffers, we argued that Republicans should present a counterproposal. The new bill that we drafted would have replaced "statistical discrimination" with increased fines and a larger mandate for the Equal Opportunity Commission.

I was asked to run the final debate on the measure for our

side, and it was the kind of experience that reminded me that women Democrats had as many problems with the men around them as did women Republicans. Our bill did not pass, but it was not the measure that received the most heated attacks from Democratic women. The final version of their party's legislation included a cap on damages in sexual harassment cases, and the women were furious. A virtual parade of female opponents lined up to speak in support of an amendment Pat Schroeder submitted to strike that provision. The Republican side was entirely silent as male and female Democrats battled it out—and the women did not prevail.

The tragedy of women's politics within the House was how frequently we were divided not by ideology, but by pure partisanship, by the pressures and politics from within our own party caucuses. Once Nancy Johnson, a Republican member from Connecticut whose husband is a doctor, was in a Ways and Means Committee hearing about medical insurance, and got into an argument with Jim McDermott, a Democrat who's also a physician. In an attempt to defend McDermott, Pete Stark, a Democrat from California, started attacking Nancy. "How can you argue with a doctor about this? Where did you get your medical education? From pillow talk?" It was outrageous—rude and sexist. And not one Democratic woman said a public word in Nancy's defense.

On another occasion, in September 1991, I was working with Congressman Jim Ramstad of Minnesota, who had written an amendment to the Higher Education Reauthorization bill to address the growing problem of sexual assault on college campuses. University administrators had a tendency to treat campus rapes more as a public relations problem, or a student personnel one, than as a crime. So they had a disappointing habit of discouraging rape victims from going to the police, diverting them to campus judicial boards instead. Jim's bill required colleges to inform rape victims of their right to go to the police and to allow them access to attorneys if they opted for a campus judicial proceeding. It also required colleges receiving federal funding to report campus crime statistics so that parents and prospective students could judge the relative danger of different academic institutions.

My job, as a member of the relevant committee, was to make sure that amendment was included before the larger bill got to the House floor, and it never occurred to me that I'd face any opposition. Who would oppose giving women information about campus rape, or allowing women to report rapes to the police? But the day the amendment was scheduled to be discussed in committee, a staffer for our chairman, Bill Ford, a Democrat, called to inform me that Ford would oppose the amendment as written. The compromise he offered me was a watering down of the amendment language that would have made the changes we sought to mandate in campus policies entirely voluntary.

Ford had bowed to pressure from the higher-education lobby, and I was not about to let him get away with being that timid. "Voluntary?" I railed when I bumped into him in the antechamber to the committee hearing room. "That's insane. We need universities to move aggressively against their star football players in some cases. They won't do that if the policies are voluntary." I looked around at the Democratic women in the room, assuming they would rise to my defense. They did not. They knew that Ford would extract his pound of flesh on their next proposals if they did. I was even more disappointed when two Democratic male members added that they wouldn't support the amendment in any case because they didn't believe there was such a thing as date rape.

I should note, in passing, that when I calmed down, I accepted Ford's compromise, knowing that it would give me a window of opportunity to go to the House floor to propose that the language of mandates be reinstated. If the entire issue of campus-rape reporting policies were absent from the legislation, under House rules, my attempt to add it on the floor could be ruled nongermane.

When word got out in the Republican caucus that I'd struck a deal with Ford, however, my name was mud. "How could you accept a lousy deal like that?" members shouted at me. I could imagine the mumblings in the corridors about how un-tough Susan Molinari was. No one seemed to consider the possibility that my deal was part of a plan. When the bills came up for consideration, I followed my script and moved for a change in the language to mandate action. There, under the bright lights of the C-Span cameras, no one was willing to vote against a bill to give rape victims full rights. Even Ford buckled under.

Sometimes it was hard to tell whether the problem was partisanship or posturing, and that was especially true in the case of Maxine Waters of California. The first time I confronted that conundrum was when my friend Peter King, who was a member of a House committee looking into Whitewater in the early days, got into a fight with Maxine during a committee hearing. Maggie Williams, Hillary Clinton's chief of staff, was testifying, and Pete got into a prosecutorial mode, asking pointed and tough questions, the type of questions Williams clearly had been briefed to expect. Henry Gonzalez was chairing, and he seemed unconcerned about Pete's line of inquiry. But Maxine Waters went ballistic. She started screaming at Pete, "You're out of order and asking improper questions and badgering the witness. You're out of order."

Pete, who's not the type to be silent in the face of attack, responded in kind. "Who are you to declare me out of order? You're not the chair. I waited my turn, and now I'm going to ask the questions I've prepared." Maxine wouldn't stop. She leaned forward in her seat and yelled, "Shut up." The room went silent. It might have been the 1990s, but in the House of Representatives, nineteenth-century etiquette still prevails. That etiquette does not permit one member to tell another to shut up in a public meeting.

The next morning Peter asked his chief of staff to call over to Maxine's office to inform them that he planned to deliver a one-minute speech about her. He calmly and coolly described the incident and called on the body to condemn his colleague from California. "Can you imagine the retribution if I, as a white male, had told Ms. Waters, an African American woman, to shut up?" Maxine stormed down to the well outraged. "The day is over when men can badger and intimidate women and marginalize them," she cried.

Watching the scene on the television in my office, I was horrified. Come on, Maxine, if you want to play with the boys, you have to expect to wind up with your face in the dirt from time to time. But Maxine did not rise to the occasion. Under House rules, her response was limited to a single minute, but she got so caught up in her fury that she kept talking even while being gaveled down repeatedly. "Do you ever see men do this to men?" she cried. Yes, I thought. They do it constantly. What is the big deal?

House business came to a halt as she raged. Carrie Meek, a Democrat from Florida, was in the chair, and turned to the parliamentarian for guidance. He was equally puzzled. Someone called for Tom Foley, the Speaker of the House, to come into the chamber and figure out an appropriate end to the chaos. Maxine stood her ground, chanting, "I will not be silenced."

◆

I'm not naive. Just the opposite. I'm a pretty hard-nosed pragmatist where politics are concerned, so I understand the power of partisanship. But that understanding doesn't erase the acute sense of sadness I still feel at all the opportunities lost, all the gains not achieved. The truth is that we agree in so many things, and all too frequently we allow our disagreements to get in the way.

The first time I felt that sadness, that acute sense of loss, was on a cruise down the Mississippi River for American businesswomen sponsored by MCI. The company had asked Lynn Cutler, who was then co-chair of the Democratic National Committee, to put together a group of twenty women, Democrats and Republicans, to talk about politics. It was designed as a huge woman-bonding event, and everyone worked to leave partisanship onshore. For three days on the Mississippi we did just that. Until we left the boat for a meeting with Geraldine Ferraro, Walter Mondale's vice presidential candidate. Instead of talking about the issues that united us, Gerry spent her time denouncing George Bush. And as we listened to her speak, we all felt this enormous letdown, Republicans and Democrats, because we'd gotten beyond that kind of partisanship, if only for three days, and we'd begun to sense the opportunity in that.

After Clinton was elected, the Women's Caucus became increasingly partisan, making any cooperation, and thus gains for women, more difficult. Some Democratic members grew uncomfortable with the number of men joining the caucus, figuring they were coughing up their $1,000 membership dues in order to impress female voters. Finally, they tried to impose a litmus test for men, which would have barred any male member who was not pro-choice. Our power had been in our ability to set aside differences on matters like abortion, but, gradually, abortion took center stage. Republican women, even those of us who were pro-choice, felt under attack for our party's platform.

I didn't want to spend my time defending the men and women in my party from assault. I was proud to be a Republican woman, and a little bitter that so many GOP women were dismissed as pawns of men or mindless airheads. The fact that the single woman on the Supreme Court, Sandra Day O'Connor, was appointed by a Republican president, never counted. The fact that Nancy Kassebaum was the first woman in the history of the United States Senate to chair a major committee because her Republican colleagues put her there was ignored.

Little by little, even while I remained active on women's issues, I moved out of the caucus. I was no more interested in spending time with women who bashed men than with men who bashed women. I was no more inclined to use my time fighting Republican-haters than I was to use it fighting women-haters.

....

Chapter Four

Learning to Party

One late afternoon during my second term in Congress, a member of my staff rushed into my office and told me to turn the television on to C-Span. The session was over for the day, which meant that members were free to speak in what we called Special Orders, a time reserved for representatives who wanted to go on at length about a topic not currently under discussion. Representative Robert Dornan of California was at the microphone, a not uncommon occurrence, speaking about abortion. Waving a photograph of a fetus in utero that had appeared on the cover of a newsmagazine, he was directing his comments to me. "And I hope that Susie Molinari is listening," he said. I did a double take. I considered the possibility that I had misheard him. Then he repeated himself. "I hope everyone is listening, especially Susie Molinari." My blood pressure skyrocketed.

A meeting of the Republican conference was scheduled for the following morning, so I called Jerry Lewis, the conference chairman, and asked to be included on the agenda. Dick Cheney, the secretary of defense, was due to appear, but Lewis promised me a few minutes before the main show began. With more than one hundred of my colleagues listening from their seats in the packed conference room, I rose to address what Dornan had done. "We've got plenty of Democrats gunning for us all the time," I said after recounting precisely what had transpired. "Do we really need to go after each other in public? Let's establish the rules. If Republicans are going to attack Republicans, if we're going to allow or encourage that behavior, let's get that out in the open.

"What Bob Dornan did was not the right thing to do, and Special Orders was not the right place to do it. If he wants to have a debate on abortion and take me on, fine. But let's make it a debate where I get to respond, instead of an ambush. If people like Bob Dornan are going to be allowed to go after pro-choice members like he did yesterday, when we cannot respond, if those are the rules, then we'll have no choice but to turn the rules back on them."

A buzz of surprise swept across the room. I'd spent almost two years establishing my reputation as a congenial, trustworthy, and hardworking team player. The time had come to remind my colleagues that they should not confuse congeniality with pusillanimity.

When I finished my remarks, Newt Gingrich, who was then our whip, asked to speak. "That was outrageous behavior on Bob Dornan's part, and we cannot allow members to treat one another that way. I suggest that every member find Bob and tell him that we will not tolerate it." Gerry Solomon, the next to speak, offered to be the first to deliver that message.

The following morning, during the time set aside for one-minute remarks by members, I stood to respond to Dornan directly. I wasn't about to allow my colleagues to defend me without standing up for myself. "I'm a member of the United States Congress," I said, "an elected official, and, in that capacity I should be referred to as Representative Molinari, Ms. Molinari, or at least Susan Molinari, Bobby. I will not be demeaned by the member from California."

At the end of the day, Dornan found me on the House floor. The wiry and balding member was atypically contrite. "Call off the dogs," he pleaded. "In the last twenty-four hours I've been told off by more members than I have during my entire time in Congress."

◆

I admit that my personal blend of good-naturedness and toughness tended to confuse people like Bob Dornan. But that was hardly the only thing people found confusing about me. My first day in office, when I officially became the junior member of the House, I broke ranks with the president who'd been so good to me and threw my support to a Democratic proposal for elevating the Environmental Protection Agency to Cabinet status, which George Bush opposed. Neither Bush nor John Sununu, his chief of staff, reacted to my seeming disloyalty, but other representatives were stunned. I was supposed to be a Bush conservative. How could I refuse to support the president?

Frankly, at the time, I didn't think of my position in those terms; I'd spent too many years being the only Republican in a legislative body to suddenly develop the habit of policymaking as a team sport. All I knew was that when you represented the Big Apple's dumping ground, you couldn't be soft on environmental protection.

Then, just weeks later, I came out in support of a $30 million child care bill sponsored by the Democrats that the president was intent on scuttling. As it happened, he was just a few votes away from being able to veto the legislation. Suddenly my telephone rang with a call from the White House. John Sununu wanted to see me first thing the next morning. The sky was dark with angry clouds, and rain was flooding the streets as I inched my way down Constitution Avenue in a cab to the White House. Strands of wet hair framed my face and dripped onto the carpet in the Chief of Staff's office, where a fire was blazing.

As always, Sununu was simultaneously pleasant and persistent. He didn't need unpleasantness to pressure members. No one wanted to get on the wrong side of him. He controlled access to the president. Two other members had been called in with me, and Sununu directed himself to us one by one, speaking to our specific concerns, offering alternative interpretations of the impact of the bill. One by one the two other members caved in to the pressure.

I, however, didn't believe that I could. I'd just come off a campaign during which I'd made an issue of the lack of affordable quality child care, and the horrors, if not downright abuse, children suffered as a result. The Republican alternative to most child care proposals was vouchers, but my experience in New York had taught me that vouchers are meaningless where women have no place to use them. Despite Sununu's intense pressure, both implicit and explicit, I would not back down.

Word of my refusal to bow to the wishes of the president reached Capitol Hill before I did that morning. Those who'd thought I was too young and stupid to be anything more than a presidential or paternal pawn were openly disconcerted. I chuckled. In a game that demands keeping the other guy off balance, being underestimated had always been my most potent weapon.

The confusion I engendered not only played itself out on the floor of the House and in the White House, but in the boardrooms of the special interest groups that love, or need, to pigeonhole the members they lobby—and they made their discomfort exceedingly obvious.

In January 1992, for example, after I'd been in office for about twenty months, the *Congressional Quarterly* announced that I was truly conservative, despite my record on abortion and gun control. Then, seven months later, the National Taxpayers Union questioned my conservative credentials because I had voted wantonly to spend money on things like mass transit.

They were joined by the National Rifle Association, which branded me a traitor for avowing conservative values and then "waffling" on gun control. I had voted against a single piece of gun control legislation while I was in the City Council, which is why the NRA had endorsed me in 1990. But I supported the Brady Bill, which the NRA despised because it mandated a five-day waiting period for the purchase of handguns. I didn't find that mandate to be unconservative. I thought it was a prudent and reasonable measure.

Liberals were no happier with my independence. In the fall of 1992 I met with Ralph Reed, the head of the Christian Coalition, after he threw his support to Republican attempts to defeat President Clinton's budget legislation. Despite our frequent public fights about abortion, we agreed, for one moment, to cooperate on tax and spending issues. Pro-choice leaders, however, wouldn't countenance my willingness to cooperate with him on any issue, and declared me an enemy of the sisterhood.

The next month it was the Jesuits, of all people, who came after me because I had attempted to amend the National Service Bill, which was a core liberal program. Funding for part of the president's National Service Corps was due to come from existing student aid programs like the Pell grants, and I thought that was a terrible idea. I'd written an amendment to withhold money for the National Service program until student aid programs like Pell were fully funded. The American Council on Education and a host of other higher-education groups applauded my efforts. But the Jesuits couldn't accept my refusal to embrace the president's bill wholeheartedly.

Then the National Organization for Women, particularly my local chapter, jumped on the bandwagon, criticizing me for my refusal to co-sponsor the Lesbian and Gay Civil Rights Bill, or for defending my father's right to take positions I disagreed with. They became openly scornful when I opposed the Equal Remedies Act, which would have uncapped the damages sexual discrimination victims can get. My disagreement with that legislation had nothing to do with my commitment to women. I just wanted more caps on damages—on all damages, no matter the gender of the victim—not less. But that distinction was lost on NOW leaders, who accused me of insensitivity to discrimination.

What did all this mean? According to the *Daily News,* it meant that I was a "crazy quilt" of conflict who veered wildly from acting like an unthinking right-wing automaton to posturing as the Republican rebel. It was all nonsense, of course. I was just doing my job. Sometimes that meant taking positions about which I felt personally passionate, like abortion. Other times it meant compromising in order to increase my leverage in other fights. Mostly it meant voting in ways I thought would serve my constituents well, and that doesn't always allow you to follow a single party line. People in rural Arkansas don't have the same interests as people from New York City, after all, so how can anyone expect unanimity within a national party? And one woman's liberal is another's conservative, so it's hardly worth trying to satisfy everyone.

My independence made life rough for my opponent during my 1992 reelection campaign, and he responded by making life as rough as possible for me. The 1990 election that had followed my arrival in Congress by just eight months had been a piece of cake; I'd handily won fifty-nine percent of the vote. The 1992 election, however, was a different matter. My opponent, Sal Albanese, had represented a Brooklyn district in the City Council since 1983, and he and his supporters ran the first truly nasty campaign I'd ever been involved in. Trying to capitalize on the anti-incumbent sentiment in the nation, he attacked me for being a political insider, an ironic accusation from a man who'd spent more time in elective office than I had. He berated me for not getting the dump at Fresh Kills closed, insisting I should have succeeded at that formidable task fifteen years earlier. That was absurd. Fifteen years earlier I was nineteen years old, and a freshman in college.

Albanese didn't have much alternative but to fling wild accusations, since he didn't have much of a positive program. So he traversed my district alleging that I was exporting jobs to Mexico, that I had Congress's worst record on the environment, and that I was a puppet of the American Medical Association. Record bashing is, of course, a time-honored tradition in election campaigns. But he crossed the line with viciousness and dirty tricks. His supporters accused me of being a lesbian, a Mafia moll, and an alumna of a drug rehab center. They tore down our campaign posters and harassed merchants supporting us.

Then came the debate between the two of us and Right to Life party candidate Kathleen Murphy. More than five hundred people packed into the auditorium at P.S. 52 on October 25 for a televised exchange that turned into a free-for-all. The evening began predictably, with Albanese painting me as a hopeless conservative, a one-dimensional paper doll cut out by my father, and Mrs.

Murphy decrying the fact that she had once supported me. "I pulled the lever for Susan Molinari and got Bella Abzug," she said. "She's a knee-jerk liberal."

There was no point trying to set the record straight, or even trying to have a civilized discussion about school vouchers and Fresh Kills, civil rights legislation, taxation policy, or a balanced budget. Albanese's people had brought in two busloads of union thugs. Every time I tried to speak, they drowned me out with jeers and boos. Even the reporters questioning the candidates had a hard time getting a word in edgewise. When I attempted to discuss the Gulf War, which I had supported, the crowd shouted me down. "Skip it," one man yelled to the cheers of his seatmates. "I want a job." When I tried to talk about taxation, they screamed, "Shut up, you whore."

I couldn't get up or lose my cool. I kept reminding myself that the debate was being broadcast live. As tensions mounted, the moderator cut off the debate and declared the evening at an end. As I headed for the door through a melee of hostility, the police in the auditorium offered to take me out the back door. "Bullshit," I said, "I'm walking out the front door," and I did, head held high. I also won with fifty-four percent of the vote.

◆

Returning to Washington for the 103rd Congress was a strange experience. The president who'd help bring me into politics had been defeated, and that loss both saddened and disempowered me. The Bushes had been friends and mentors to me. Shortly after I arrived in Congress, I found myself stuck in hearings on my mother's birthday, a birthday she was spending in the hospital. My father was out of town, and I was desperate to find some way to cheer up my mom. I picked up the phone and called Barbara Bush. "I can't believe I'm doing this," I said as my way of apologizing up front, "but it's my mom's birthday and she's in the hospital. I can't be there to cheer her up and neither can my dad. She's an enormous fan of yours. Do you think you could give her a call?" Fifteen minutes later, my mother phoned in a state of pure exhilaration. Barbara Bush, an incredibly busy First Lady, had taken the time to wish her Happy Birthday.

George Bush was equally warm and accessible. As a former member of Congress himself, he understood the importance of his relationship with legislators. Although I complained about it at the time since I'm not one who wakes up at the crack of dawn, ready to race off to meetings, he routinely invited small groups of us in for breakfast and would sit chatting about the issues before the House, or problems we were facing. If I had a question or a problem, if I needed his support on a bill or a program, I always knew I could turn to the president.

The sense of loss wasn't just personal. Our Republican congressional minority lost the clout and leverage of the White House. The ascension of Bill Clinton to the presidency fundamentally changed the terms of the debate on scores of issues, for worse and better, in my view, from health care to abortion. And dozens of old friends had retired, or were defeated. I was the sole surviving Republican on New York City's thirteen-member delegation.

Ironically, however, those losses for friends and my party were also a gain for me. If Republican votes were critical to something the mayor of New York cared about, he suddenly had no choice but to turn to me. If he was blocking something I cared about, I suddenly had leverage that I could use as political muscle. Furthermore, those same changes in Congress, which opened up dozens of committee seats, also created the possibility that I could gain some real power inside the House. The name of the game in Congress is committee assignments. Without good ones you can spend your life on the Hill and not accomplish much for your district, or have any real influence. With the right ones, you can become a rising star.

The rightest of the right is the Appropriations Committee, which divvies up all federal dollars, and I'd had an eye on a seat there since my arrival in Washington. Committee assignments were made every two years by the Committee on Committees (no kidding, that's really what it's called), which party leaders create before the opening of the new session. That committee makes preliminary assignments, which are then ratified by the party caucuses. While seniority is not the only factor considered, it is extremely hard to buck.

I'd asked for a seat on that committee in 1990, even though I knew that as a freshman I didn't have much chance of getting one. In 1992, however, I thought I had a shot because Bill Green had been defeated, leaving what people thought of as a New York Republican appropriations seat vacant. My rival for that appointment was Jim Walsh, a Republican member from Syracuse. He'd also been after an appropriations seat for years, and, as we headed into the assignment season, lost no opportunity to remind other members that he'd served in the House one year longer than I had.

I thought that I could mount a convincing campaign against him anyway, and I mounted it on every conceivable front. Green, I argued, had belonged to the city delegation, so his slot belonged to a city, not a state, Republican. I was, of course, the only one left. Furthermore, I reminded all relevant parties, I'd also done my duty putting a friendly female face on House Republicanism. It was time for my reward.

If all else failed, I believed I had an ace in the hole. The member in charge of committee horse trading for the Republican side was Gerry Solomon. He and my dad were both marine veterans of the war in Korea, had served together in the state assembly in the 1970s, and played handball as partners in House tournaments.

The powers that were arrived in Washington on December 7 to negotiate committee assignments, and Solomon immediately announced that he planned to make a bid for an extra seat for New York—one to replace Green and another to recover the seat lost when Jack Kemp left Congress. In public he suggested that if given only one seat, he preferred either Sherry Boehlert, a five-term member from Utica, or Walsh, to me. I wasn't worried about Boehlert, since I knew he would never pass muster with the Republican conference. A liberal maverick, he'd already failed once, in 1988. I was certain the outcome would not be different a second time around. Walsh remained a bigger problem, but committee staffers assured me in private that I did not have to worry. By then I was not so naive as to be placated by a private political promise, and my skepticism turned out to be amply justified. With Solomon's support, Walsh was handed the seat.

The following October, Bob Michel announced that he would step aside as House minority leader in 1994, and Solomon wanted the position badly. His rival was Newt Gingrich of Georgia. The differences between the two men were more form than content. They were both solid conservatives, but Solomon was a nonconfrontational kind of guy who worked comfortably with the Democrats. Gingrich, on the other hand, was the leader of a group committed to transforming House Republicans into a more activist force. His strategy was aggressive confrontation.

It's bad form in the House not to support a member from your own state for such an important position. But I believed that Newt would energize us. I passed on the opportunity to speak on behalf of Newt when he made his announcement, but I declared my support for my colleague from Georgia—much to the dismay of Solomon's friends, who'd assumed I'd vote like Guy's daughter.

I should probably note that there was yet another complication to the Solomon-Gingrich affair. If Gerry Solomon was one of my dad's best friends, Newt was his nemesis, having engineered the worst setback of his political career. Just after his second term in Congress, my father was offered a position on the investigations panel of the Public Works Committee. He wanted the job, since it would make him the ranking Republican, which gives you much more power than an ordinary member. But he worried that he might wind up investing two years on the committee only to be bumped by someone more senior, which would probably be Newt. He approached party leaders to discuss his concerns, but they reassured him that no member would treat him that shabbily.

My dad wasn't convinced. Newt was one of the voices of reassurance, and my dad didn't trust him. So he asked the Georgian to give him a letter of agreement about his position on the panel, which Newt did without protest. My dad threw himself into his work as the subcommittee held hearings on airline policy and air traffic controllers, Superfund sites, toxic dumps, and organized crime. He was in his glory flying around the country in real harmony with the committee chair, Elliott Levitas, a Democrat from Georgia.

His activities did not endear him to his Republican colleagues, since he ruffled feathers right and left, but nothing untoward happened until he targeted the aviation industry. He and Levitas began aggressive investigations of airline safety and, after Reagan fired the air traffic controllers for striking in 1981, sponsored a bill authorizing their reinstatement. That seemed to cross some invisible line.

As committee assignments were being doled out for the session beginning in 1986, my dad heard rumors that Gingrich was going to claim seniority and bump him from his position. He dismissed them, knowing that he had Gingrich's letter of agreement in his files. Newt would never go back on a written agreement, he assumed. But on the final day of negotiations, Newt called to inform him that the rumors were true. "You can't do this," my dad said. "We have a letter of agreement." Newt feigned ignorance of the letter. My dad sent over a copy. It did nothing to change Gingrich's mind.

My dad tried to challenge Newt's action, and Nancy Johnson

from Connecticut and Clay Shaw from Florida did what they could to support him. The notion that one member would make an agreement with another and then renege violated the whole concept of collegiality on which so much of House workings depend, after all. Nonetheless, when the votes were counted, the members were unwilling to uncut Newt's right to assert his seniority.

My dad suspected that he'd been targeted by Newt for becoming too cozy with the Democratic chairman, and that Newt had been prodded into the attack by Delta Airlines, which was in his district. No matter the reason, he was not about to take the humiliation lying down. His chance for revenge came one day when Newt was on the floor attacking the Democrats for missing votes on some key bill. When we were still in the minority, that was Newt's favorite sport, which made him somewhat less than popular both with the Democrats and with Republicans who honored real collegiality. My father watched the performance on television in his office, and the tirade jogged his memory. He grabbed the *Congressional Record,* ran down to the House floor, and requested time to speak. He rose and, in the most flowery language possible, seconded the concerns of the gentleman from Georgia. Anyone who missed that vote should be roundly condemned, he said. But I'm confused, he continued, pulling out the *Congressional Record* for the day of the vote in question. "I can't imagine that Mr. Gingrich would attack people on the other side of the aisle if he himself had missed the same vote. So I'm sure there must be some mistake, since that's what the *Congressional Record* indicates."

A group of Democrats were watching and listening, and they merrily ripped Newt to shreds. My dad stood in the corner and enjoyed the fun. As he was leaving, Newt called him over. "I thought we'd settled that problem," he said. "Settled?" my dad replied. "You bumped me, got the position, and I'm out. Is that what you call settled?"

He smiled and walked out. Like father like daughter.

◆

By my second full term in Congress, I was ready to have a life outside my office, and that life gradually came to revolve around Bill Paxon. After my breakup with John, we began seeing more and more of each other, falling into a comfortable routine of popping into each other's offices, which were near each other, and going out to dinner with mutual friends. Bill knew that I was hurting from the end of my marriage, and he was there for me as a friend. I wasn't ready for anything more. I didn't want to get involved. I didn't trust the closeness.

Plus our lives were complicated. We were both frantic with committee work and obligations to our constituents, and Bill was in the middle of redistricting. Everyone knew New York was about to lose three congressional seats, and most people were already writing his political obituary. So while I licked the wounds of my failed marriage and learned how to be an effective member of Congress, Bill was in the thick of trying to save his political career.

That career wasn't just a job to him. It was his entire life. When I was still trying to figure out what to study in college, he was ignoring his college homework to plan his first run for Congress. He grew up in a small town out in the farm country near Buffalo, which made him more a midwesterner than a New Yorker. Politics was his family business. His dad was a lawyer who had became active in the Republican party and wound up as a county judge. His mother, the real political animal of the household, was a force in the party in that region of the state.

In high school, while other boys were reading *Mad* magazine or *Playboy,* Bill was studying issues of the *National Review.* Other kids dressed up like sixties wanna-bes; Bill hung a Nixon poster in his school locker. He licked envelopes, volunteered on campaigns, and waited for the day he could run for office himself. Bill was just out of college when he decided that day had come, and he announced his intention to run for a seat in the Erie County legislature. The county Republican chairman did everything possible to dissuade him. The party needed to win the seat, and the chairman wasn't sure a novice in his early twenties could do it. He was so desperate that he asked Bill's mother to run instead, then called Bill and told him his mother had agreed. Crushed, Bill called home and asked his mom if it was true that she had decided to run against him. She was incensed. "He called, but I said no," she said. "It's ridiculous. You're going to run, and you're going to win." For years he's joked that if his mother had made a different decision, she'd be serving in Congress instead of him.

Bill won that first election, and five years later he made his bid for the state assembly and won again. His grand plan, however, was to get to Washington. Even while he plodded through the snows of Albany, he was plotting his next move. He figured that Jack Kemp, who represented Buffalo, would eventually run for the presidency and that he could take Jack's seat. The only problem with the plan was that it presupposed that Kemp would remain in Congress until the mid-1980s, when Bill thought he'd be ready. When Ronald Reagan was nominated in 1980 and the rumor spread that Jack was under consideration to be his vice presidential running mate, Bill was shattered. His plan seemed ruined. Reagan's decision to tap George Bush, then, made Bill's career. By the time Kemp left the House in 1986, Bill had built up his base and established himself with nine years in the assembly. He sailed into Congress as a disciple of Kemp's, another true believer in cutting taxes and fostering economic growth.

Bill was an early and ardent conservative who was advocating welfare reform and privatization long before those positions became part of the national debate. He fought the unions over the privatization of a county hospital in the late 1970s, when he was still in his county legislature. He proposed limiting welfare benefits in the early 1980s, when he was still in the New York State Assembly.

Bill was precisely the kind of man I'd avoided my whole life. He was entirely too nice. As the wounds from my first marriage healed, however, nice gradually became more attractive. He was secure and strong enough to make me feel stronger. And he never felt threatened by me, which successful women will understand is a major miracle. Maybe it's because he was raised by an incredibly strong mother, but when wonderful things happen to me, he's always excited with not a hint of jealousy or resentment. I get to bask in his unselfish joy.

Neither of us remembers precisely when our casual dinners became dates, and we were probably "going out" long before I realized it. When I did, I panicked and broke up with him. Bill, however, found a perfect way to get me back. One morning he called to tell me that George Bush had invited him to a state dinner for the president of Brazil. Did I want to be his date? How could I resist? I'd been in the White House plenty of times, but I'd never been to a state dinner.

We arrived at the White House feeling very grown-up. But when we reached the receiving line, Mrs. Bush pulled Bill aside. "Do you know who you're with, Paxon?" she said. Bill was very formal. "We're grateful to be at this dinner," he replied. Barbara Bush interrupted. "No. I mean as your date. You take care of her."

Barbara Bush wasn't the only matchmaker in our orbit. Congressman Ray McGrath, an old friend of my father's, was a wonderful, gregarious guy from Long Island. He clearly had his eye on Bill and me as a couple long before I was ready to contemplate the possibility. Whenever he saw us together on the floor of the House, he'd grab our hands and start sermonizing, "Dearly beloved . . ." and offering to marry us right there in the midst of the debate.

For months after Bill had decided to marry me, I gave him an impossibly hard time. The first time he mentioned marriage was one New Year's Eve in New Hope, Pennsylvania, when I asked him if he had any wishes for the coming year, and he responded, "That you'll marry me." I did not even reply. But as things happen, by the time I was ready, in the summer of 1993, Bill had stopped talking about marriage. He'd spent ninety-nine percent of our relationship pursuing me, then he kept me waiting for months. I obsessed over the problem. Doesn't he want to marry me? Aren't we going to get engaged? But Bill is a planner, and he had decided, for some reason even he doesn't remember, to wait until the end of the session, which was in August.

On the afternoon of August 5, I was in a meeting in the Speaker's office, when Bill sauntered in casually. He bantered awhile about whatever issue we were discussing and then excused himself to go back to the House floor. Almost as an aside, he asked me to meet him there when I was done so that he could catch me up on the day's goings-on. When I caught up with him, he steered me over into a corner where the Florida Republican members usually sit. A defense spending bill was being debated, but most members were watching it from their offices, so the place was pretty empty. Then Bill got down on his knees, held out a ring, and asked me to marry him. He caught me totally and completely off guard with what I later learned was a well-orchestrated plan.

He had, in fact, thought carefully about where and how he should propose, and had chosen the House floor because that's where we had gotten to know each other. He had chosen the hour because he knew that his friend Michael McNulty, a Democrat from Albany, would be in the Speaker's chair. Mike had been forewarned, and was ready to gavel me down if my answer was no.

An hour earlier, knowing that I was in a meeting, Bill had called my parents to ask for my hand in marriage. He knew enough about the Molinaris to realize that he had to cut it close because we are incapable of keeping secrets from each other. Asking permission is the kind of old-fashioned gesture that Bill finds entirely modern. But he knew enough to update it to include my mother. In fact, he did call my father first, but my father suggested that he play Molinari family politics by calling my mother and pretending that he was asking her first.

So there I was on the floor of the U.S. House of Representatives, and Bill Paxon was on his knees offering me a ring. I said yes as quickly as possible, then demanded that he get up off the floor immediately. We sat there for a few moments, caught up in the moment, then I raced back to my office to call my parents and compose myself. We agreed to meet at the next vote, which was pretty typical of our lives.

The minute I got back to my office, I took off the ring and hid it in my pocket. I couldn't wear it yet. I needed to think about it—not about getting married, but about wearing the ring and making it public. My friend Barbara, who ran my office in Staten Island, panicked. "For God's sake, Susan, at least put it in the safe," she said. I couldn't. I needed it with me but not on me. When I returned to the floor with an empty finger, Bill didn't know what to think. By the final vote of the day, however, it was back on my finger.

A few staffers had noticed Bill down on his knees on the House floor, so word of our engagement began trickling out. That night we went out to dinner at a little Italian restaurant to celebrate with some friends, and a reporter sitting nearby overheard the fuss and saw the ring. The trickle became a torrent. The following day a blurb appeared in the paper speculating that we had decided to get married. There was no way of getting out of it. We had to make a public announcement. We did so first on the House floor, and that group of political creatures couldn't resist grabbing the moment. Elliot Engel, a Democrat from the Bronx, made a full speech. "The Bible says be fruitful and multiply. I wish them many healthy, happy children. And may they all grow up to be good Democrats."

Bill and me in our first postwedding kiss—on a bridge near the inn where our reception was held. HARRY HAMBURG

This is what we really like—Bill, Susan Ruby, George, and me. HARRY HAMBURG

Just Bill, George, and me doing my favorite thing —cuddling up on the couch, eating Chinese food. HARRY HAMBURG

On the campaign plane with Bob Dole, August 1996.

Visiting with Albanian children in Kosovo in 1993.

The passing of the torch,
with my father the day I
was sworn in as a member
of Congress. HOUSE OFFICE
OF PHOTOGRAPHY

My eighth-grade
graduation, with
my father.

With the foreign
minister of Bosnia,
Haris Silajdzic
(center), and
Representative
Peter King (left).
HOUSE OFFICE OF
PHOTOGRAPHY

Testifying before the Glass Ceiling Commission, October 1991. HOUSE
OFFICE OF PHOTOGRAPHY

My going-away party from the House, in the Ladies Reading Room
(left to right—Marge Roukema, Nancy Johnson, Sue Kelly, Deb Pryce,
Tillie Fowler (hidden), Joanne Emerson, Barbara Cubin, Jennifer Dunn
(partly hidden), Jack Quinn, Scott Klug, Steve Largent, and, at my side,
Ileana Ros-Lehtinen. HOUSE OFFICE OF PHOTOGRAPHY

Paired off against DeeDee Myers on *Equal Time,* interviewing Mayor Rudy Giuliani. DIANE BONDAREFF/MAYOR'S PHOTOGRAPHIC OFFICE

Mugging it up with Steve Forbes at the Republican National Convention, August 1996. MIKE FALCO/*STATEN ISLAND ADVANCE*

On the podium at the Republican National Convention, August 1996. MIKE FALCO/*STATEN ISLAND ADVANCE*

Introducing President George Bush at the fund-raising luncheon at the Shalimar on Staten Island, when he appeared to help launch my first campaign for Congress.

Hard at work in my office in the House of Representatives.

With Bill Paxon just after our engagement, in the office of Speaker of the House Newt Gingrich

Fighting for the crime bill, with (left to right) Rick Lazio, David Levy, Dick Zimmer, Jim Ramstead, John Kasich, Mike Castle, Peter King, Deb Pryce, and Ron Macht. HOUSE OFFICE OF PHOTOGRAPHY

With my mom,
Marguerite.

My favorite
picture of my
daughter,
Susan Ruby
Paxon.

Me and
my doll.
SAN DIEGO
UNION

Then we called the press together for an announcement on the Capitol lawn. "The audience was a small one," Bill said of the engagement, "but it was the only one I cared about." I couldn't resist a little New York bite. "We showed the American people that something productive actually does occur on the House floor."

Since Bill's was the first proposal ever made on the House floor, the press went wild. The story ran on the evening news on three of the five major networks. C-Span junkies who'd been glued to the tube during Bill's proposal because it occurred during a budget debate called and sent telegrams. The world press wrote dramatic headlines: "Gridlock Breaks for Wedlock." "Doing Their Bit for Family Values." "Two Representatives Play House, New Unity in Republican Caucus."

Time declared us a power couple, along with Bob and Elizabeth Dole and Andrew and Kerry Kennedy Cuomo. *Roll Call* issued a chilling reminder of what can happen to members who wed by recounting the story of Andy Jacobs and Martha Keys, Democratic members who married in 1976 after a whirlwind romance and wound up divorced. *Good Morning America* booked us for an interview in the Senate Press Gallery. Fox aired us from the front lawn of the Capitol. The big question was how we coped with our political disagreements on things like gun control and abortion. The answer was entirely unnewsworthy; like most couples, we talked mainly about what we were having for dinner and how to get out of town for the weekend.

After Bill and I made our engagement public, Jay Leno devoted one of his nightly monologues to his fantasy of our wedding. "Imagine being the bride, standing at that line of people waiting to kiss you," he quipped, "and then you see Bob Packwood and Ted Kennedy coming at you." That suggested precisely the problems we faced in putting together a wedding. We spent weeks agonizing about where and how to get married. We couldn't hold the wedding in either Buffalo or Staten Island without insulting each other's constituents. Some friends suggested that we get married on the House floor instead, and Bill raised the alternate possibility of a wedding on the lawn in front of the Capitol, or even inside the dome. I wasn't having either plan. If our engagement was incredibly public, I was intent on making sure that our wedding would be entirely private.

We decided, then, to get married in New Hope, Pennsylvania, where I had spent so many happy weekends as a kid, a town Bill had also learned to love. We turned for help to our friend Jim Greenwood, who represented New Hope in Congress, and, with his assistance, planned a three-day wedding weekend for the July Fourth holiday.

We squeezed discussions with the florist in between budget negotiations, and planning meetings with the caterer in during the early wrangling over the crime bill. Bill, who was running to the National Republican Congressional Committee, the group that channels money and advice to Republican candidates across the country, was in the thick of the push to increase our numbers in the fall elections. Phil Gramm chided him about the fund-raising potential of our wedding. "Are you planning to sell tickets to the wedding, the reception, or, better yet, the honeymoon?" he asked. Bill paused. "Hmmm, that would have some real fund-raising potential." I kicked him.

Our press secretaries fielded phone calls from media wanting to cover the "event." Presents poured into our offices and homes. Three weeks before the wedding, Bob Dole rose to the floor of the Senate to address our impending marriage. "I have checked the laws of our land very carefully, Mr. President, and can find nothing that prohibits two members of Congress from marrying," he said. "But just to be safe, I want my friends to know that I stand ready to propose an amendment to the Robinson-Patman Anti-Trust Act to render the Paxon-Molinari merger a combination in the public interest, and not in undue restraint of trade.

"May they have many happy years together, and may their votes never cancel each other's out."

On July 3, my maid of honor, Julie, my father, and I pulled up in front of Our Lady of Carmel Roman Catholic Church in Doylestown, Pennsylvania, where 130 friends and family members were waiting. One person was missing. Two days earlier, my friend and mentor—the architect of much of my political career—Mike Petrides, had died. Dozens of our guests had rushed directly from the funeral to the wedding.

For at least forty-five minutes, the duration of the ceremony, no mention was made of politics. I cannot, however, say the same for the reception at the Black Bass Hotel in Lumberville, or the barbecue we threw the next day. Too many members of the press were making punk jokes about the wedding tent and the Big Tent of the Republican party. Too many of our guests were die-hard politicos who can't imagine a conversation that does not include the word *Republican.* The only person who eschewed such discussion was the one man who generally can't resist talking politics, my dad. The only thing that seemed to be on his mind that day—the only thing he even mentioned to the press—was when I would pop out a grandchild.

Politics, however, did cast its pall over our plans. Since Bill was running the NRCC, and the elections were only four months away, there was no way he could get away for a honeymoon. My schedule was no more accommodating to romance. The crime bill was about to come up for a vote, and I was expected to be at the center of those negotiations. I had also just announced that I would run for a position in the Republican conference leadership in the fall, and I didn't intend to break my record of never having lost an election.

My decision to run for that position was probably Bill's fault, because he'd been pushing me for two years to map out my future, a future he was sure would include the presidency. My lackadaisical attitude—about the condition of the house, the filling of the refrigerator, my clothes, or my career—drove him crazy. He's the kind of guy who spends weekends cleaning out the garage, for fun.

The leadership race was Plan B, actually. Bill's Plan A was for me to leave Congress, then run for and become governor of New York. Conventional political wisdom dictated that that would be a disastrous move, since the sitting governor, Mario Cuomo, was considered unbeatable. But Bill was convinced that New Yorkers were ready to vote for someone new, that Cuomo could be unseated by the right Republican candidate, which was me.

He wasn't the only person tossing around that possibility. As early as February 1993, when pundits began speculating about who might take on the governor, my name cropped up in the press. My dad, who loves the intrigue of fueling political speculation, couldn't abide being upstaged, and kept telling journalists, "Molinari and Molinari would be a good ticket, but we can't agree which of us would be which." I said nothing. Congress was still too rewarding.

Then, in April, the press discovered that the GOP had commissioned a statewide name recognition and popularity poll, and that I wound up in the top six. What surprised most people was that I ranked high among people from upstate, which is pretty unusual for a politician from the city. Even more surprising was the fact that I had beat out my father, who'd landed smack in the middle of the pack. Suddenly, the idle speculation became pressure to at least consider a run for the statehouse. I refused. My only fantasy about life beyond the House centered on what would happen if Al D'Amato, New York's perennially contentious and controversial senator, ran for governor and gave up his seat in the Senate. That was an intriguing prospect. But governor? No way. I announced I would remain in Congress.

That announcement didn't quash the speculation, since politicians are notorious for announcements that have nothing to do with their real plans. My dad diverted some of the attention by throwing out the possibility that he would run. And, as New York's infamous tabloids began a frenzied competition over rumors about his intentions, we decided to have some fun. For the annual dinner of the Coalition of Italo-American Associations, for example, we designed a full routine around the notion. The script called for my dad to rise to make a mock announcement that he was running for governor, which would be my signal to grab the mike and announce as well. He did, but I didn't, which brought the group to their feet in laughter. But I couldn't help but throw in my own quip, "If Bill and Hillary can be president, why can't Guy and Susan be governor?"

In fact, by the summer of June 1993 I had begun thinking seriously about throwing my hat into the race. Bill had pored over the numbers and was convinced that we could move into the governor's mansion if I would only make up my mind. I wavered and offered a dozen reasons why it was a bad idea: He countered them point by point. "We're at a critical point in our personal relationship," I insisted. "I'll quit Congress and move to Albany with you," he replied. "I wanted to have a baby." "Who says a governor can't give birth?" "Other Republicans really want the job." "Come on, you can beat them handily." "I've already lived in Albany and don't care to repeat the experience." "Living in Albany as a college student isn't exactly the same as living there as the governor of the state."

Finally, he beat me down and I called a meeting of my inner circle of advisers to discuss the possibility seriously. My dad and Mike Petrides agreed to meet at my house on Staten Island. Julie Wadler, whose fund-raising skills would be essential, promised to fly in from Washington, D.C. The evening of the gathering, I was a nervous wreck, racked by indecision. Did I want to be governor? Could I be governor? When Bill left for the airport to pick up Julie, I took refuge in the bathroom, trying to imitate something a CNN hair stylist had done with my hair. Unlike her, however, I was using a cheap plastic brush, and it got hopelessly tangled in my hair. Just then the doorbell rang, which set off the dog, who started barking like crazy. All I could think was "How am I going to convince people that I'm qualified to be governor of New York with a brush sticking out of my hair?" I panicked, pulled out a pair of scissors, cut the brush out, and ran to the door to begin discussions about my political future with a patch of hair missing from the top of my head.

I loved the fantasy of being the first female governor of New York, but I still wasn't sure that the job itself played to my strengths. Policy was more my forte than administration. But as Bill made his pitch, even those who'd been totally lukewarm about the idea became more enthusiastic, or at least got caught up in the fantasy. Everyone agreed that the governorship was winnable. Julie offered the only real note of caution. She thought we could raise the necessary money, but she warned me that for the first time I'd have to be involved in my own fund-raising. I'd always hated the idea of picking up the phone to ask people for money. The prospect of doing so didn't thrill me, but neither did it deter me. By then I'd bitten dozens of bullets.

Although I still hadn't said the magic words, by the end of the meeting the conversation had moved from "if" to "how." We tossed around ideas about endorsements, campaign themes, even timing. We were on such a roll that when the meeting broke up, Bill, Julie, and I almost naturally hopped in the car to go out to celebrate my new career. We did shots of tequila in one bar, then moved on to another bar to hang out. Halfway through the evening, Bill, who'd had as much to drink as the rest of us, got so caught up in the fantasy that he called a friend and asked if he might be interested in running as my lieutenant governor. When he came back to the table and announced what he had done, I went berserk. "I'm not even governor yet, and you're already trying to run the state," I screamed in front of a good chunk of Staten Island. "Well, forget it. I'm not running for governor."

The bartender freaked and suggested to Julie that she get Bill and me out of there. We went home and passed out. In the morning, I was more sober, both physically and politically. And I was not running for governor.

◆

Bill and I hadn't been married a month when I was thrown into the first real test of my ability to play in the big leagues, an opportunity handed me, ironically, by Bill Clinton. The president had declared himself tough on crime during his first State of the Union address. We Republicans weren't hopeful that he'd propose meaningful measures to back up his rhetoric, but we applauded the rhetoric nonetheless, since it was borrowed right out of our handbook of the major problems confronting the nation. Our praise of his speech threw us in an odd conflict with the Democrats, who had begun attacking their own president as a demagogue within seconds of his departure from the Capitol.

The two weeks prior to our wedding, the House began to tackle the specifics of the president's bill and, in preparation for negotiations with both the Senate and the White House, we went through our ritual motions to instruct. Those motions offer the members who will negotiate the final bill clear guidance on programs and issues the House wishes included in the legislation. As we prepared for debate on those motions, Newt asked me if I would take the lead for our side, knowing that I was eager for the inclusion of my long-standing proposal for a law that would allow jurors in rape cases to hear evidence about prior sex offenses committed by the accused.

I'd been advocating that change for years, and the Senate, under the leadership of Bob Dole, had already approved the measure. House Democrats, however, had rejected it, bowing to the pressure of the American Civil Liberties Union. Rapists don't generally violate women in front of a gang of witnesses, so I believed that juries needed every possible piece of evidence about the histories of men accused of sexual assault.

When I presented that proposal as a motion to instruct, the Democrats lined up at the well to oppose me. They sang a single refrain: Such a law would jeopardize an accused rapist's right to a fair trial. I answered each refrain by citing the story of a woman who'd been raped by a man who already had a history of similar sexual assault.

Under the gaze of the C-Span cameras, House members overwhelmingly voted to instruct our negotiators to include my provision in the final crime bill. But when the package appeared in early August, that provision was notably absent, as was another bill I had coauthored, one mandating HIV testing for accused rapists. The final measure I was looking for to protect women and children from harm—a federal version of Megan's law, a New Jersey bill that gave residents the right to know if a convicted child sexual abuser moved into their neighborhood—had been watered down beyond recognition. As written, the bill specifically limited neighbors' right to know to situations in which such information was necessary to law enforcement efforts. That wasn't good enough. I wasn't worried about cops; I was worried about children.

Those exclusions were hardly the only problems with the president's crime package. As promised, he had included a ban on assault weapons, which was guaranteed to provoke the full wrath of the National Rifle Association. Virtually every Republican member was irate at the micromanagement of the anticrime effort implicit in his proposals, a kind of unified approach that would have forced police in rural Arkansas to adopt the same strategies as those in New York City. Conservative talk radio hosts like Rush Limbaugh lit into him for including an array of social programs like midnight basketball leagues and dances that were allegedly designed to fight gang violence. And that was just the conservative side.

His left flank was furious that the president had included funding for the hiring of 100,000 more police officers, when they believed that crime should be fought with social programs rather than force. The Black Caucus was still chafing over Clinton's early refusal to include a provision they'd proposed that would have allowed death row prisoners to challenge their sentences as racially biased. Their members almost unanimously dismissed the crime bill out of hand.

While other Republicans crafted amendments to increase spending for prison construction, my staff and I worked on amendments to address my concerns about women and kids. But we were cut off at the knees when the Democrats decided that they would permit no debate on Republican amendments to the crime bill. They did so by writing that prohibition into the rules of the debate that they proposed for our discussion of the package. Those rules are written for every piece of legislation that comes before the House. Usually, however, they do not prevent the minority from input into the legislative process.

Strutting with the new sense of power provided by their capture of the White House, however, that's precisely what the House Democratic leadership did, forcing us to vote yea or nay. It was a critical miscalculation. Votes on the rules of debate are generally pretty pro forma, and follow straight party lines. But when the rules were considered on August 12, much to everyone's surprise, fifty-eight Democrats, including ten members of the Black Caucus, broke with tradition and voted against them, along with virtually all the Republicans, stopping the crime bill in its tracks.

The black members were protesting the entire thrust of the package, but the remaining Democratic turncoats were trying to scuttle the package in order to avoid voting on the assault weapons ban. They did not want to anger either the National Rifle Association and its constituents, or the first Democratic president of the United States in twelve years. So they voted against the rule in the hope that they could kill the crime bill before it even made it to the floor for consideration.

I also voted against the rule, although for the opposite reason. I supported the assault weapons ban. I was instantly denounced throughout New York City. Rudy Giuliani, who'd been campaigning for the bill at Clinton's side, blasted all the naysayers in the vote as indifferent to the needs of urban residents. Police Commissioner William Bratton singled me out, accusing me personally of not knowing what my constituents needed. The local press branded me a sellout who'd voted against the rule for the greater glory of Newt Gingrich. Strangely, they made no such accusation against Charles Rangel, a Democrat from the city, who voted as I did.

The rule vote blocked all action on the crime bill, leaving the new president stunned and humiliated. He had staked his reputation on four elements of the legislation: the assault weapons ban, life imprisonment for three-time violent offenders, crime prevention programs, and the hiring of 100,000 extra police. He vowed not to accept defeat. He took to the radio and television and blasted the NRA and the Republicans, hoping to whip up public pressure for a reconsideration of the bill. To no avail. He called in the dissident Democrats, but they refused to budge. He was left, then, with no choice but to turn to moderate Republicans.

On August 16 he got around to me. I was in my Staten Island office when the White House switchboard rang, and I expected ten minutes of presidential pressure. Instead, he was startlingly accommodating. He bemoaned the absence of a full version of Megan's law and my provision for unshielding rapists in the legislation, then asked for my advice. It was just the window of opportunity for which I and a group of moderate Republicans had been hoping. "Well, sir," I suggested not all that tentatively, "I think there's a possibility that we can find common ground here." I suggested that he talk to the House Republican leadership about sending a negotiating team to work out compromise legislation.

Meanwhile, John Kasich, Rick Lazio, Mike Castle, and I approached our leadership and asked for permission to be that team. Newt was adamantly opposed to the crime bill, even the new version that we envisioned, but he bowed to our request. We identified a core group of forty Republicans we believed would support a crime bill that would include the president's four provisions if seven key changes were made in the package: severe reduction in social spending, the inclusion of funds for prison construction, the creation of block grants to the states that would allow local law enforcers flexibility in fighting crime, the reinstatement of my two provisions, and Megan's law, along with some more technical modifications.

As an awkward alliance of more than one hundred liberal Democrats and conservative Republicans met in the Capitol to lay out a strategy to block whatever moves the president might take to push through the crime bill, down the hall we began a three-day, round-the-clock marathon bargaining session with the nation's leading Democrats—Senator Joe Biden, the chairman of the Senate Judiciary Committee; majority leader Richard Gephardt; Speaker of the House Tom Foley, and Leon Panetta, the White House Chief of Staff. Each of the four of us was in charge of a specific area of the changes. Mike Castle, the former governor of Delaware, took the lead on the block grants. Kasich, our money guy, bargained the funding reductions. I, of course, stayed with the women's issues.

We knew that the key to our success would be holding our band of Republicans together. We couldn't afford to lose even one of our forty, since Democrats were deserting the president at a record rate. Late the first night of the negotiations, Jack Brooks, a Democrat from Texas who chaired the judiciary committee, spent hours wrangling with us, trying to weaken the assault weapons ban. We held our ground and he stormed out of the smoke-filled room into the arms of a pack of reporters. Bill Hughes, a New Jersey Democrat, fought me tooth and nail on unshielding the histories of accused rapists. When I refused to cede ground, he also departed.

Throughout the weekend, the White House caved in to our requests one by one, until Mike, Rick, and John were satisfied with their gains. But Joe Biden kept blocking my rape provision. Rather than discuss the merits of the proposal, he took refuge in a technical argument. The Judicial Conference, the nation's board of leading judges and lawyers, had to offer its opinion before laws about rules of evidence could be changed, he insisted. "Where's that written?" I countered, knowing full well that he was referring to tradition, not law.

As the other members of the negotiating team paced the floor waiting for resolution of that single issue, Biden offered me a compromise: We'd include the rape provision, but with the caveat that it could not take effect until the Judicial Conference approved it. I was no dope. I knew the Judicial Conference would not approve that change in the law and, furthermore, that my leverage would disappear the moment the crime bill passed. "No dice," I responded.

The press was literally at the door of the conference room where we were negotiating, waiting eagerly for news that an agreement had been struck. I held my ground. Joe Biden and I were the only two people left in the room. "Why don't you just claim victory and go home," he told me. I laughed and held my ground. I knew I was holding up a major piece of legislation that the president was desperate to pass, but I also knew that that desperation was my only leverage. Finally, Biden made me a final counteroffer: My provision would be included but would not take effect for nine months. Biden presumed that the Judicial Conference would disapprove of it, which they did, and, before it could take effect, revoke the provision. What he did not presume was that nine months later, Republicans would be in the majority, controlling what bills were called up.

Biden bit in the wee hours of the morning on Monday, and we had a package that could be taken to the floor. The Democratic leadership of the House was unhappy, since they'd been cut out of the negotiations. Even though we had acted with Newt's consent, few Republicans were much more pleased. When I walked onto the floor for the final vote, one member grabbed me by the elbow and, in a rage, accused me of causing his "death and destruction." Bob Dornan, the ultraconservative from California, took the well and berated the four of us for bailing out Clinton's presidency. The editor of the *Washington Times* labeled me "the prom queen" of the moderates, who had been manipulated by Clinton. Our district offices were inundated with hate mail from members of the National Rifle Association.

The day of the final vote, I was asked to close the debate for the Republicans, a position usually reserved for a senior member. Bill begged me not to speak. He wasn't just opposed to the legislation we'd negotiated; he feared that my involvement with it might spell political suicide. He wasn't crying wolf. His political instincts are sharp as a tack. In the House of Representatives, when you make a play for power, you play to your party caucus. By breaking with ours, I seemed to be throwing myself into the political sea. The Republican modus operandi of that moment was defensive: If the Democrats were for it, we had to be against it. But I didn't believe that approach served either the party or the country on an issue as important as crime. I opted to swim against the Republican tide. Bill was certain I would pay.

He wasn't wrong. With our band of Republicans holding together, the crime bill passed the House. For weeks after, Castle, Lazio, Kasich, and I were ostracized by other Republican members.

Members turned their backs on us in conference meetings and vowed to block our legislative initiatives. We became pariahs. Newt finally called in the most irate members and ordered them to cool down. They cleaned up their acts in public, but none of us was naive. The lust for payback was almost palpable.

....

Chapter Five

Two from the Heart

L et me be clear: Serving in Congress isn't always an exciting job. You spend most of your congressional days wading through issues that touch you and your district only tangentially. You wind up devoting an inordinate amount of time to hearings and briefings, to writing and rewriting House rules, voting on procedures that govern every debate, even adjournment. You get the picture.

No matter the issue, I could get caught up in the excitement and energy of the political fight if one erupted. I got worked up—downright passionate—about the closing of the dump, and the toll on the Verrazano-Narrows Bridge, because those things had a real impact on the quality of life of every one of my neighbors. But two issues dominated and shaped my congressional career that had nothing to do with political advantage or positioning, and were not governed by my commitment to following the lead of my constituents. A politician's career is shaped by dozens of forces—from political strategizing to political popularity. Sometimes, however, even if not frequently enough, it is guided simply by her sense of what is right.

Abortion

When George Bush announced that he would come to Staten Island to campaign for me in 1990, chaos erupted. Volunteers scurried to arrange a luncheon for the president and donors, to inform the media of our plans and to coordinate security with the Secret Service and the local police. Prominent Republican politicians in the city adjusted their schedules so they could join the entourage. My fund-raiser began lining up donors to pack the event. And I picked up the phone with particular pleasure to call Sister Charlotte.

On Staten Island, everyone expects those kinds of public events to begin with a benediction by a Catholic priest. In a delicious moment of feminist triumph, I decided to replace the man in black with a woman in black. Sister Charlotte had been appointed principal of St. Joseph Hill Academy High School while I was still in grade school, and became my surrogate mother, friend, and role model. Asking her to deliver the benediction was my small way of thanking and honoring her. It was a quiet gesture. I didn't send out a press release extolling her virtues or promoting the importance of women to the Church. That wasn't necessary; the point would be obvious without any folderol. I smiled with pride when she rose to the podium and blessed the gathering.

Two days later, Barbara Palumbo, my chief of staff and another Hill alumna, opened the mail and found a note from Sister Charlotte. "Don't ever ask me to do anything for you again," her message read. She'd enclosed a few nasty letters, samples of what she'd received from pro-life families at St. Joseph Hill complaining about her appearing on a stage with me and the president of the United States.

I was devastated. I certainly hadn't intended to cause Sister Charlotte problems, but I was shattered by the way she handled the situation. I wouldn't have expected her to stand firm and offer the complaining parents a lesson in tolerance, although I would have applauded that act of defiance. But why couldn't she have picked up the phone and talked to me? Hers was a terrible, hurtful way of handling the situation, and one that still rankles me whenever I think about it. Which is more frequently than I would like. In the eight years since that incident, I have never been invited back to speak at St. Joseph Hill, and that letter has become my symbol of how people have let their strong beliefs about abortion alienate them from anyone who disagrees.

I studied the abortion wars up close well before I entered politics. My father has always believed passionately that life begins at the moment of conception, and no argument has swayed him from this conviction. My mother has always been just as committed to the opposite position, that a woman's right to choose is fundamental to her autonomy. So while my father crusaded against the right to choose, my mother sent money to the National Abortion Rights Action League and cheered on Kate Michaelman.

I listened but remained silent about abortion until I got to college, then sent my father a five-page letter explaining why I agreed with my mom. That letter is the one piece of family memorabilia I wish I had kept. Since my father didn't save it, I can't begin to reiterate how I explained my position. Much of my argument was based on my belief, which has not changed much over the years, that the right to control your own body is essential to your dignity. That position was clearly influenced by the fact that I had friends who'd had abortions, and I couldn't imagine how they could have had any meaningful control over their lives without the right to make that choice. Furthermore, the era of illegal abortions—of dirty back rooms, doctors without sterile instruments, and women dying of complications—wasn't all that distant. Banning abortions, I knew, would not stop abortion. It would simply return us to those grim realities.

Over the years, reporters and politicians alike have sought a further explanation of my position on abortion, seemingly expecting a tearful tale, or a confession about an abortion to justify my willingness to suffer political consequences for my pro-choice stance. I have neither to offer. All I know—and I know it with full certainty—is that making abortion illegal will create more problems than it will solve.

In the years since I laid out my disagreement with my father, we have discussed the issue, like so many other Americans. We have fought about it, again like so many other people. We have not budged each other a single inch, which made us remarkably like the two sides in this debate nationwide. In the Molinari household, as in the nation, the battle lines were drawn early, and nobody crossed over.

Unlike my family, however, where we have agreed to respect our differences and move on, America remains a bloody battlefield on which pro- and anti-choice forces hurl epithets and recriminations at one another, usually to no avail, and to the detriment of both sides. I learned this the hard way, and not just from Sister Charlotte. Shortly after I was elected to Congress, the New York Foundling Hospital asked me to be the guest speaker at their annual fund-raising luncheon at the Plaza Hotel. When that invitation was made public, anti-choice activists threw up picket lines in front of St. Patrick's Cathedral with placards saying DON'T INVITE SUSAN. Nasty phone calls and hate mail flooded my office. Even though the affair wasn't scheduled to be held on archdiocesan property, even though the event had nothing to do with abortion, the protests and pressure mounted until the *New York Post* actually ran a story with the headline "Holy Row." Finally, under pressure from the archbishop, I assume, the nuns just canceled the luncheon.

It was a horrendous ordeal. Abused and battered children were sacrificed to my position on abortion. Why? What sense did that make? It certainly didn't change my feelings about abortion, just as it didn't change the Church's position. It didn't change anything but the bottom line for the foundling hospital and the way I felt about the Church. I did something about the former: I launched a fund-raising drive and, with the help of Andrew Stein, then president of the City Council, raised more money than the luncheon would have yielded. But there was nothing I could do about the situation. Every time I went to a Catholic event, I worried. It was not paranoia. Pro-life Catholics were demanding my excommunication, and Catholic clergy weren't exactly supportive of my God-given right to form and follow my own conscience. One Sunday morning I attended a special Mass given to celebrate the rebuilding of a Staten Island church that had been demolished in a fire. John Cardinal O'Connor, the archbishop of New York, was presiding. I sat through the Mass terrified that he was going to single me out for condemnation. Nobody should be made to feel that way for taking a sincere position.

It wasn't just the Catholic Church. For years I had to contend with the most intransigently intolerant members of the extreme right branding me a killer or "Bella Abzug without the hat." I tried to turn the other cheek, and, mostly, I succeeded. I came close to losing my cool on only one occasion, when I was appearing on television with Gary Bauer of the Family Research Council. Toward the end of the program, as we moved into idle chitchat, Lynne Cheney, the moderator, asked how my daughter, Susan Ruby, was doing. At that point she was just a month or so old, and I prattled on like new mothers tend to do. Gary Bauer interrupted me and said, "And she had a right to life."

I started to get up to hit him. How dare he use my daughter for his political purposes! Even in my hysterical state I knew that slugging him would have been politically unwise, but political calculations didn't enter into my decision to refrain from violence. Bauer's daughter was sitting right in front of me in the audience. She shouldn't have to suffer for her father's ignorance, I thought. So I cooled myself down. But Gary Bauer should know—and I hope he reads it here—that that's the only thing that saved him from being decked on national television.

Mostly, my commitment to a woman's right to choose abortion provoked nothing that dramatic. It was just a constant barrage of niggling insults. Every Saturday afternoon for years, the pro-life crowd would show up in front of my Staten Island office waving photographs of aborted fetuses. Campaign after campaign, they'd follow me to conventions and fund-raisers and speaking engagements screaming murderer. The Right to Life party always fielded a female candidate to oppose me, and she would inevitably heap me with vitriol at every debate, in every news interview.

Even when I was smack in my battle with the base closure commission to save the Staten Island home port, they kept at me. I'd arranged for the chairman of the commission to visit the facility, and my staff and I spent weeks making sure the trip would be letter perfect. Just after his helicopter landed and we were loading into the van that would take us around, however, Barbara Palumbo called frantically from my office. She's gotten word that antiabortion protesters were planning to disrupt the visit. As it turned out, the threat was disinformation, one of dozens of acts of harassment directed my way. But each time, my blood pressure rose and I was forced to steel myself against the possibility that the threat might turn out to be real.

In June 1991, when I began working to reverse the Supreme Court ruling upholding a ban on abortion counseling in federally funded clinics, Respect Life, a group not even based in my district, launched a postcard campaign to pressure me into changing my position. Interestingly, they put no such pressure on Democrats who shared my views, as if Democrats, who weren't seen as treasonous, had less impact on national abortion policy than did I. The Staten Island Pro-Life Action Group threatened to ruin my career. My staff lived with years of crank phone calls telling us to go to hell. The venom was heaped even on my father, who was branded a traitor for raising a pro-choice daughter.

I, better than most, understand that not everyone in the pro-life movement is like Gary Bauer. The anti-choice movement is not a single, undifferentiated, faceless mass. There are many people, including my husband and my father, who are opposed to abortion but have no wider agenda when they advocate that women lose their right to choice. But there are too many others who use abortion and religion to hide their misogyny, and who have an agenda that goes well beyond ending abortion. They are "pro-life" and anti–everything else, from birth control to sex education and day care.

The difference between these two anti-choice groups was obvious every time a bill came into the hopper. The one opposed abortion. Period. The other voted to close down family planning clinics entirely, insisting that birth control pills stop beating hearts. They tried to redesign welfare in order to punish young single mothers. They turned every discussion about birth control, which grown married women need to know about, into a morality battle over frisky sixteen-year-olds.

It is difficult to overestimate the impact that this issue has had on American politics. Conservatives branded women like me moderates even though we were entirely conservative on almost every issue but abortion. How can we allow a single position to define politicians and politics? And on dozens of issues that had nothing to do with abortion, the discussions inside the Capitol never make it to the heart of the matter. They were cut short because members were terrified of the reaction from the Right to Life community. So dozens of wonderful programs, from family planning to meaningful welfare reform, went down the tubes because they are considered too risky.

The political side of the abortion war reached its ugliest and most demoralizing pinnacle for me before and during the 1992 Republican convention. A group of us began organizing months before Houston to try to force a change in the party platform. We weren't advocating replacing the antiabortion plank with a pro-choice one. We just wanted a plank that respected the right of Republicans to disagree. That's all. Sixteen of us from the House— Olympia Snowe of Maine, Nancy Johnson of Connecticut, Sherwood Boehlert of New York—circulated a letter urging delegates to rescue our party from those who didn't really believe in the fundamental Republican principles of limited government and the right to privacy. We hoped that by reminding Republican leaders that ours is the party that recognizes diversity and the ability of individuals to make their own decisions, we might sway at least a few votes.

We were careful not to do anything that would provoke more division, since that was the other side's tactic. We rejected, for example, a Favorite Daughter candidate campaign lofted by grassroots Republican activists. They argued that such a strategy would demonstrate to the party how much support a pro-choice Bush could draw in the electorate. I agreed with the point they were trying to make, but I could not hurt George Bush that way. I might have been unhappy with my political family's behavior over this one issue, but it still was my family.

In the end, we were powerless to change the abortion plank because the convention was designed and staged by the most militantly conservative wing of the party, which is not notorious for its tolerance of divergent points of view. Short of an ugly floor fight, we had no chance of making a dent in their control, and few of us were willing to risk that kind of ugliness when we were relatively certain that we still would not prevail.

I arrived in Houston disturbed not only by the reality that the party platform on abortion would not be changed but by my exclusion from the podium. I had fully expected that I would be invited to speak, even if in one of those six A.M. time slots that guarantees that no one but your mother will listen. After all, I'd been an active supporter of George Bush's for years, and had gone on the stump hyping the role of women in the GOP. I was disappointed by my exclusion and didn't mind admitting it. I was worried that my position on abortion had consigned me to the floor.

But once I arrived at the convention, it was neither the abortion plank nor my exclusion that demoralized me. It was the tone of the convention itself. The same people who had hijacked the abortion plank hijacked the podium and broadcast their message loud and clear: Women belong in the home. Professional women wandered the convention floor in a daze, begging me and other female members of Congress to do something, anything. "They're telling us we're not worthy," they cried. "They're spewing hate."

This was not the language of reasonable people who are opposed to abortion but have no wider agenda. I had heard what I considered to be reasonable antiabortion language coming from my father, a man who has never demeaned me as a woman. I'd heard it from my Catholic husband, who was spending half his life being called Mr. Molinari, picking up the dog and the kid and the groceries so that I could excel. None of what happened in Houston was about the right to life. It was about the right to diminish the lives of women. It was a lonely and bleak time for a pro-choice Republican woman.

I should note, however, that not all of my lonely and bleak times as a pro-choice Republican were due to the misogyny of conservative extremists. I remember as keenly, and with as much pain, the attacks from my friends in the pro-choice movement. During the 1994 election season, I endured endless criticism from women in the National Organization for Women and the National Abortion Rights Action League because I was campaigning for anti-choice candidates. I admit that I was guilty of campaigning for anti-choice candidates. I refused to be a single-issue campaigner. Forgive me, but that's bad for America.

Anyway, what did they want me to do? Campaign against my husband and my father?

The attacks became more vitriolic when I supported a move to cut off funding for the United Family Planning Agency as long as that group gave money to China for abortions. Molinari is selling out, NARAL and NOW leaders declared. I was livid. For me, supporting choice means supporting a woman's right to refuse abortion just as strenuously as defending her right to have one—a position with which the Chinese do not agree. Just as I believed that the pro-life community did itself a disservice by refusing to support measures that would reduce the number of unwanted pregnancies, I believed that the pro-choice community did itself, and women, a disservice by refusing to denounce and work against forced sterilization and forced abortion overseas.

That was a painful break, but I knew with every bone of my body that I was right. The more difficult moment was the vote over partial-birth abortion. The debate on this procedure was harder and uglier than any abortion debate I'd ever heard, because such late-term abortions are grizzly procedures that fall dangerously close to infanticide. I cannot judge to what extent my ultimate decision to support the ban was influenced by the fact that I was pregnant at the time and knew without a doubt that things felt different at eight months than they did at three. I do know, however, that seventy Democrats and twenty-five of our forty solidly pro-choice Republicans joined me in supporting the ban. But that was small consolation. When the pro-choice community denounced the ban, I was the traitor they singled out. Daniel Patrick Moynihan, Patrick Kennedy, and Dick Gephardt—all Democrats—voted with me. They got off unscathed.

My bottom line is that abortion policy is, and always will be, a divisive debate in this country. But women need legislators to use some of that energy and passion on other issues as well, like day care and child abuse, programs to increase literacy, reliable family planning, and improved health care. And I am hopeful that that is going to happen. Abortion, I believe, is losing its political potency, at least at the federal level. Perhaps that's because both sides have suffered enough politically. Democrats have alienated millions of members of their traditional constituencies over the issue. The extremists in the Republican party are on the run because their message is turning off a new generation.

Bosnia

If Gary Bauer is the man I've most wanted to hit, Slobodan Milosevic, the president of Serbia, is the man I've most wanted to see tried for genocide. In 1991, the patron saint of ethnic cleansing in the former Yugoslavia whipped Serbians in Bosnia, Croatia, and Kosovo into frenzied excitement over the possibility of a Greater Serbia. More than a quarter of a million people lay dead as a result.

I'd hated Milosevic from afar for almost five years, and battled against him in the Balkan wars on my home turf on Capitol Hill, when I finally confronted him face-to-face. It was December 1995, and Congress was considering President Clinton's proposal to send twenty thousand troops into the region to guarantee the Dayton Peace Accords. I'd been asked to lead a fifteen-member congressional delegation to survey the situation on the ground. We had one long weekend to prepare our report.

On December 1, I boarded Secretary of State Warren Christopher's government plane and set myself up in the executive cabin for the long flight to Belgrade, caught between fear, excitement, and pride. The fear was simple: I was three months pregnant and flying into a war zone. The excitement and pride were predictable: I'd battled George Bush, demanding that the United States bomb Belgrade into a parking lot if the Serbians refused to halt the genocide. I'd lashed out at Bill Clinton for his indifference to mass rape and "ethnic cleansing." I had finally succeeded in pushing the House of Representatives into lifting the arms embargo that had given the Serbians free reign in the region. Finally, I was in a position to influence directly U.S. foreign policy in the region.

When we arrived in Belgrade, an army of congressmen with our staffs, the Serbians offered us every consideration due an official delegation from the United States, and it was a far cry from what I had found on my two prior journeys to the region. We were installed in a luxurious suite at the Hyatt in Belgrade, an odd counterpoint to the devastation we had flown thousands of miles to witness. I almost took refuge there when it was time to climb into the car that would take us to our meeting with Milosevic. The thought of holding a civil and courteous meeting with a man I considered to be a modern-day Hitler was repulsive. I'd spent half the flight considering a boycott, and was still wavering. But I'd been sent to do a job, and that job included that meeting.

Milosevic was charming, which only made matters worse. It's always easier when the enemy is overtly evil. The purpose of the gathering was to ascertain whether American troops could be safely deployed on the ground, and Milosevic presented himself as an eminently reasonable statesmen. Sandor Levin, the ranking Democrat on my team, asked the Serbian leader directly, "How can we be sure you'll hold up your end of the accords?" Milosevic leaned forward and, in a serious tone that might have seemed utterly sincere to a person who didn't know that he had been the architect of genocide, replied, "I give you my word."

Balkan leaders like Milosevic didn't have particularly proud histories of living up to their promises. Even worse, just before our arrival, the Bosnian Serb military leader Ratko Mladic, who'd been excluded from the Dayton negotiations because he was under indictment as a war criminal, had declared that he would vigorously oppose any move to unite Sarajevo under the control of the Bosnian government. "We cannot allow our people to come under the rule of butchers," he'd declared. "A new and just solution must be found."

Milosevic's calm promise filled me with bile. I left the meeting both nauseated and infuriated, and walked right into an impromptu press conference. Levin stood there reiterating Milosevic's assurances. I was as candid as humanly possible. "I'm not optimistic," I said. "He can't be trusted."

For the next two days we traveled the region, meeting with the presidents of Croatia and Bosnia. They knew me from those years when no one else in Washington would talk to them, so they understood my skepticism. But their position was pragmatic. The accords might be unjust and unfair, they argued, but they were probably necessary. A flawed settlement seemed to be better than the bloody alternative.

I still wasn't convinced as I donned my flak jacket and boarded a military transport plane for the flight into the airport at Sarajevo, a city once the symbol of a peaceful multiethnic world. It lay in ruins. After three years under siege, there was no electricity or heat. To the backdrop beat of sniper fire, we drove in our armored car to the marketplace that had been the scene of two of Sarajevo's most gruesome massacres—direct shelling by the Serbians on the one place civilians were most likely to gather. We watched children playing amid the rubble, children no longer able to smile. We stopped at the American Embassy, where a small staff lived and worked in the fortified structure in the middle of a war zone.

I was in a trance: So much destruction, so many lives lost, and all so unnecessary.

◆

When I flew to Croatia in January 1992, my first trip to the region, I didn't have politics on my mind. I just knew that a friend on Staten Island, an Albanian whose family lived in Kosovo, had told me about the terror that was gripping their lives. That first journey was my Balkans 101. The war was in its infancy, and the Bush administration was dismissing it as the kind of civil war we certainly would not want to get entangled in. But as we drove outside Zagreb, I saw entire blocks of apartment buildings with their windows blown out, and children playing between the sandbags and the rubble. I saw soldiers using old police pistols and rigging World War II handguns onto broom handles so they could defend themselves against Serbians armed with the modern equipment they'd inherited from the Yugoslav army. In the war zone itself I met soldiers headquartered in a blown-out department store. Ducking sniper fire, they took me on a tour of the ruins of their homes. Sharing cigarettes and slugs of slivovitz, they told me the stories of their families, stories that made the Balkan wars more than a distant nightmare. Our driver was a young blond boy, a musician who'd exchanged his guitar for a gun only three weeks earlier. When I returned to Croatia a year later, he was dead, along with tens of thousands of his countrymen.

By the time I returned to the United States, I was convinced that President Bush was wrong, that this was no ethnic civil war. It was a Serbian land grab pure and simple, and the United States was standing by feigning "neutrality" while the death toll—already at ten thousand—rose. I was hardly a foreign affairs expert, as numerous State Department types reminded me. But you didn't need a Ph.D. in Balkan history to understand that families were being driven out of their homes, children were being murdered, and women raped. I didn't need to be a professional diplomat to know that the United States had a moral obligation to do something, no matter what the president and his foreign affairs advisers said.

I did not advocate that we send ground troops into the region. Quite the opposite. I believed passionately that the Bosnians and Croatians and Albanians in Kosovo could, and should, defend their own homelands. Self-defense might be expensive, but it is the surest path of dignity. I just wanted the United States to recognize Croatian independence and to end the arms embargo that had been imposed by the United Nations on the region with our enthusiastic support. That embargo might have made sense had the hostilities been a simple civil war in which both sides controlled relatively equal force. But the Serbians had plenty of arms, which they were using to create their vision of a Greater Serbia. The Croatians and Bosnians who were attempting to protect their homes, on the other hand, didn't have access to the armories of the former Yugoslav army. They were, quite simply, defenseless.

President Bush was firmly opposed to both those actions, and I never really understood why. He argued that U.S. recognition would fuel the war, but that never made much sense to me. Germany and the Vatican had already offered recognition, and everyone I met—from the archbishop of Croatia to members of the Croatian Parliament and representatives of the Croatian Jewish community—believed our recognition would be key to their survival. Furthermore, I figured, if helping people who were being invaded and exterminated fueled the war, fine. So be it.

I also wanted the United States to take more aggressive action against the Serbians by performing surgical air strikes on Belgrade. I reasoned the powers in Belgrade were egging on the Serbians in Croatia and Bosnia—encouraging, arming, and financing them— and that they needed to understand that those actions would carry a price. Bring the war home to Serbia, I demanded. What better way to convince the Serbians to back off than to demonstrate that the most powerful nation on the planet was unwilling to countenance murder? I met with Vice President Dan Quayle and national security adviser Brent Scowcroft to promote that concept, but they treated me with complete disdain—a grunt and guffaw that said "Sure, you think you're some kind of expert." No matter the reality—the reports of massacres and the displacement of thousands of people—they would not consider the conflict as anything but a civil war without good guys or bad guys.

Serb aggression became my not-so-quiet crusade in Congress and on the Hill, and I gradually pulled in a series of friends and colleagues. Finally, the House Republican conference appointed me to chair a six-member task force on the crisis, which gave me some degree of leverage in advocating a change in U.S. policy. When Bill Clinton was elected, I was momentarily optimistic since, as a candidate, he had attacked George Bush viciously for failing to counter Serbian aggression. Once Clinton captured the White House, however, I learned about the distance between a Clinton promise and a Clinton delivery. (It wasn't until almost three years later that he stepped up to the plate.)

In February and March 1993, our task force—which included four other New Yorkers, Bill Paxon, Peter King, Ben Gilman, and Elliot Engel—wrote to Clinton urging him to lift the arms embargo, arguing that the administration's position was a de facto recognition of Serbian territorial gains made through military force and ethnic cleansing. The president didn't budge. He countered that U.S. action might escalate the situation and lead to Russian intervention on behalf of Serbia. That policy was both shortsighted and cold. His concern about escalation had come too late for the quarter of the Bosnian population that had been expelled from their homes, or the more than 100,000 Bosnian Muslims who'd been killed.

Instead, he opted for humanitarian relief—the dropping of food and supplies to embattled Bosnian villages—but that plan backfired. The drops served as bait for the Serbian troops, and Bosnian representatives begged us to do something to stop them. We approached Secretary of State Warren Christopher with that information, which we had received from entirely reliable sources. Christopher would not accept that assessment. No one but he and his followers were permitted the least input into what was already clearly a disastrous foreign policy.

Bill, Pete King, Elliot Engel, and I finally decided to fly to the Balkans to study the situation ourselves, and to use our presence to create the kind of publicity that might pressure the White House to live up to Clinton's campaign promises. We used our departure press conference to issue five demands of the president: sign an executive order increasing support for the activities of groups like the Red Cross; press for the United Nations to redeploy troops to Macedonia to prevent the crisis from spilling over its border; send observers to Kosovo and Sanjak; enforce the economic sanctions already placed on the Serbians; lift the arms embargo against the Bosnians. Finally, we pleaded with the president to meet with us when we returned.

Our plan was to travel to Kosovo, but since Elliot Engel wanted to go to Albania first, Bill, Pete, and I decided to start in Croatia and then meet up with Elliot in Macedonia. We toured refugee camps in Split, visited Zagreb and Mostar, then tried, unsuccessfully, to get into Dubrovnik. The horror we had envisioned from our comfortable offices on the Hill was mild compared to the devastation we witnessed. Thousands of people—ordinary human beings—had returned to their homes from work one day thinking about the kids and dinner, only to be rounded up and thrown out of their homes by their neighbors. Women in tattered dresses told of being separated from their husbands. Children wandered around silently, numb from the shock.

From the camps we traveled to Macedonia and drove into Kosovo on Easter morning. The Grand Hotel there was anything but grand, although it was the Hyatt compared to the homes of most Kosovons. A classic example of Stalinist architecture, it boasted no locks on the doors, no heat or hot water, no beds other than cots, and, often, no electricity. Even worse, Commander Arkon was installed on the top two floors. A war criminal wanted by Interpol, Arkon had been appointed by the Serbs as the Kosovon representative in their Parliament. His presence did not make for a good night's sleep.

Kosovo itself was chilling: Schools and the university were closed, the hospitals were shut, and fear hung over the region like heavy fog. The leaders of the Albanian community, who repre-sented the majority of the Kosovon population, could not come to our hotel to speak with us. Albanians were not permitted to enter the Grand. So we drove around behind the concrete sports center to the garbage dump, where we found the one-room shack that was the headquarters of the Albanian resistance group. We listened to their stories about the systematic exclusion of Albanians from edu-cation, civil service, and meaningful employment. Albanians, we were told, were being rounded up at random and detained.

As a condition of our visit, the Serbians had insisted that we meet with representatives of their occupation forces, and we found the provisional governor in a formal room in City Hall. We had decided to attempt a policy of constructive engagement, the kind of diplomatic nicety the State Department would have liked. But when he began denying everything we'd been told—in fact, most of what we had seen, as well—I couldn't control myself. No, that's not entirely true. I decided not to control myself. I confronted the Serb with everything I had heard and believed, and felt somewhat better for venting my spleen. My actions were irrelevant, of course. The Serbians weren't about to stop jailing Albanians just because some congresswoman from Staten Island yelled at them.

After six days of meeting with government, political, and religious leaders, of interviewing refugees and aid workers, we flew back to the United States more convinced than ever that the United States had to do something to stop the Serbians, to show the same resolve in Bosnia that George Bush had demonstrated in the Persian Gulf. Our demands were more specific than ever: air strikes against Serbian-controlled airports, railroad, energy sources, and ammunition dumps; the cutting of diplomatic ties to Belgrade; an end to the arms embargo to convince the Serbians that they did not have carte blanche to break cease-fire agreements and murder civilians; the immediate transfer of UN troops from Bosnia and Croatia, where their mission had been a failure, to Macedonia and Kosovo, which we believed would be Serbia's next prey.

To sway the conscience of the president and the nation, we went on television to talk about Kosovo, where ordinary people were being plucked off the street and jailed for no reason other than their ethnicity. We issued statements about the plight of the Croatians, who were so overwhelmed with Muslim refugees that the government literally had nowhere to house them. Push the Serbians into peace, we demanded of the president. Make them answer for the fall of Srebrenica, we insisted. The American people seemed inured to suffering. The White House had no comment.

All through the summer I tried to keep up the pressure, calling on the world community, and the United States, to remember its contempt for international indifference to the slaughter of the

Jews during World War II. In August, when a group of Clinton's foreign policy advisers quit in protest over his refusal to take action in Bosnia, I used the word genocide. Still the administration did not budge.

In the fall I tried a new tactic. Six months earlier, in part at our urging, the United Nations had authorized the formation of an international war crimes tribunal to prosecute those responsible for the atrocities in Bosnia, with the inclusion of rape as a war crime. But nothing had happened: no tribunal, no prosecutions. I contacted Catharine MacKinnon, one of the nation's most controversial feminists and a professor of law at the University of Michigan. MacKinnon had recently taken on the cases of a group of Bosnian women who had been raped by Serbians. I asked her to join me at the United Nations to lobby the ambassadors for the prompt convening of the tribunal.

In the face of reports about rape camps, I was convinced that the feminist community, at least, would rally to the support of the women of Bosnia, especially given the activism of MacKinnon, who is smart and incredibly well prepared. The Serbian military, in pursuit of a Greater Serbia, routinely, as a weapon of war, raped Croatian and Bosnian women up to ten times a day until they became pregnant with Serbian babies. But most of the feminist community showed little interest in our battle. When asked about our UN activities, the co-president of the Staten Island chapter of the National Organization for Women didn't even deign to address them. Instead, she said simply, "I don't think she [Molinari] is sophisticated enough for Washington . . . it's like she's right out of the cornfield.

"Is she going to be the cutesy of the House forever?"

By then the White House was so entrenched in its rhetoric and inactivity that when the Bosnian ambassador, a Muslim, flew to Washington to plead for help, he was spurned by Clinton and wound up meeting with me, Senate majority leader George Mitchell, and minority leader Bob Dole instead. It was a shameless act of contempt that was superseded only by the indifference of Boutros Boutros-Ghali, the secretary of the United Nations, the following month.

The world press had discovered, and reported, that UN troops in Sarajevo had been regular patrons of a Serbian-run brothel six miles north of Sarajevo, where Muslim and Croatian women were being forced to work as prostitutes. According to those accounts, the troops had even transported captive Muslim and Croatian women in their armored personnel carriers and jeeps. The secretary general's reaction—that he would investigate the charges—was entirely inadequate. Added to the inaction of the president, it pushed me over the edge. "The spineless bureaucrats tell us that Bosnia is too complicated a situation to solve," I said in total exasperation. "In reality, Bosnia is not complicated, prosecuting war crimes is not complicated, doing what is morally right is not complicated. It just takes will and strength of character."

The dawn of the new year, 1994, offered no improvement in the situation in the Balkans. In fact, things actually deteriorated when the president began to talk about creating peace by partitioning Bosnia. My disgust reached an all-time high. How could we reward Serb aggression by giving them land they had stolen? Even worse, the president offered to lift the economic sanctions against Serbia itself if that government would participate in peace negotiations. Bribing murderers to end their killing sprees did not seem to me a noble foreign policy. It was one of the few times in my life that I've actually been ashamed of my government.

Clinton knew what to do. When Serbian forces laid siege to Sarajevo, he demanded the withdrawal of Serb artillery around the city and backed that demand up with a promise to send U.S. planes on air strikes against Serbian positions if that deadline expired. His actions worked. The Serbs backed off. But the president refused to apply that same strategy to Mostar and other Muslim enclaves.

Month after month I barraged the White House with the same demands: Lift the arms embargo, authorize air strikes, and stop the genocide. And, gradually, our small chorus of voices became a clamor. In May, the Senate voted to lift the arms embargo. Unfortunately, after considerable pressure from the White House and State Department, the Senate backpedaled in a separate resolution by urging that it be lifted only if our Western allies supported such a move.

I refused to countenance such a halfway measure. I didn't care if our Western allies were willing to permit genocide in Bosnia. I was not. Finally, in June 1994, I believed we had the votes necessary in the House to do what the Senate had been too timid to do: Lift the arms embargo entirely. The moment was ripe; the Serbians had just rejected a plan to end the war. We tacked the lifting of the embargo onto a defense budget bill, which would force the president to either end the embargo or veto the entire package.

"Let us be clear," I said during the floor debate, "the war is going on in Bosnia whether or not we see it on television." The concentration camps, I continued, "still have an open-for business shingle."

The president fumed that such a move would throw U.S. foreign policy into disarray. Hours before the vote, he sent Defense Secretary William Perry, General John Shalikashvili, Chairman of the Joint Chiefs of Staff, and Deputy Secretary of State Strobe Talbott to Capitol Hill to warn members that the measure would imperil U.S. relations with Russia, wreck NATO, and draw the United States inexorably into the conflict. Those warnings made little impact. The bill passed by a wide margin. The victory was Pyrrhic, however, since it got tied up in endless reconciliation negotiations with the Senate, and stalled.

The lifting of the embargo wasn't my only goal. I wanted those responsible for the atrocities committed in Bosnia and Croatia—the ethnic cleansing, the mass rape, the murders—punished. Unfortunately, the United Nations tribunal had postponed more investigations than it had completed. I begged the White House again and again, in public and in private, to put pressure on the UN to move forward with the trials. But the administration was lukewarm about those trials, at best. In fact, testifying before Congress, Secretary of State Warren Christopher said that all parties in the conflict were equally responsible for the atrocities. That was not true, and Christopher's error was not based on misinformation. The CIA had already documented that ninety percent of the atrocities committed in the region had been committed by the Serbs. Surely Warren Christopher had full access to those reports.

By August 1995, Bob Dole had convinced the Senate to join the House in ending the arms embargo unconditionally. I was relieved, but still furious that we had delayed a full year. So I was bitter when I rose to speak on the measure. "We gave them a year," I said. "A year of more bombings, a year of more bloodshed, another year of children being viciously taken from their parents, another year of women being raped and men being tortured. . . . We've heightened our complicity by insisting that the Bosnians do nothing. Fathers forced to rape their daughters at knifepoint. Do nothing. Concentration-camp victims forced to drink their own urine to stall dehydration. Do nothing. Mothers forced to watch their babies beheaded in front of them. Do nothing. . . . No more delays. The Serbians have not stopped in their quest for blood. The UN cannot save a town, a life, or a hope.

"Our actions are all too reminiscent of what Neville Chamberlain wrote fifty years ago as he dismissed Nazi aggression. 'How horrible,' he wrote, 'how incredible it is that we should be digging trenches and trying on gas masks here because of a quarrel in a faraway country between people of whom we know nothing.' His words sound very similar to the speeches we've heard here today. It was tragic then. It is tragic now.

"No more delays."

Even as we debated a unilateral end to the embargo, Clinton was continuing his war of appeasement by throwing his weight behind the Dayton Peace Accords, which were, essentially, a partition treaty. I loathed the idea of sanctioning the partition of a country that had been divided by invasion. I was convinced that the land apportionment left the door open to further Serbian expansion. And I hated the treaty most of all because it let war criminals like Rodvan Kardzic and Ratko Mladic off with a slap on the wrist. Their only penalty for mass genocide would be that they could never again hold public office.

Worse yet, the president—the same president who'd spent three years justifying a foreign policy that left thousands of Bosnians, Croatians, and Kosovons to the viciousness of the Serbians on the grounds that he did not want the U.S. pulled into the war— was proposing that we send twenty thousand troops to back up those accords.

It was as a result of that proposal that I flew to Belgrade for my meeting with Milosevic. Neither before nor after that visit did I support the troop idea. Not only did I deem it imprudent, I believed it to be unnecessary. I was convinced that the Bosnians and Croatians could guarantee their own peace if they had access to weapons. Nonetheless, I ultimately declined to oppose Clinton's plan to send troops. By the time the measure arrived in the House, American soldiers were already on the ground; I could not support any action that would have demoralized them. Furthermore, I knew that the House action would be no more than symbolic. Bill Clinton had decided on his course of action, and we were not going to dissuade him.

I can't look back and claim to have made a huge impact on

the Balkans. I was heartened in 1994 when Henry Kissinger admitted on national television that I'd been right when I'd told Dan Quayle and Brent Scowcroft that we should bomb Belgrade into submission. But being heartened didn't change the fact that almost three million people lost their homes, and a quarter of a million their lives. I knew I was right at the time, just as I knew I was right for the four years I pushed and lobbied and complained. And I'm both sad and angry that so few people listened, not because my ego needs to be stroked, but because a change in U.S. policy would have saved lives.

While I didn't have the influence I might have liked, I did manage one concrete achievement that left me with the kind of personal pride that surpasses politics. During my trip to Kosovo with Bill, Pete King, and Elliot Engel, I heard from the Albanians about two aid workers from the French group Equilibra who had been jailed by the Serbs on some trumped-up charge. When we met with the Serbian governor, I inquired about the men. They are criminals who had a radio, he explained. "Have they been charged?" I asked. "Not yet," the governor responded. "Are they being well treated?" I pressed. "Absolutely," he countered.

I was too angry at everything I had seen up to that point to leave the matter there. "Prove it," I dared him. "Let me see them." The governor grudgingly responded, "When?" I didn't skip a beat. "Now," I responded. We drove directly to the jail, where I demanded to see the prisoners. "Come back in the morning," the jailers insisted. The kind of fury that can be foolishly wanton grabbed hold of me. "Now," I said yet again, plunking myself down on the nearest chair. "I'm not leaving until I see those two men."

The air grew heavy with tension as I leaned back and made myself comfortable. There are times when you can't resist drawing a line in the sand. The jailers got the message that I had reached one of those times. The puzzled prisoners were brought out to speak with me, and I left with some minor sense of satisfaction. That night, however, while we were at dinner, the two young men came into the restaurant. They'd been released just after our meeting.

Not much, but not bad. I didn't save the Bosnians, Croatians, or Albanians. But two lives were better than none.

Chapter Six

The Spoils of War

On November 1, 1994, all I wanted to do was stay home in Staten Island and celebrate. I'm a chronic worrier, but even a hysteric couldn't have been too concerned about a reelection in which the competition was an unknown who'd spent only $20,000 on his campaign. The polls showed me crushing Tyrone Butler, Bill was in his district in Buffalo, and I was ready to put election '94 behind me.

Really ready. For two months Bill and I had been barnstorm-
ing the nation, stumping for candidates in eighty-four districts.
Half the press covering those forays portrayed me as the loyal wife,
traveling the nation to provide solace to her husband, who, as head
of the National Republican Congressional Committee, was the
leader of our crusade to increase the number of House Republicans.
The other half painted my travels as yet another indication that I
was Newt's good little girl. They were all wrong. It was a power
play, pure and simple.

Earlier that year, after I'd decided not to run for the governorship of New York, I'd started thinking about trying for a position in the House Republican leadership. Really, I'd been thinking
about making that move for several years, but as a kind of fantasy.
I'm one of those people who just can't leave well enough alone. If I
was going to continue playing the game, I wanted to play in the big
leagues.

In the House of Representatives, that means being elected to a
position of party leadership. I had announced my intention to run
for vice chair of the party conference, the fifth-ranking slot, and the
road to victory would be paved with the IOUs I could collect by
helping Republican candidates all over the country. I needed those
chits because my opponent for the position was Cliff Stearns of
Florida, a dyed-in-the-wool conservative and antiabortion activist.
His friends hated me both because I was pro-choice and because I
had supported the assault weapons ban. They'd been champing at
the bit for an opportunity to pay me back for my role in the crime
bill, and my run for leadership was the perfect opportunity. There
was nothing subtle about their motivations. Duke Cunningham of
California actually came up and said to me, "I'm not only going to
vote against you, I will work against you because of the crime bill."

Even before the 1994 election campaign was in full swing, I
had started working with potential candidates who came to Wash-

ington for briefings and training. Bill had been recruiting them for two years, and he regularly turned them over to me for encouragement and advice. Every time a female aspirant came to town, Bill would send her to meet with me on what it was like to run as a female Republican. I'd try to rope other women members into joining us to talk about everything from fund-raising to the downside of wearing heels. But usually the only takers were my friends Deb Pryce and Ileana Ros-Lehtinen, the other two members of the Short Blond Caucus. It became a joke among candidates and aspiring candidates: "Do you have to be a short blonde to win a seat as a Republican woman?"

But in the last few weeks before the election, Bill and I upped the ante, flying from city to city, sometimes hitting three or four states in a single day. We offered to go anywhere as long as the airline we were booked on offered a plane with two engines and two pilots, which wasn't always that readily available. One evening we wound up leaving Minnesota for Omaha, Nebraska, in a two-engine Cessna, which did have two pilots, although their average age was about eighteen. Once we got in the air, the ride was incredibly bumpy; both pilots had forgotten to retract the flaps. Then the heater didn't work, so we had to turn around and wait two hours while it was fixed. Finally, on our approach into Omaha, the pilots worked themselves into a frenzy because they simply couldn't find the landing lights the air traffic controller had specified. They clearly saw landing lights, but they didn't begin to resemble the ones they were hearing about. Bill heard them fretting and complaining and looked up. "Hey, guys," he said. "I think you're looking at the wrong airport. That's the Strategic Air Command base you're heading for."

In the West, people looked at me like a Martian when I gesticulated like a wild New Yorker. In the South, I was never sure that anyone understood a word I said since no one else was slurring entire sentences into single words. And in every small town, the sight of a female member of Congress was as exotic as the appearance of a bearded lady.

I was Dorothy journeying to Oz, and I never doubted for a second that I wasn't in New York any longer. In one district, the candidate warned me that the press hated him and would probably pepper me with tough questions. After our press conference, he apologized for the hostility. I hadn't noticed any. That's what comes from spending your life dealing with the New York press corps. In another district, the journalists who approached us were, in reality, members of the candidate's staff posing as reporters to make us feel that somebody cared that we'd come.

One evening we landed in Medford, Oregon, to campaign for Wes Cooley. The night before his campaign breakfast, Bill and I didn't sleep. The bar in the Holiday Inn blared country music incessantly. When they took a break, the din was replaced by the roar of tractor-trailer engines racing in the parking lot. So I wasn't in the greatest mood at seven A.M., when we walked into Cooley's event. The candidate began by introducing his guests, which included a committee of local people, Bill, and me. When Cooley got around to explaining who we were, he said, "We got two congressmen here with us today, and one of them is, well, a girl. Yep, they've got Congress girls now in Washington." I smiled, dug my nails into Bill's thigh, and applauded politely.

By election night I couldn't decide whether to be tense, excited, or just relieved that I didn't have to worry about my own race. Bill was predicting a Republican sweep, but I am constitutionally incapable of that level of optimism. But I knew that the potential was there. Every poll indicated that the American people were fed up with Washington, with an economy that offered less for their children than they had, and with the sense that politicians in Washington were ruled by self-interest and special interests rather than the good of the nation. Clinton had come into office promising a new agenda, a new approach to the nation's problems. He had not delivered.

We Republicans had targeted voter frustration with a single clear message: No more business as usual. And in May, six months before the general election, we realized we had struck a chord. In a special election in Oklahoma, our House candidate, a rancher, beat an opponent who'd had years of experience in Washington as chief of staff for a Democratic senator. Suddenly Bill smelled the possibility of a much wider victory. One special election remained in which to test the waters, a race in a largely rural district in Kentucky. That should not have been much of a race, since the Democratic candidate was the party leader in the Kentucky State Senate and the Republican a part-time minister who owned a Christian bookstore. But the Oklahoma victory suggested that our strategy of nationalizing the election, of turning it into a referendum on business as usual, might actually work. With the support of Newt, Bill decided to go for broke in a final test of that possibility. He hit up dozens of members with large campaign war chests for contributions to the campaign, then used the money to buy television air time for what became the most famous ad of the election season. The visual was a computer-generated graphic in which the face of the Democratic candidate, Joe Prather, dissolved into the face of Bill Clinton in a process called morphing.

The message was simple: "If you like Bill Clinton, you'll love Joe Prather." The House Republican conference had erupted in laughter and shouts of delight when Bill screened the spot for the group. Voters in Kentucky were just as impressed. Joe Prather was roundly defeated.

For election night Bill had arranged for dozens of counters and poll watchers to phone in results from across the nation. Newt had told the press that we would pick up enough seats to capture the majority. Although Bill had tried to rein in expectations lest the press treat our gains as a disappointment, he, too, was filled with optimism. I didn't know what to think, so I concentrated on what would happen with the governor's race in New York State.

Rather than stay home in Staten Island, Jim Mazzarella, my press secretary, and I decided to drive into Manhattan to see what was happening at state Republican party headquarters, which were in the Hilton. We drove into town in my Jeep Wagoneer with my dad, stopped for a quick dinner, then headed over to the Hilton. Even six months earlier, no one had held out much hope that we could capture the governor's mansion in Albany. Mario Cuomo, the three-term incumbent, was a national figure in the Democratic party, a man of stature and eloquence. Our candidate, George Pataki, was a young, relatively unknown assemblyman from an area just north of New York City. But in the weeks before the election, the poll numbers showed that Pataki was gaining on Cuomo. By election night the race seemed too close to call.

It still was when we arrived at the Hilton. But just as we were pulling up, my friend Julie Wadler called from the National Republican Congressional Committee office in Washington, where she was monitoring the returns. Things were looking good nationally, she said. Very good. We were winning seats we shouldn't be winning all across America. As we entered the Hilton ballroom, hundreds of reporters looked down from a ledge above the stage with that hunger that seizes media folk when news is breaking. In a flash, word spread that Sue Molinari had arrived. They descended on me in a swarm. I'd never been in that kind of frenetic situation before, with cameras being shoved into my face and dozens of reporters throwing questions at me in a pack. Then again, I'd never before been on the verge of being a member of a history-making majority.

Jim sorted the reporters into a line, and I spent the next hour moving up and down it, commenting on what seemed to be happening. The Republican party was sweeping the nation. With a confidence I would not have anticipated even thirty minutes earlier, I was predicting that before the night was out, we might well be the party in power in Congress, the first time Republicans would be in control since 1952.

Between interviews Jim fed me the numbers coming in from Bill and Julie. Bill had spent most of the day in his district in Buffalo. But by seven P.M. he was back in his NRCC office after a trip on a private plane that was so packed that he'd been forced to use the toilet as his seat. Early reports from all those districts where I'd spent the past two months were amazing. We weren't just winning more seats than we'd expected. We seemed to be winning every seat. I could almost smell victory. The energy was getting higher and higher. We already had a Republican mayor in New York. Congress was falling into our hands. And, as the night progressed, it appeared that even the governor's mansion would be ours. Even in my fog I began to feel the promise of a sea change, for America and for me.

Before the night was over I became a member of the new Republican majority. Sixty of the candidates Bill and I had campaigned for won their elections. We defeated the Speaker of the House, Tom Foley, Dan Rostenkowski, chairman of the Ways and Means Committee, and Mario Cuomo, the governor of New York. We gained fifty-two new seats, eleven new statehouses, and nine million more votes than we had received in 1992.

Those of us who had worked in the minority, who had always thought of ourselves as the minority, had never had the chance to try out our ideas, even to have our programs be given serious consideration. For forty years we had learned to be grateful when Democrats agreed to co-sponsor our bills, or when television producers gave us five minutes on television. The unexpected win was like a giddy drunk. On that one night we went from being nobody and nothing, second-class congressmen, to being in charge of the U.S. House of Representatives.

◆

Four days after the election, Bill and I flew to St. Bart's for a long-delayed honeymoon. We'd rented a villa on the beach and had planned to spend a romantic and leisurely ten days concentrating on nothing but each other, the sun, and some great food. Unfortunately, St. Bart's had telephone service.

Taking charge of Congress meant designing a new leadership structure, appointing committee chairs, hiring staff to run offices, and finalizing a new legislative package. We had barely two months to get ready. Although the Associated Press did not declare our ownership of the House of Representatives until three in the morning after election day, by then, Bill, a member of Newt Gingrich's inner circle, was already in the middle of an endless conference call with Newt, who was in Atlanta, and the other members of the Republican leadership.

Newt needed one thousand planning meetings, and Bill was expected to participate in each one. In the four days between the election and our departure for St. Bart's, while I called to congratulate the newly elected freshmen who would decide my race for the vice chair of the conference, Bill raced from one meeting to another, making lists, preparing reports, laying the groundwork for the transition. Once we were installed in our villa overlooking St. Jean Bay, nothing changed.

Reporters wanted to interview us, our staffs had dozens of questions, and Newt's staff set up leadership meetings that included conference calls with Bill that lasted three, five, even six hours a day. Bill looked longingly at the sun and the sea from inside the living room. The cord on the phone in our villa wouldn't stretch far enough to allow him to sit outside. It was hardwired in, so he couldn't even replace it with a cord long enough to allow him to walk to the refrigerator for a beer.

Once or twice during one of Newt's long-winded exegeses on Napoleon or Alvin Toffler, Bill tried leaving the line open and sneaking out to the beach with me. But someone would bring the discussion down to practicalities and ask Bill's opinion, which led to some embarrassing silences. Our greatest frustration, and fortune, was that the telephone system was a mess, with every call to Washington routed through Guadeloupe and Paris. The line would crash just in the middle of a critical discussion and it could take six or more attempts to reestablish the connection. Once in a while Bill would pretend that the line had crashed so that he could take me out to dinner. Or he'd plead "interference" on the line, which was usually caused by my beating a can against the phone.

We couldn't escape. One afternoon, we decided to escape to a desolate corner of the island. We found a seaside resort that served lunch on the beach, and parked ourselves in chairs with the water lapping up to our feet. Finally, I thought, we were getting our honeymoon. I looked up into the distance and spotted Martin Hoke, a member from Ohio, strolling toward us. I couldn't resist a lobbying break. I needed his vote in my race for leadership.

The stakes in that race had risen dramatically with our victory in November. Sitting in leadership when your party is in the minority is interesting, but being in the leadership of the party that controls the House places you in the center of the storm, and at the apex of power. I'd announced my candidacy the June before, which seems early for a December election to anyone who operates in the real world. But in the surreal universe of partisan politics, that was actually late; Cliff Stearns of Florida had been in the race for months by then.

The election for leadership positions was scheduled for Tuesday, December 6, and the minute Bill and I got home, we pulled out all the stops in the last stage of our campaign strategy. I already had a long list of the chits that I'd garnered by helping out candidates with my presence and campaign contributions. I'd finagled an appointment to the steering committee of the Committee of Committees, hoping that members' desires to curry favor with me in their quest for choice assignments would give me an added boost. That final week, my job was to solidify my votes.

Then, the weekend before the elections, Cliff's minions went on the attack. The freshmen, who would swing the vote, were all staying at the Hyatt, and every night they received a letter from someone like Paul Weyrich, a veteran conservative activist, or Gary Bauer, the head of the Family Research Council, criticizing something I'd said on television five years earlier. The Right to Life Committee issued communiqués painting me as the national spokeswoman for the "pro-abortion" movement because I'd been one of only a handful of Republicans who'd supported Clinton's efforts to restore federal funding for abortion. They made me out to be a fanatic indifferent to the needs of Americans to protect themselves because I'd supported the assault weapons ban. My leadership in the crime bill fight made me even more vulnerable. I suddenly became a sellout who had saved the president, just as Bill had predicted more than a year earlier.

I countered by attending every event held for the freshmen, who were key to the election. Bill and I slipped our own letters under their hotel room doors. I worked the phones all weekend, calling in my chits, or at least trying to. I had no way of knowing whether they would be honored, since the vote would be taken by secret ballot. I knew I could count on most of the moderates, who numbered about forty; there was no way they were going to vote for Cliff. And I hoped that many of the seventy-three freshmen, even those opposed to abortion, would remember that I'd been there for them during the dark days. But Bill has the perfect adage to describe those kinds of situations: In Washington, if you want a friend, get a dog.

The day of the election, I thought the numbers were leaning in my direction, but, frankly, there was no way to be sure. In those situations, people always slap you on the back and say, "Honey, I'm with you." But when voting is by secret ballot, those sorts of promises come easily. I picked three conservative members to deliver my nominating speech, including one of the leaders of the freshman class. Then I sat back and tried not to let them see me sweat until John Boehner, the conference chairman, announced my victory.

I'd been determined to become a player and, for better and for worse, my dream had come true. When Congress returned from break in January, I ranked ninety-second in seniority among the Republicans, and number five in the Republican leadership. I was thirty-six years old.

◆

How can I describe what the changeover from life in the minority to life in the majority felt like? Imagine having lived in Alaska all your life and abruptly waking up one morning in Florida (with all due respect to Alaska), or living in a cave and moving to a glass house on a hill. Not a single member of our conference had served in the House under a Republican majority. Not a single one of us had ever chaired a committee, or run a major debate on the House floor. The only Republican member who'd ever seen Republicans in the majority was Bill Emerson, who'd served as a congressional page in the 1950s. We'd spent decades as outsiders. We'd alternately begged the Democrats to consider our legislation and adopted the time-honored, traditional minority stance of naysaying. All of a sudden we mattered. Our ideas might actually turn into programs, our proposals might actually become law.

Tom DeLay, our whip, moved into an office that, rumor had it, had been Thomas Jefferson's. Other friends found themselves in suites lit by heavy chandeliers, original to the building, or offices still pockmarked with bullet holes from the Civil War. The

Speaker's suite commanded a riveting view down the length of the mall to the Washington Monument. Treasure troves of the nation's most important art were opened to us to hang on our walls.

Our offices were inundated with memoranda and planning documents, and our staffs were overwhelmed with conflicts in scheduling, moving, and media requests. Our press secretaries were no longer working the phones, begging the media to pay attention to us; journalists suddenly couldn't get enough of us. They tracked every negotiation over committee appointments and the selection of the new chairman. It was one of the mixed blessings of victory.

Our freshmen, all seventy-three of them, were constantly getting lost and rushing in late to meetings. There were few political insiders in their group, a new breed who didn't know their way around Washington, and they were indifferent, if not hostile, to most of its traditions. They plotted their revolution in the cafeteria, in conference meetings, and on the lawn of the Capitol. Their first sign that something really new was happening, that it was not all rhetoric, came the day Newt essentially scrapped the seniority system and announced the appointment of those freshmen to major committees and fewer senior members to chairmanships. The Old Guard, the Republican Old Guard, was being isolated, and power concentrated in the hands of the Speaker-to-be.

I finally, after four years, won my slot on the House Budget Committee and was appointed chair of the Railroad Subcommittee. The implications of my graduation from bit player to starring chair were awesome: One of the first items on the agenda for the new session was the revamping of Amtrak. I became the would-be architect of the rail system's future.

As we geared up for the opening session of the 104th Congress, Bill began to worry that the Democrats would tie us up in parliamentary maneuvers that we, who had no experience being in charge, would be helpless to counter. He envisioned even greater chaos because seventy-three of our members, the freshmen, had no idea how to behave on the House floor. So the leadership appointed Bob Walker of Pennsylvania, a genius at floor maneuvers, to lay out hypothetical situations and countermoves to prevent the new opposition from amending us to death, or from delaying consideration of legislation we had promised the electorate we would pass on our first day. He produced a script and we actually went to the House floor to rehearse being in charge.

◆

On January 4, 1995, it was too cold to be outside just so television crews could conduct interviews with Republicans posed in front of the Capitol. But that didn't stop them from demanding that I do so. In the frenzy of excitement that was the first day of the new session, the first day of *our* session, I couldn't say no, although the microphones almost froze to my skin. The Capitol was like an enormous political carnival with network anchors roaming the halls, talk radio hosts set up in the rotunda, and members' children racing around the House chamber. A sense of history being made hung over a place already heavy with history.

Just after twelve-thirty we gathered in the House chamber for the election of a new Speaker. The was no doubt as to the outcome, since Newt was unchallenged. But after forty minutes of voting, when his election became official, shock ignited the Republican members. "Newt! Newt! Newt!" we chanted. Speaker Richard Gephardt declared the end of the Democratic era and handed the gavel over to Newt Gingrich. Newt pulled out his own gavel, an oversized one. "This is a Georgia gavel I got this morning, done by Dorsey Newman of Tallapoosa, who decided that the gavels he saw on TV weren't big enough or strong enough," he explained. "So he cut down a walnut tree in his backyard and made a gavel."

Tradition demanded that we remain in session briefly, that opening day be a kind of pro forma session leading to a quick adjournment until after the president's State of the Union address.

We did not adjourn. We stayed in session until we had passed every piece of legislation we'd designed to change the rules of the House, fulfilling the first promise in our Contract with America. Hour after hour we tackled reforms that even Democrats agreed were long overdue. We cut the number of committees, slashed committee staffs by a third, banned closed committee meetings, ended voting by proxy, and imposed term limits for the first time in the nation's history—on our chairmen and the Speaker of the House. In fourteen hours and twenty-four minutes we accomplished what members on both sides of the aisle had talked about doing for decades.

Just before midnight, in between votes, we gathered in Newt's new suite of offices—his leadership team, children, and close friends. It wasn't a giddy or raucous celebration—no champagne, just Newt's favorite, Foster's lager "oil cans." We were numb with the enormity of what we had accomplished, and what we had promised to accomplish over the coming ninety-nine days. I was numb at the position I had finally reached. There sat Newt, the Speaker of the House of Representatives. And there I sat, in the leadership of his House.

Newt Gingrich was like no other Speaker the House had ever seen, and, at that point, no one was sure precisely what that would mean. Unlike the rest of us, he hadn't entered Congress thinking he would do some good or gain some power. From the day he was elected in 1978, on his third try for public office, he had been planning for that night. While other members talked about legislation, Newt talked about extending freedom and Alvin Toffler's Third Wave, about cyberspace, de Tocqueville, Winston Churchill, and regaining control of Congress to undo the New Deal. He didn't give us memos to study, but reading lists in history and military strategy.

Newt's the type of man who loves plans and systems, and for

fifteen years he created task forces, arranged informal meetings, and founded new organizations to advance his agenda for Republican control of the House. The first, Project Majority Task Force, convened just five months after he entered Congress, was a stunning, and classic, example of Newt's vision, and arrogance. He barely knew his way through the back corridors of the Capitol, yet was already plotting the revolution. He stormed into the NRCC, then run by Guy Vander Jagt, and demanded that he begin strategizing an end to Democratic domination of the House.

I don't want to make it sound like Newt laid the groundwork for the Republican revolution carefully, because that simply is not his style. He laid the groundwork, but he was too much of a loose cannon to be careful. He slashed and burned his way through the conference, stepping on toes, creating enemies, and alienating every member of the leadership on both sides of the aisle. Nonetheless, his vision of our regaining the majority, a possibility most people never took seriously, was like a magnet.

The force of that vision might not have been enough if Newt were really the conservative ideologue most Americans believe him to be. But, in fact, he is just the opposite. No matter what his personal beliefs are, he is the single most pragmatic politician I've ever met. He knew we would never win a majority as long as the party was at war with itself, as long as members threw verbal and political bombs at each other, for example. So he forged a single conservative idea—the dismantling of the Big Government—around which we could rally, and then, much to the dismay of his early conservative supporters, offered moderates a seat at the table if they would board his train.

To Republican members, especially to those of us elected in the late 1980s, Newt wasn't so much the conservative alternative to a moderate establishment as the activist alternative to an establishment of older members who often seemed defeatist. He overwhelmed everyone with his ideas and energy, even with his view of himself as a genuine revolutionary. He believed in the power of ideas, and threw them out with dizzying speed in late-night telephone calls, on tapes, and at lectures.

By 1989, when the position of Republican whip opened up, he had a firm cadre of followers. Minority leader Bob Michel, who was no fan of the Georgia upstart, had no desire to see Newt in that position, but Newt was able to send both conservatives and moderates like Nancy Johnson and Steve Gunderson, precisely the people to whom he'd offered that seat at the table, to ask Michel to remain neutral in the election. Michel bowed to the inevitable, and Newt slipped in by two votes.

By October 1993, when minority leader Bob Michel announced his retirement from Congress, Newt was the heir apparent. In fact, by then he had been the leader-in-waiting for almost four years. Nonetheless, he took no chances. When he announced his intention to run for the job—a full fourteen months before the election would ever be held—he staged it as a preemptive strike. Seventy-five members appeared at his side, and dozens more, including me, announced that we would support him. The only question left at that point was how to make sure that Newt became not the minority leader, but the Speaker of the House.

Bill agreed with Newt that the 1996, if not the 1994 election, was winnable for Republicans nationwide if we played our cards right. And in fact, we played from a dozen decks simultaneously. Bill's job as chairman of the National Republican Congressional Committee was to make sure that we had enough money to be in the game. That seemed like an impossible task in 1992, which explains why no one ran against Bill for that chairmanship. Between 1981 and 1992, the NRCC had poured $260 million into House races, yet we had actually lost sixteen seats. The field staff was bloated; the group was $4.5 million in debt. When he took over, Bill was told that the NRCC fund-raising list included a million names. In fact, it contained 100,000 names, and the average age of the potential donors was seventy-eight.

Bill brought his chief of staff, Maria Cino, over as executive director, and the two of them changed all the rules. They pared the staff down to twenty-five and informed members that they could no longer expect the routine $5,000 campaign checks they'd been accustomed to receiving. Incumbents who wanted financial support had to prove that they really needed help to stave off a serious challenge.

If that wasn't bad enough, Bill demanded that members with fat war chests recycle the wealth for the "greater good." No one had ever made that request before. He startled them even further by assessing them dues: $2,500 for freshmen, $5,000 for other members, and $7,500 for members in positions of leadership. At first people laughed at the concept, but Newt put on the pressure, reminding members that loyalty would be a criterion in the selection of committee chairmen in the future. More than a million dollars suddenly flowed into the NRCC's coffers.

As we got closer to the 1994 elections, Bill and Newt upped the ante even further. In the middle of July they asked every member either to donate $148,000 to the NRCC from his or her own campaign funds, or agree to raise $50,000 for the group over the final fourteen weeks before the election. John Boehner and I led off the spree of giving. Another $5 million came in to finance the races of the candidates that Bill had carefully recruited and trained.

Money wasn't enough, of course. We needed to use it to convince the American people that the time had come to throw the Democrats out. The plan for doing so—for nationalizing the election—came together gradually in late 1993 and early 1994, and became concrete in the morph ad the NRCC ran in Kentucky in May. That strategy grew out of a simple suggestion by John Kasich of Ohio, the ranking Republican on the budget committee. Kasich was fed up with spending his time wielding an ax at Democratic budget plans and suggested that we forget about tradition and present our own budget to the Congress. It was classic Kasich, the son of a mailman, who seems alternatively innocent and brash.

The very concept of doing things in ways they had never been done, of going against the grain, is precisely the kind of approach Newt loves. He's got a deep rebel streak that inclines him toward upsetting even the best apple carts. The notion of nationalizing the election, which defied the conventional wisdom that all politics are local, then, was irresistible. In the end, Newt went Kasich one better. Why just the budget and deficit reduction? Why not welfare reform, tax policy regulatory reform, an entire plan for smashing Big Government and repealing the New Deal?

The notion of presenting a single, coherent vision of what Republicans would do if they were running the House wasn't an instant hit. Unless you're a real politics junkie, you probably don't understand how revolutionary the concept of presenting a minority platform was. I'm not talking content—that comes later—but approach. House tradition dictates that members in the minority respond. They snipe about majority proposals, and whittle away at them. They posture, complain, and sling rhetoric. They do not, however, present full-fledged alternatives. It just isn't done.

"Why would we want to give the Democrats something to attack?" people argued when the idea was first fielded. Kasich countered, "How can we ask voters to make us the majority party if we don't show them what we stand for?" A member like Bill, who was skeptical at best, would shoot back, "But we're the minority and are powerless to pass our own program." A Young Turk like me would respond, "Who wants to vote for professional naysayers?"

That was the mood when Republican members went to Salisbury, Maryland, on retreat in January 1994. Up to that point, our retreats had been more show-and-tell than times for serious discussion. The year before, we'd gathered in Princeton, New Jersey, and the place was crawling with lobbyists. That was not my idea of a productive retreat. When the Salisbury session was announced, I refused to attend. I wasn't inclined to waste my time on another dog and pony show for contributors.

But Salisbury was different. Rather than gathering at a fancy hotel paid for by special interests, conference members convened at a small state university over a grim and rainy weekend without lobbyists or donors. Everyone was sick of spending their days on the attack—although we all relished our victories against Clinton's nationalized health care plan and economic stimulus package. The prospect of being positive rather than negative, of showing the voters that we weren't playing a game of sour grapes because we weren't in power, began to gain deep-rooted appeal. By the time Bill and the other members returned, it was clear that we had the broad outlines of a plan.

Through the late winter and early spring, though, the idea still had no concrete foundation. How would we present to the American people, in all states and districts, a coherent view of what a Republican-led House of Representatives would do, and ask them to endorse that plan by sending us enough Republican representatives to put us in power? What would be in such a plan, and how could we possibly get members to agree on it? Would voters buy it, or would they dismiss it as hokey?

Bill and his staff at the NRCC decided to find out by polling sample voters with different scenarios. The early results were not encouraging. People weren't impressed with the prospect of Republicans saying: Kick out the Democrats and give us a chance. They were so cynical that even the idea of a specific plan didn't hit much of a nerve. What about a signed contract? they were asked. Even then the people polled remained skeptical. Finally they tried one last approach: What if we offered you a signed contract with a provision saying "If we don't fulfill it, kick us out of office"? That struck a chord.

The problem, of course, was forging such a contract, with boiling scores of ideas and proposals down to ten concrete points on which we all—incumbents and candidates—could agree. In the spring, the job of making that happen was assigned to the staff of Dick Armey, our majority leader. They designed a survey form with sixty-five items in twelve categories and mailed it to sitting members and candidates. They met with the moderates and conservatives, and with the major groups that traditionally support Republican candidates. It should have been a nightmare, since the party included people who wanted more environmental regulation and others who wanted no regulation, environmental or otherwise, whatsoever; people who wanted no controls on women's access to abortion and others who wanted to throw abortion doctors in jail; people who opposed any form of gun control and others who believed that the Brady bill didn't go far enough.

That's where Newt's political genius proved itself. He held up the magic figure of sixty percent as the level of agreement we'd have to achieve on any item. He fended off Dick Armey's attempts to include a plank on school prayer by laying out precisely how that proposal would play in the *Wall Street Journal.* When members were at loggerheads, he'd put them on a task force together and give them twenty-four hours to come up with a compromise. He committed people into submission. He might be mercurial and even petulant, but Newt Gingrich knows how to build a team.

In the end, we culled out of the repertoire of Republican proposals the ten that were, I believe, at the core of our beliefs, including a balanced budget, reform of the way the House worked, welfare reform, a real war on crime, support for families with children, relief from a crushing burden of regulation, legal reform, term limits. We were not agreeing to support all these proposals, just agreeing that they were important enough that we owed the American people a vote on them.

No one was entirely happy, of course. I was, and remain,

incredibly uncomfortable with the provision of our welfare reform program that would require a mother to identify her child's father in order to get assistance. It puts a heavy burden on a woman who might not know who the father is, or who might not want the father to know about the kid, or might need to protect herself from the kind of abuse that the courts don't handle very well. I was opposed to term limits.

I believed that more women's issues should be included, especially a provision for more access to day care for all Americans. I argued that such a provision would be a concrete demonstration of the value that we placed on families, many of which had few options if they wanted their children in safe and protected environments. That proposal actually made it into discussion, but we could not agree on how to fund it. In the end, I lost that and a number of other battles to the argument that singling out women's issues, or children's issues, or any other subgroup's issues would defeat the point of our contract. I bowed to the consensus that we should concentrate on reforms that would affect every American.

September 27, 1993, the day of the unveiling of our Contract with America, was amazingly bright and sunny, following on the heels of three days of miserable Washington rain. Members and their staffs swarmed onto the west side of the Capitol, as eight buses pulled up with candidates and their families. Bill and I joined the other Republican incumbents and challengers, 367 strong, piled onto a three-tiered stage to unveil our Contract with America, to sign and proclaim our plan for dealing with the nation's most pressing problem. In doing so, we offered the voters a deal: Give us at least forty-two more seats, and within one hundred days of the opening of the 104th Congress, we will present and vote on a plan to balance the federal budget within seven years; a tax reform package that provides parents with a $500 tax credit for each child in the family and cuts capital gains taxes; a crime package emphasizing enforcement rather than social spending; and a comprehensive program of welfare reform. We promised that on the first day of the session we would begin by putting our own House in order with a set of real operational reforms. For voters who didn't see the event, we bought an ad in *TV Guide* that laid out our contract in clear language.

A demoralized and fractious Republican conference had been forged into consensus and unity. But we had no idea whether the American people would care, or whether they would even know what we had done. If the electorate responded, which history suggests that it did, we Republicans probably can't take the full credit. The Democrats fell directly into our trap. They seized on the document as if it were manna from heaven, and began attacking us for our proposals. In the process, they nationalized the election for us.

◆

The contract was not a simple election ploy. When we won the 1994 election, it became our blueprint. We didn't need to scramble and strategize what we would do during our first months in office, or how we would prove that we'd been serious when we'd declared no more business as usual. We had a clear set of promises to guide us and believed that if we did not deliver on them, the American people would throw us out in the blink of an eye. We'd invited them to do that, and it was not a prospect we relished.

It wasn't just the American people we were worried about; it was the Democrats. They were still off balance from the surprising election returns, and we needed to break the logjam and shift power back to the states quickly before the president could recoup. We needed to change the terms of the debate definitively before the Democrats in the House could learn how to be effective in the minority.

The political marathon that followed was its own unique form of insanity. Committee hearings that usually took months were concluded in days. As soon as one bill was sent to the floor, we began voting, even while the next part of the package was still in committee. We were driven. We had revved the engine of the train up to such a high speed that we had no time to consider, to rethink, even to go grocery shopping and remember how real people live. Gotta go, gotta move.

Most days I began before breakfast and got home, exhausted, well after the eleven P.M. news. All day I juggled: a subcommittee hearing on some Amtrak legislation scheduled at the same time as a budget committee meeting, both interrupted by floor votes, bill signings, and interviews with reporters. I watched the leadership staff work like human computers, getting bills drafted, keeping track of their flow through the committee structure and guiding them onto the floor. We stayed on the floor voting until midnight, and returned to our offices in the morning to find unshaven and bleary-eyed assistants who hadn't been home at all. Some of the freshmen declared that they would not move to Washington, yet another sign of their often arrogant independence. Newt gave them permission to live in their offices, and they worked around the clock.

First it was the Congressional Accountability Act, which mandated that the same laws that we passed for the rest of the country would apply to us. It passed unanimously on January 17 and was signed into law six days later. Then came a bill to curb unfunded mandates, which was a nod to the Republican governors. We'd been passing legislation for years that required the states to do X, Y, or Z without giving them any money to pay for our bright ideas. They wanted us to stop. The Democrats put up a token opposition, primarily in the form of dozens of amendments. But we were on a roll. The bill passed the House on February 1.

Then we turned our attention to a new crime package, our attempt to take back the issue as our own after the president's crime bill of 1994. We held a slim margin in the House, and could not afford to alienate either moderates or conservatives lest our momentum stop. The crime bill was the first test of our unity because it had no provision for lifting the assault weapons ban, a major conservative demand. The NRA was livid, and we feared that their pressure could bring the whole house of cards tumbling down. Leadership meetings were tense as we worried about holding our conservative flanks in check. We dispatched Newt to negotiate, as we did repeatedly during those first months. We all knew that he was the glue holding us together. The opposition was squelched for that moment. The bills slid through the House virtually unscathed.

If the NRA brought us grief from the right flank, the next bills, governing regulatory reform, ran us into trouble on our left. We all agreed that the federal government was overregulating the country, but one person's "unnecessary" regulation is the next person's salvation for the environment. And it was, in fact, our members concerned with the environment, rather than labor or consumer affairs, who balked at the proposals. In leadership meetings we pored through lists of members, checking and rechecking who might bolt. We called in skeptical members, pleading with them for yet another show of unity. Most simply folded and opted to vote with the majority, assuming that the measures would be stopped in the Senate. But we knew we were close to the edge, and that the endless meetings and internal lobbying sessions really were.

I won't go through the list measure by measure. Suffice it to say that by February, most of us were staggering around the Capitol. We were at that point of exhaustion where you feel entirely in command although you are moving and thinking like an automaton. Members would fall asleep on the floor in the middle of votes, or show up to vote with temperatures of 102. Spouses complained. Marriages frayed. The freshmen, who had hit the ground running before they had even moved into their houses, or sold their businesses at home, had to learn to live by bells that were ringing more frequently than they ever had in the history of the nation.

Bill and I were living in a town house on Capitol Hill, not far from the Capitol itself. Our living room became the place where exhausted members would stop when they were too exhausted to drive home. Members and staffers who lived in the neighborhood would come by for a beer or a relief from the adrenaline. Most of the time we were too punch drunk from lack of sleep to have organized parties or dinners. We finally descended into the total silliness of the bunker mentality. We reached the nadir one night, when a dozen or more people were lazing around our living room and heard a voice singing outside. It was Dan Frisa, a member from Long Island, singing "When the moon hits your eye like a big pizza pie, that's Molinari."

By the fifty-day mark, members started worrying that Newt, who seemed impervious to fatigue, would proclaim a second-one-hundred plan, like the old Soviet Five-Year Plans that went on for half a century. Newt promised to rein himself in, and Bill tried to cheer everyone up with a party. He rented out Head's, a Hill restaurant and hangout, but hardly anyone showed up. Members needed the night off to sleep or take a bath.

Bill and I not only had our committee responsibilities, our constituents to attend to, and our staffs to manage. As members of leadership, we spent twenty to thirty hours a week in meetings. The laundry piled up, the refrigerator stayed empty, my hair grew out, and I was down to jogging twice a week at best. Some evenings I'd throw on my sweats and go out for a run, only to be interrupted by the blasting of my pager warning me of an impending vote. We survived on Chinese takeout and pasta, and I swilled dozens of Mountain Dews, since they had more caffeine than Coke or Pepsi.

There were momentary distractions from the political sweatshop, of course, and the best laugh was provided by Sonny Bono. Bono, of course, was the brunt of a gazillion jokes when he was elected, both inside and outside the Capitol. Once he arrived in

Washington, he became even more infamous for his impatience with the congressional process, even the speedway version we'd imposed. During endless hearings of the Judiciary Committee, on which he served, he'd try to speed things up by ordering in pizza and then withholding it until the marathon session ended, hoping that the enticing aroma would cut down on the verbiage.

But few of us had seen him in action until the annual congressional dinner held by the Washington Press Club Foundation on January 25. That kind of event isn't just for members and the Washington press corps. Colin Powell was there, along with Tipper Gore, Janet Reno, and Barbara Walters. Bianca Jagger showed up with Bob Torricelli, a member from New Jersey. Newt mingled with David Brinkley, Peter Jennings, and Sam Donaldson.

Bill and I were too tired to do much more than suffer through the dinner. Fred Thompson, a lawyer turned actor turned senator, told a few jokes. ("I still have a lot to learn about Washington. Yesterday I spent some of my own money.") John Ashcroft sang and Kay Bailey Hutchinson did a stand-up routine. By the time Sonny stood up, we were tired. We just wanted to go home.

He ad-libbed for twenty minutes, and brought the crowd to its feet with his imitation of Phil Gramm telling a crowd, "You can't eat corn if you ain't a pig." He made fun of himself and the other freshmen for their excessive dependence on maintenance workers for directions. And he brought down the crowd with a dead-on description of our new Speaker: "If you look at Newt, he's always smiling, but then he says something to rip your head off."

But such moments of relief were few and far between as we squeezed the tightest and most complex legislative agenda in the nation's history into a few short weeks. Fights broke out between the moderates and the freshmen over a bill that would mandate a supermajority for any legislation that would increase income taxes, and between those who believed that we should tackle the deficit before we lowered taxes and those convinced we should do both at the same time. When we began talking about welfare reform, the Christian Right insisted that we build a provision in to block grants to the states that would prod them into creating programs to reduce illegitimacy. The Catholic bishops balked, sure that such measures would encourage abortions.

As the Democrats regained their equilibrium, they began flaying us with a vengeance, painting our tax scheme as a sop to the rich and our reductions in the rate of growth of social spending as attacks on the poor. But we were too deeply enmeshed in our schedule to figure out how to counter that portrayal of us as a modern-day merger of the Grinch and Scrooge. We tried—God knows, I talked myself blue in the face on the radio and on television to remind voters that reductions in growth weren't cuts and that a crushing deficit could be fatal. I was the female face that we hoped would reassure Americans that we weren't really horrible people.

But there was no time to stop and lay out strategy. We careened from near-disaster to near-disaster. We squabbled and horse traded and twisted each other's arms until they were black and blue, but our coalition held. Committees held hearings, bills were marked up, and we ran to the floor, yet again, to vote.

On April 7, the ninety-third day of the session, we reassembled on the Capitol steps. It was almost spring, although few of us had noticed that buds were appearing on the city's cherry trees. The banner behind us read PROMISES MADE, PROMISES KEPT. We had pledged that we would vote on all ten provisions of the Contract with America, and we had fulfilled that pledge. It was a time to celebrate, but no one had the energy. We were relieved to be done. We were proud that we had stuck together. We were even awestruck at our accomplishments. But we could do nothing more than go home and sleep.

◆

On the personal front, the good news that arose from those first hundred days, and beyond, was that I finally shook off the image that I was nothing but a puppet of my father's. The bad news was that I still wasn't taken seriously as a free agent. Day after day I'd open local and national newspapers and read that I was moving to the right because Bill was pulling me into more conservative positions, or because I was kissing Newt's fanny. Although the American Conservative Union continued to criticize my voting record as too liberal, liberals accused me of becoming a "femi-Newtie." We hadn't been in the majority a month before Brooklyn Councilman Anthony Weiner compared me to a rented mule. And Pat Schroeder charged, "Everything changed when Newt took over. Her values just kind of melted down."

I admit that I wasn't lobbing grenades at the Speaker's office. And I never faced Bill down on television or during a public debate. But I honestly can't think of a single issue on which I changed my position. The problem was that people thought of me as a moderate because of my stands on abortion, gun control, day care, and family and medical leave. But the Contract with America and those first hundred days were not about those social issues. They were about balancing the budget, cutting taxes, regulation, court reform, and crime, issues on which I had always been conservative. From the start of my political career I disagreed with but one of the ten items that became the contract, term limits, and I never wavered from that position.

The problem is that the pundits and opinion makers confuse having an ideology with fitting neatly into someone else's predetermined philosophical category, and they are not the same thing. I'm ideological on all the issues, from NAFTA, abortion, and the assault weapons ban, which I support, to affirmative action, which I don't. I believe in forcing the government to move on combined sewer overflows to save our beaches and our oceans. I believe that the worst way to deal with teen pregnancy is to attack teen moms as immoral, when they're the ones home raising the kids while the fathers, who are racing around partying, get off scot-free. I think that our nation's attitude toward kids is a disastrous war between those who think that parents have the right to exercise total control over their kids, which inevitably includes abusing and battering them, and people who think everybody deserves five or six chances.

There has to be common sense. There has to be a middle ground, and that is the wellspring of my ideology. The reality is that our ascendancy to the majority, and the forces that impelled it, moved the political playing field to the right, which means, per-force, that the middle ground in the nation moved with it. But what I did during most of the Contract with America days was precisely what I have always done: Try to create consensus. The job of politicians is to govern, after all, and governing in our type of democracy means forging compromises and delivering.

My role as a member of the House Republican leadership, then, was to pull my colleagues back from ideological rhetoric into the real world in which our constituents lived—or, in my short-hand, to educate the boys. At one point, a committee was consider-ing a bill that would have outlawed adoption by single people. At the next leadership meeting I raised a red flag.

"Do we really want to go on record as saying that single people can't adopt?" I asked quietly. Everyone looked at me with puzzlement. "Doing so suggests that we don't believe that single mothers, or single fathers, for that matter, can be good parents. Do we really want to send that message? Anyway, do you think it's a good idea for a party that opposes abortion to bar single people from adopting kids?" As usual, they hadn't thought beyond the rhetoric. I brought them back to reality, and the group switched its position.

When the Violence Against Women Act came up for funding, I found myself in a similar position. The men at the table with me wanted to oppose it on budget grounds. They were so caught up in the idea of holding the line against spending, they were unable to focus on the implications of what they were advocating. That day I didn't even try to argue the merits of the programs funded by the Violence Against Women Act. My goal was to ease the opposition. "Look," I said, "you're going to be forced to vote on this issue in front of the C-Span cameras, and you're going to vote for funding it because otherwise it will seem like you don't care that women are being beaten up. So why not become champions of the issue so that you can take credit for it?" Those simple words—which hardly took a genius to utter—seemed to bring the wisdom of the heavens down on my colleagues. They agreed not to block funding of the bill.

I thought those positions were no-brainers. But, at times, the conversations in leadership meetings became almost surreal. Just after it was revealed that Dick Morris had been whispering sweet political somethings to his prostitute, a male member came into a leadership meeting and suggested that we subpoena the woman. The excuse for that action was our need to know what national security secrets Morris might have revealed to her. The reality was that he wanted us to prolong the embarrassment of both Morris and Clinton. Usually I contained myself and sat back to let the guys talk an issue to death before intervening. But that day I could not restrain myself. The prospect of U.S. marshals knocking on her door, and the tumult that would ensue if she refused to go along quietly, was too absurd. I could hear David Letterman's jokes about Republicans' needing subpoenas to get prostitutes.

"That's so dumb," I said. It slipped out of my mouth before I could close it. Come on, guys, I said. Everyone else is attacking your opponent. You're already winning.

My job as my party's champion of women's issues sometimes

meant seizing that politically advantageous turf from the Democrats, the high form of political hardball. Toward the end of my tenure in Congress, for example, Vic Fazio, a Democrat, introduced a bill that would create a breast cancer stamp, a stamp that would be slightly more expensive than your ordinary postage, with the difference earmarked for breast cancer research at the National Institutes of Health. The Senate sponsor was Diane Feinstein. The chairman of the Post Office and Civil Service Committee was blocking the bill because the post office wasn't wild about the logistics of the proposal. Vic came to me for help. I pushed the idea in leadership meetings until the Speaker got behind it—with a single caveat: that I become the bill's sponsor. That's the kind of political power play that's standard operating procedure in Congress, which didn't make it any easier for me to break the news to Vic that the Fazio-Feinstein bill was about to become the Molinari-D'Amato bill. But, hey, I thought, at least a good idea would become a reality.

I found Vic on the floor and broke the news to him. As we were talking, a colleague approached and asked him what was happening. "I'm getting a lesson in being in the minority," he said. I like to believe I was a wonderful teacher.

Chapter Seven

A Mom in High Places

After the storm of the hundred days, I was ready to collapse. We'd run a marathon that had frequently felt like the Bataan Death March. My friends on the Hill went home and slept even as Newt's inner circle began mapping out the strategy for the next wave of the assault. I knew that as a member of the leadership I was supposed to be concentrating exclusively on Round 2, but I've never been very good with supposed-tos.

I was consumed with the Battle of Amtrak, which fell into my lap when I became chairman of the Railroad Subcommittee. If the federal budget was going to be balanced, Amtrak's subsidies would have to end, and it was my job to figure out how to make that happen without destroying the nation's rail system. The most ferocious of the budget slashers didn't care. The ultimate free market crowd, they proposed cutting the system off immediately and letting private business pick up the profitable parts. I thought I could find a more reasonable approach, a slow phaseout, which would give Amtrak a chance to survive on its on.

That prospect wouldn't have seemed so dim if Congress hadn't saddled Amtrak with a series of labor regulations in the 1970s that were straining the budget and making the kind of downsizing and streamlining that corporations need periodically virtually impossible. Dozens of stations and service lines needed to be closed, but Congress had mandated that any worker laid off would be guaranteed six years' pay. It was a crazy and irresponsible provision that had been built into the union contract for almost two decades. Almost as hurtful was a proviso that all maintenance would be performed in Amtrak's own union shops. Those shops, however, were inefficient and absurdly expensive boondoggles that couldn't compete on the open market. I was convinced that both of those provisions would condemn Amtrak to an early death.

Amtrak's unions seemed oblivious to the change in the political winds and refused to make any concession that would save the near-bankrupt system. So as I searched for a compromise that would buy Amtrak time to reshape itself so that it could survive independently, I ran into the stone wall that is the labor lobby. I became a broken record, telling labor and their surrogates in the House, over and over again: "One thing is certain, Amtrak will not survive without some radical reforms." They wouldn't budge. I called their bluff, asking the secretary of transportation, Federico Peña, for a liquidation plan for the railroad. They responded in kind. Sonny Hall, the head of the Transport Workers Union, sent out a press release accusing me of plotting "germ warfare" against the union. When they mounted a concerted lobbying effort that moved even Republicans into their camp, I knew I was stymied. It was the one time while I was in Congress that I was utterly thwarted.

In the midst of those negotiations, I went on the stump for Bob Dole, whom I'd endorsed in February. The press was all atitter with speculations that I was trying to position myself for the number-two slot on his ticket, which was a ridiculous concept. If Dole wanted a pro-choice woman, Christie Todd Whitman, who had a much higher profile, would have been the logical choice. And I thought that Colin Powell or Bill Weld, the governor of Massachusetts, would be much stronger choices. I hadn't even fantasized about the vice presidency. I signed on to the Dole campaign because I liked him and trusted him. He had been the Senate co-sponsor on my Sexual Assault Prevention Act, and had faced down Joe Biden, the Democratic chair of the Senate Judiciary Committee, and the ACLU, to push it through. He'd been my Senate counterpart again in pushing for an end to the arms embargo in Bosnia. He was remarkably comfortable with strong women, so I admired him, and owed him.

But even as I twisted arms to forge an Amtrak compromise and led the charge for Bob Dole in the House, I was distracted. All those affairs of state were heady and important, but mostly I was thinking about having a baby. Okay, I know that it's passé or hopelessly sappy or some other way out of fashion, but getting pregnant became more important to me than shrinking the size of the federal government, ensuring the quality of rail transit in the Northeast, or the future of the Republic. So sue me.

I'd always wanted children, but hadn't had much opportunity to get pregnant. How do you have a kid when you don't even have a date? And who wanted to date a woman who would go out on a romantic drive in a convertible and spoil the moment by demanding that the car stop so she can figure out what the new smell emanating from the dump is? I'd comforted myself with my dog, George, a mostly Labrador retriever I found starved and half dead on the day George Bush was elected president.

George and I had been inseparable for seven years. He slept with me, jogged with me, and went to the office with me. He was a fixture at the women's gym, and a notorious presence to every member of the Capitol police force. If I dared leave home without him, he'd sit staring at the door until I returned. Most people in and around my office suite loved George, who'd spend most of the day curled up on the floor by my desk. The only problem was that he has an almost pathological suspicion of men in uniforms and begins barking and growling if one comes into view. More than once he'd get loose and chase a Capitol policeman or postman down the halls of the building.

When Bill and I got married, I warned him straight out: Don't ask me not to sleep with the dog because I will always sleep with the dog, even on the nights you sleep on the couch. I insisted that he install a bowl for George in his office across the hall from mine so that I could park him there if I had to run off. But despite my affection for George, after Bill and I had been married for almost a year, I was ready for a human child. After all, I wasn't exactly a kid.

We stopped talking about getting pregnant and started trying to have a child over the summer of 1995. I became obsessed. If my period was thirty minutes late, I'd call Julie and demand that she run to the pharmacy and bring me an EPT kit. Before she left town on business, she'd bring extra test kits over to keep me sane.

The first hint that we'd succeeded was delivered by an unlikely prophet in an unlikely locale. In August, Bill and I went to Jerusalem with a dozen other legislators on a trip set up by Sheldon Adelson, who owns the Sands Hotel, for the American-Israel Public Affairs Committee, a major lobbying group. I'd been to Israel in January 1991, on the eve of the Gulf War, when Bob Michel, who was then the Republican minority leader, asked a group of us to meet with the Israelis, the Egyptians, the Saudis, and American military commanders to assess the situation on the ground.

That second trip, however, was focused on the resolution of the Israel-Palestinian conflict, an issue with which Bill had been involved for years. Prime Minister Yitzhak Rabin had struck an agreement with Yasir Arafat of the Palestinian Liberation Organization in 1993, and we both had deep misgivings about the prospect of Israel's giving up the West Bank and the Golan Heights.

We traveled the country meeting with both Israeli and Arab leaders and citizens living on the political fault lines. We visited the Western Wall, where I tucked wishes sent by dozens of Staten Island Jews—and a few of my own—between the ancient stones, following a tradition that has endured for centuries. Then, one night, Sheldon arranged for us to take a cruise on the Sea of Galilee. The sky was jet black, the stars popping out in their brilliance as we drifted across the lake that had been home to Jesus. A band was playing wonderful Israeli music, and everyone was dancing. Suddenly, Sheldon, who's a boisterous guy not known for his subtlety, turned to me and said, "You have a glow. You must be pregnant." Bill and I laughed. What could Sheldon possibly know?

Only later did we realize that Sheldon had been right. I'd just become pregnant, at the King David Hotel in Jerusalem. If our child turned out to be a boy, we agreed that we would call him David.

There was no way we could keep my pregnancy secret, especially since Staten Island had been waiting for such an announcement for years. That concern was not spontaneous. My father had been nagging me about grandchildren relentlessly. When I turned thirty-five, he'd sent me a birthday card that read, "You're thirty-five, you're not president of the United States, and I don't have a granddaughter." And he felt no need to keep the nagging a private joke. Whenever he went to a public event, he'd brag about me and then complain that I still hadn't given him any grandchildren. Week after week, month after month, year after year, Staten Island heard about Guy Molinari's discontent. There I was, a member of Congress, the highest-ranking woman in the House of Representatives, and people would stop me while I was walking the dog not to complain about government policy, but to berate me, "Hey, Sue, give your father a grandkid already."

I admit that I wasn't as comfortable with revealing every detail of my biological functions as Bill was. When he was born, the Buffalo papers had all covered the great event, and his mother had kept scrapbooks with pictures of him in the hospital. So it seemed normal to him that our kid would get the same kind of coverage. I, on the other hand, felt a sudden shyness about revealing the size of my growing waistline.

◆

Three months into my pregnancy, all hell broke lose in Congress when we faced off with the president over the budget. On election day almost a year earlier, House Republicans had pledged that we would present a plan to balance the federal budget, and we fulfilled that promise with a proposal to cut taxes by $245 billion and bring the nation's fiscal house to order within seven years. As soon as he saw it, Clinton threatened to veto the bill. His alternate proposal, which he said would balance the budget within ten years, would actually have left the government with a $200-billion deficit. Even Democrats in the House didn't support it and talked about offering their own seven-year alternative.

Polls indicated that the country was solidly behind balancing the budget as soon as possible, and our plan was to reduce the deficit quickly, so that in 2002 the federal budget would generate an actual $1-billion surplus. We'd included tax reductions both for families and business and, wherever possible, saved money by changing federal entitlement programs into block grants to the states. We knew there were some bullets that would be tough to bite, and even tougher to digest—an increase in Medicare premiums, a slowing of the growth in Medicaid spending, workfare, and a phaseout of crop subsidy programs. But we thought that the election of the Republican majority was a mandate from the American people to cut back on the size of government.

We had worked out many of the details of our budget proposal at a conference retreat in May at a Xerox training center in Virginia that we all called Xerox U. It was a far cry from the resort hotel many members expected. Imagine the world's largest college dorm connected in a maze with meeting rooms, classrooms, a cafeteria, and gym. Everything was color-coded, which only seemed to increase the confusion. I was sure it had been designed by some Skinnerean psychologist who was secretly studying our behavior as we got lost going from the cafeteria to our meeting room, or from the elevator to our bedrooms.

At night everyone gathered in an enormous recreation room that offered an open bar, a pool table, and a piano. Martin Hoke, a member from Cleveland who's a terrific pianist, grabbed center stage as he led sing-alongs. But—woe to my party—everyone stood around belting out show tunes or patriotic songs. No one but me seemed to know the words to anything by Billy Joel or Elton John. So perhaps it was the surreal atmosphere of our own fight over the budget—a fight led by John Kasich on the one side, and Bill Archer on the other, over whether we should concentrate on cutting taxes or cutting the deficit—that warped our sensibilities. We were thinking only about what would be right for America in the long run. We were remarkably blind to how it would all play out politically.

Most important, we never got around to discussing Bill Clinton, and we sorely underestimated him. Ordinary politicians posture and pontificate and then sit down and negotiate. So when the president threatened to veto our proposed legislation without even seeing it, we thought he was playing the tough guy in preparation for negotiations. When he announced that he would let the government run out of money before accepting our plan, we assumed he was staking out a bargaining position.

We were wrong. The president refused to negotiate. He'd meet with representatives from our side, deliver a monologue, and leave the meetings. He refused to return phone calls. Instead, he took to the airwaves and declared that Congress's refusal to pass the necessary legislation would shut down the government.

We were stunned. We weren't refusing to pass the necessary legislation. We had already passed it—a series of bills that would have allowed the government to operate while we worked out a final budget agreement. Clinton was refusing to sign it because the same bill mandated an $11 per month increase in Medicare premiums and a pledge to balance the budget within seven years.

The Saturday before the federal government was due to run out of money, the president delivered a radio address accusing the Republicans of putting the nation at risk. We laughed. Risk, we said. He was the one who was refusing to negotiate and whose budget plan was a statistical sleight of hand that would keep America in debt. We were trying to pull the nation out from the mire of debt, which was just what voters said they desired.

Since I was a member of the Budget Committee, I could hardly duck the negotiations, the strategizing, and the media barrage. But I also couldn't duck the fact that I was pregnant, and that my doctor was on Staten Island. Early on, he barred me from flying and suggested that I take Amtrak on my trips home. Given my relations with Amtrak's unions, that didn't seem like a great idea. So I'd finish up an all-day budget session, load George into my Ford Escort, race to New York, and see the doctor. On my way home I'd be glued to the radio for the latest updates, so that I could park my car in the basement of my office building, leave George in the office, and be ready to add my two cents to the discussion of what the president was trying to accomplish.

By Monday, the day before the shutdown would take effect, however, we were chastened. Early polls indicated that the president's spin had captured the nation's fancy. Our entire plan had been built around the unquestioned assumption that the American people would support us. We rushed to retrench. Members filed into our caucus room for a stormy meeting on how to respond to the president. Most of us thought we should drop our other demands and offer to give the president stopgap funding to keep the government open if he would pledge to balance the budget within seven years. The freshmen wanted to stand fast. I talked myself blue in the face about realism and living to fight another day. Only half of them agreed.

In the long run, it made no difference. We presented the president with that offer, but he ignored it. He went back on the air and accused Republicans of turning their backs on the nation's values. He, of course, played the defender. "I will fight it today," he said. "I will fight it tomorrow. I will fight I next week and next month."

On day one of the shutdown, the president spoke to the nation about proposals we'd modified two days earlier, ignoring entirely the compromises we'd offered. He painted us as Scrooges intent on impoverishing the elderly, decimating the environment, and driving our children into illiteracy. Unite behind me to stave off Republican blackmail, he pleaded—and the nation listened.

We were stymied. We couldn't imagine how to proceed in the negotiations because Clinton seemed intent on ignoring every offer we sent to him. We could think of no way to end the impasse without capitulating entirely to the president's demand that we just give him the money he wanted and shut up.

Newt launched a public relations counteroffensive, explaining that our budget proposal included a forty-five-percent increase in Medicare spending over seven years. He laid out our plan in detail to demonstrate that it would increase total government spending by more than $3 trillion. The crisis had erupted, he argued, because the president was holding out for the fourth trillion. That explanation made no impact on the poll numbers. In leadership meetings, we considered every possible move in the elaborate chess game and finally decided that our best one would be to pass an actual balanced budget and send it to the White House so that the American people could see, concretely, what we were proposing, and who was being obstructionist. But even as the Senate and House debated and passed the measures, Clinton vowed, "The budget is dead on arrival when it comes to the White House and, if the price of any deal is cuts like these, my message is no deal."

By the time we finally reached an agreement with the White House that would reopen the government and keep it solvent for a month, the damage had been done. Although the president had, in fact, agreed to work out a seven-year balanced budget plan, nobody was listening to the details. The spin had become truth, no matter the reality.

Although many of my colleagues would never admit it, we had been hopelessly naive about Clinton's skill as a politician. He was masterful at twisting public opinion to his own end. In December 1995, for example, he publicly bemoaned the fact that House Republican moderates were letting extremists control the party. It wasn't true. Those moderates—and he was talking about people like me—fully supported the Republican position. So a day later, we—twenty-five notorious nonconservatives—called a press conference to explain that we weren't being used or manipulated by anyone, that the party plan was our plan. Our announcement barely dented the public consciousness. In the public eye, we all became dupes and pawns.

The month set aside for final budget negotiations sped by

with no progress on the deal, and we headed into Shutdown 2. I knew it was time to cut our losses. Only the freshmen, still imbued with an unrealistic sense of their own power, held out. But Clinton had beaten us with extraordinary political savvy, and there was no point in turning a bad situation into a catastrophe.

In the lull between the first and second budget crises, the press ran some stories about my pregnancy. I was only the third member of Congress to give birth while in office, so I still had a certain celebrity status. Had I had a sonogram? Did I know the sex of the baby? Would I announce it to the press? The answers were yes, yes, and no.

What they didn't ask me was what pregnancy was like, and the truth was that it was damned inconvenient. I'd rise to speak at a campaign breakfast for Bob Dole, or enter negotiations with the president of Bosnia wondering if I'd be hit with a heavy bout of morning sickness. I felt the first kick of the baby while I was on *Larry King Live* debating politics and Bosnia, and tried to remain coherent even while I wondered whether people could see my stomach moving. I managed to run out to buy a layette even while I was dashing around the House to find enough support to uphold the assault weapons ban. I donned oversized sweaters and waddled through floor debates on a bill close to my heart—my National Senior Citizen Pet Ownership Protection Act. (Okay, I know it seems terminally cute, but it is precisely the kind of legislation that can make a real difference in the lives of the elderly who, up to that point, were forced to choose between their pets and living in federally subsidized housing.)

Like any other expectant parents, Bill and I were consumed with the logistics of adding a baby to our lives. We realized, as everyone does, that it wasn't going to be easy. Since we both often worked until nine or ten P.M., we each needed a changing table and all the appropriate accoutrements in our offices. Obviously, we needed to outfit the nursery at home, but we didn't have just one home. We each had to maintain a home in our respective districts, and spend most weekends there to meet with constituents. So we had to outfit three nurseries and pack away a carload of travel equipment.

By the end of April, we were as ready as parents ever are, which meant that the nursery was perfectly decorated, a pink elephant was on display on the chest of drawers, but we still didn't have bedding for the crib and the curtains we ordered still hadn't arrived. We even had a plan for what to do with George, who had enjoyed seven years as an only child. I figured I'd feed Susan and George at the same time. I'd take them both with me when I jogged or went to the office. Sounds crazy? If you think so, you've never had a dog.

On May 10, the day of a critical House vote on a bill I had written to ease adoption, I went into labor. Bill spent half that time in my hospital room watching soap operas, and complaining that the hospital TV system did not include C-Span. Between contractions, I nagged him to call the office or turn on the radio to check on the vote on my bill. By the time we heard that it had passed, I was in my eighth hour of labor and had another piece of politics to distract me. An article appeared in that morning's *Daily News* about the treatment I was receiving in the hospital. According to that report, I was basking in the lap of luxury, eating off bone china and drinking out of crystal goblets. I read that news while chewing on ice that had been given to me in a urine cup. I'd had nothing to eat for half a day.

After twelve hours, my doctor delivered our daughter by cesarean: Susan Ruby Paxon—Susan for my wonderful Mama Sue, and Ruby for Bill's paternal grandmother, a suffragette who had died two years earlier at the age of 107.

The public reaction was overwhelming. Bob Dole called to congratulate us, George Bush dropped us a note from Kennebunkport, and my offices in Washington and Staten Island became virtual kiddie department stores filled by my constituents, who knitted booties and sweaters and blankets. They sent me trinkets from Tiffany's, hand-woven baskets, and a stuffed animal that was almost my height.

Meanwhile, the nonpublic, so to speak, jumped on Susan Ruby Paxon as a dream media opportunity. That sounds opportunistic, and it probably is, but feeding the press is part of the job. So my dad made sure every reporter in New York knew he was looking for a priest to baptize his granddaughter a Republican. Rudy Giuliani stopped by to deliver a stuffed toy lion emblazoned with a Team Rudy button.

Once I left the hospital, I stayed in touch with my office and the progress of legislation, but I was distracted. I just lay there looking at Susan Ruby with utter wonder. Forgive me this unbearably goopy passage, but you can't expect me to write about my life without indulging in my love affair with my daughter. She transformed me. It felt like there weren't enough hours in the day to watch her and hold her. I'd lay in bed and play with her, take her out jogging with me, and sing her to sleep with "Born to Run." It was heaven.

The thought of going back to work—of getting dressed and driving off and maybe not seeing her until six P.M.—was awful. Or having to leave her in my office while I went to a meeting, especially on those nights that we voted until ten or eleven P.M. We'll figure it out, I reassured myself. We'll cope.

We did a test run on June 5. Bill and I loaded the car up with Susan Ruby's crib mattress and bags filled with disposable diapers, herded George into the backseat, packed Susan Ruby into the car seat, and drove to the Capitol. George, who was always trying to lick the baby, or swipe her stuffed animals, was banished to Bill's office. The press followed us around Capitol Hill while we introduced Susan Ruby to Congress. We stopped by to visit Bob Dole, then went to the Speaker's office for an afternoon leadership meeting. When Newt reached for her, I felt a momentary pang of concern. He'd just been on *The Tonight Show* with a baby pig who'd squealed his lungs out the minute Newt tried to hold him. I worried that my little girl would react no better to the Speaker of the House.

We never found that perfect nanny we dreamed of. Our lives and schedules were too chaotic for anyone else to be included. Bill and I swapped her back and forth during the day as we raced from meetings to votes and public appearances. When we worked late, she'd sleep in her stroller next to my desk, or in the corner of whatever conference room I was meeting in.

Susan Ruby's presence wasn't as odd a sight as it might have been even a decade earlier. Enid Green Waldholz, who'd arrived in Congress pregnant, had given birth six months earlier and also set up a full nursery in her office. Bill Orton of Utah brought his son, Will, to the Hill on the days that his wife worked. Chet Edwards's son was a fixture in the Capitol. Members were used to seeing Rick Lazio holding one of his daughters in his arms during debates, or chasing the other one down so that she wouldn't take over the well. One day, those of us on the Republican side spotted a young boy in our midst. He was wailing and crying that he had lost his father. We frantically looked around among the members, trying to figure out whom he belonged to. Finally we realized that he'd crossed the aisle from the Democratic side, where his father, Elliot Engel, was searching for him.

Some of the older members were less than comfortable with the new face of the House, fearing that the presence of kids injected a loss of dignity to the institution. Most, however, not only enjoyed them, but instinctively understood that they served as a reminder that our work was something more than rhetoric. When I needed to go to the well to speak, or to go up to write in a vote because I had, as usual, forgotten my electronic voting card, I'd hand Susan Ruby to our whip, Tom DeLay, to my friend Ileana

Ros-Lehtinen, or Tom Coburn, a member who's also an obstetrician.

By July we had developed a routine that was what passed for normalcy—something akin to the controlled chaos most new parents live with. Fortunately, with the elections approaching, things were relatively quiet in the House. And I managed to find time to devote to Bob Dole's campaign, which seemed a good idea, since I was one of the national co-chairs. My responsibility was to keep track of Dole's support in the House, but I also served on his "Clinton accountability team," an eight-member squad dedicated to poking holes in presidential factual misdirection and debunk Clintonian rhetoric.

As my media presence increased, the pundits who spend Sunday morning pretending they are seers ratcheted up the speculation that I was running for vice president. Again, they were wrong. There were only two things I wanted from Bob Dole: to watch him be sworn in as president and to be given a place on the podium of the convention in August. By July, I was beginning to get nervous about the latter prospect. Dozens of members had already been asked to speak, and I was not one of them.

I reassured myself that the silence was nothing personal, that it had nothing to do with my positions on abortion or the crime bill. I tried to comfort myself with the knowledge that Dole wanted to fill the convention proceedings with ordinary people, and a member of Congress doesn't count as ordinary. But I was still pouting. Even a bad slot would be better than nothing, I thought. At least I'd emerge with a photo of myself on the podium. But those concerns vanished the minute I saw Susan Ruby, who seemed to thrive on the constant attention she was receiving.

The guard of the House played with her on their breaks. In the midst of the most intense possible political battles, Nita Lowey or John La Falce, who were always on the opposite side of those issues from me, would grab her, sit down on the floor, and play with her. Time and again the cold wars melted when she'd walk down the aisle. I wasn't the only one she grounded.

Susan Ruby's presence on the floor also gave my mother a chance to watch her granddaugher grow, day by day. Before a floor debate, I'd call home to give her the head's-up, then walk my daughter over to an area in clear view of the C-Span cameras and ask her to wave to her grandmother. My friend Ileana Ros-Lehtinen used to kid that with C-Span, you're never too far from home.

We planned Susan Ruby's christening for mid-July in Akron, the small town outside Buffalo where Bill grew up. Bill's parents still hadn't seen their granddaughter, and we expected a quiet event for close friends. Saturday night, after the baptism, my folks headed home for Staten Island, and Bill's mother offered to baby-sit so we could go out to dinner with friends. It was to be our one moment of relaxation in a hectic schedule, since the next day we were off to Rochester, where Bill would officially announce his intention to run for reelection.

We gave Bill's mother our beeper number, just in case. Then I threw on a pair of jeans and sneakers, grabbed one of Bill's sweatshirts, and we headed out for the evening to a local joint in Williamsville. We relaxed and, for the first time in almost a year, I actually had a few drinks. Then, just as I was about to dig into a plate of penne, Bill's beeper went off. We panicked. Susan, something's wrong with the baby. Bill checked the number. The call was from a member of his staff. Just what we need, I thought, some political crisis.

"I'm listening to *Larry King Live* and I think Bob Dole just announced that Sue is going to be the keynote speaker," the staffer yelled into the phone. We didn't even have time to react to the news before Bill's beeper went crazy. The next call was from Dole's handlers, and they gave us direct orders: Go to the nearest pay phone and call *Larry King Live* to accept the invitation.

I stuffed some penne in my mouth and raced to the pay phone, which was sandwiched in a corner between the kitchen and the bathrooms. I tried to compose myself and concentrate, but waiters were screaming, pots were banging, toilets were flushing, and Bill was running around the bar like a crazy person announcing that I was on the phone with Larry King and Bob and Elizabeth Dole.

"I had two envelopes, one marked running mate and one marked keynote speaker," Dole said. "Maybe I chose the wrong one." Even in my less than focused state I didn't miss a beat. "I accept," I answered.

By the time I finished thanking Dole and accepting the invitation, dinner was over. My press secretary, Jim Mazzarella, was already in my Washington office, demanding my attention. He'd always thought of himself as the Maytag repairman and was suddenly receiving twenty messages every five minutes. We raced home, and I headed directly to the phone to call my parents. My father wasn't home. Just when I needed to talk to him, he was out eating pizza with Rudy Giuliani. I beeped him. No answer. Everybody beeped him. But he was clearly in one of those moods when no one could disturb him. When he finally got home, my mother told him to call me before even checking his messages. "I'm going to be the keynote speaker," I announced, feeling the weight of the moment when the child becomes her parent's equal. It was the only time I've ever heard my father at a loss for words.

The following morning was chaos as I raced from one camera crew to another to feed the appetite of the network morning shows. When Bill and I arrived at the airport, reporters swarmed around us. I'd dealt with the press before, for years. But I'd never been the eye of a media storm. We set up a spontaneous news conference, and I answered questions while holding Susan Ruby in my arms. She slept quietly through the din. Reporters honed in on the issue they had been pumping up in the press for weeks: abortion. Would I mention it in my speech? There was no doubt in my mind that I would not. Dole's selection of a pro-choice woman to deliver the keynote was his declaration of inclusiveness. I didn't need to shove that message down anyone's throat.

The reaction to my selection was both thrilling and predictable. The *New York Post* ran a front-page story headlined "Susan to the Rescue." The pro-choice Republicans who'd been made to feel like second-class citizens in Houston in 1992 broke out the champagne. The most extreme wing of the extreme right—the conservative chauvinists, if you will—bemoaned the decision as a sign that Dole might be moving in the wrong direction. And the National Abortion Rights Action League, seemingly convinced I should throw myself on a sword to advance the cause, berated my decision not to mention abortion from the podium.

I refused to get sucked into that vortex. I had a speech to write, and no idea what I was going to say, or what tone I should adopt. Everyone else did, of course. Former Clinton speechwriter David Kusnet told the press that the speech should be conversational, not oratorical, and that I should avoid pounding the podium at all costs. James Fallow, who'd worked with Jimmy Carter, suggested that I should not be afraid to be florid and put on a show. Bush's writer Tony Snow opined that I should relax and not try to be Mario Cuomo. Tony Dolan, who'd worked for Ronald Reagan, added to the list of who I shouldn't try to be: Winston Churchill, Ronald Reagan, or "Barbara WaWa."

It never occurred to me to be any of those guys. I didn't want to craft high oratory, a ponderous exegesis on the state of the nation. I wanted to deliver a positive speech, a speech about the kind of world I wanted Susan Ruby to live in, the kind of speech that would make me, as a listener, cry. The problem was that I had only three weeks to draft it, and Dole's campaign staff was anything but helpful. They sent me a speechwriter who turned out negative drivel about listening to America on the car radio. I fired him and demanded a woman.

But it was impossible to concentrate. Dole's campaign manager had decreed that selling myself was as important as the speech. So Jim set up a war room to schedule meetings with the press, and we made time to fill every request. Reporters followed me around the Capitol. They watched me play with Susan Ruby in my office. They declared me a player and asked me about my political goals. I answered endless questions about abortion. When I wasn't spewing out my guts to them about my life and dreams, I tried to find time to write, to be a member of Congress, and to spend time with my daughter.

Lost in the hundreds of messages Jim received every day was one that came in from Andrea Bernstein of the *New York Observer*. He didn't return it. The *Observer* wasn't important enough to waste time on and he knew that its liberal muckraking bias guaranteed a less than enthusiastic story about me or Bob Dole. Then Andrea called again, and again, leaving a more detailed message. Once he'd deciphered what she wanted, Jim walked into my office and closed the door. Andrea claimed that old friends of mine from college had told her that I'd smoked pot while I was a student. The paper planned to run the story. She was calling to offer me a chance to comment.

I had, in fact, tried marijuana while I was at SUNY, but I couldn't figure out how Andrea could possibly have known that. I'd smoked only with a few friends, almost two decades earlier. I couldn't imagine who was feeding her information. But it didn't make any difference. It was time to come clean and own up to mistakes I'd made while in college.

I called my father for advice and comfort. No lectures or recriminations. We talked politics, practical politics. We agreed that I should ignore the *Observer* and wait to see if any legitimate news organization picked up their story. For two days we held our collective breath. Then a reporter from the Reliable Source column of the *Washington Post* called Jim and asked the question. I couldn't duck a reporter from the *Post*. So I placed the second horrific phone call of the week and acknowledged, regretfully, that I had smoked pot in college at least a half dozen times. It was a dumb kid mistake, I said, the kind of rite of passage adolescents seize upon to prove their independence.

As I took a deep breath to place the final dreaded phone call, I seized on the hope that the press wouldn't pounce on the story full force. Surely by now, after the revelation that the president had not inhaled and that both Clarence Thomas and Newt Gingrich had, my minor dabbling with pot would be a nonstory, I told myself. Even as I did, I knew that was a pipe dream. Not long before, the president's spokesman, Mike McCurry, had made the same admission, and Gerry Solomon had flayed him for expressing no regret. I fully expected that every Democratic spinmeister in Washington would use my admission as payback.

My dad tried to calm me down by passing along the local reaction. One woman came up to him on the street and said, "I wish it was only pot with my son and daughter." Another waved him down and said, "Big deal, smoking pot, everybody's kid smokes pot." That didn't make it any easier for me to call Bob Dole. He had honored me with his trust, and I had set off the kind of flap no candidate appreciates. I tried not to infect him with my distress. "Well, at least I got abortion off the front page," I quipped. He was incredibly gracious.

Things calmed down quickly, and I began to regain my focus as we headed for the final push before I left for San Diego. Every day I'd lock myself in my office to write and edit, then rush off to meetings and run back in time for another interview. In the midst of the frenzy, the last thing I wanted to worry about was what I would wear for my speech. As you probably know by now, I'm hardly a clotheshorse. Give me a pair of jeans and a T-shirt and I'm a happy woman. But I'm not naive. I knew that commentators would give as much airtime to my look as to the content of my speech, so I rounded up some friends and went over to Emily's on Staten Island.

Everyone went crazy pulling out dozens of suits that had that traditional convention look—pink or royal blue numbers with the kind of funky necklines that are supposed to make women look serious. I stood in the dressing room, trying on whatever was shoved at me, although I felt like I was getting ready for a masquerade ball. Finally I spotted a beige Emanuel Ungaro wool suit. It felt perfect. It felt like me. Everyone else was horrified. Get something brighter, in fuchsia or at least a spring color, they insisted. I bought it anyway.

Even that purchase became a political football, of course. That's the nature of American politics. The Democrat opposing me in the November elections seized on the story of my purchase the minute it hit the papers and derided my spendthrift ways. A $600 suit, he said. I buy mine at Marc Jeffries for $200. "And your tie is old and your shoes need to be shined," I responded.

My last task before I left for San Diego was the only real pleasure of those three weeks. Jim surprised me by booking me on Rosie's show, knowing that both my mother and I loved her. Rosie O'Donnell is one of my heroes because she's just herself, which seems heroic these days, and the show was my own special time-out. We compared children and joked about men in politics. Nothing weighty or overly serious.

Finally, on August 8, I boarded the plane, leaned back in my seat, and began to relax. I had a speech I believed in, a highly personal appeal to working families. I would talk about my great-grandfather, who'd opened a barber shop in Queens and whose love and devotion had led his grandson and great-granddaughter to seats in the United States Congress. I was happy with the remarks

I'd crafted to reach out to America's women, to moms stretched to the breaking point because they were trying to hold down jobs inside and outside the home. It felt true. It was definitely from the heart.

The reverie didn't last long. When I called to check in with Jim, he told me that New York One, a local nonnetwork news station, had called, and they were reviving the marijuana question with a vengeance. Four years earlier, in the course of asking me about Supreme Court nominations, a reporter for a small Staten Island cable television station had asked me if I'd ever smoked pot. I was flustered and ended that line of questioning the stupidest way possible, by lying.

New York One had gotten hold of a copy of the tape of that show and was about to broadcast the story. I couldn't decide whether I should walk into the bathroom on the plane and flush myself down the toilet or call the reporter and ask what kind of drugs he'd tried in college. I wanted to lash out that the reporter, who had worked for one of my father's opponents, was pursuing a vendetta against me. I did none of the above. I couldn't. No matter the reason for the report or the motivation of the reporter, what he said was true.

By the time I reached San Diego, I was a mess. The front page of the *Daily News* was set. It read: "Career up in Smoke." To make matters worse, everywhere I went I had to dodge someone ready to criticize me for either being pro-choice or for not being pro-choice enough to use my platform to roast my own party. I did the best I could to contain the pot fiasco. I expressed my contrition for the lie, which was sincere. And I let Jim be the attack dog. "For the past two weeks the media and Democratic opponents have been scouring the state of New York for dirt on Susan Molinari," he said. "Basically, if this is the best they can come up with, then they should just grow up."

Meanwhile, I tried to focus on preparing myself for Tuesday

night, which wasn't easy. The campaign had given Bill and me a suite of rooms in the Marriott Hotel, but it was hardly a refuge for quiet concentration. The telephone and fax machines rang constantly, and people kept storming in to tell me that I had to add this or change that. The Dole campaign had refused to pay for my speechwriter to fly out with me, and I was relieved that I'd paid the freight myself, since everyone was started tearing into my prose. Every time we tried to accommodate the criticism, the speech got longer. Then they'd start screaming that I was running over ten minutes, which would be a disaster. My dad thought I should tell everyone to go to hell and insist on more time, or at least plan to run long, which he knew the other speakers would do. That wasn't my style.

From time to time, something ridiculous would happen, which is always what I need when I'm under stress. In this case, it was the arrival of my old friend Danny, who flew out to San Diego with a horde of Staten Islanders to watch the hometown girl on the podium. Danny is notorious for dressing up as Captain America, and he arrived at the convention in full regalia. Suddenly people were stopping me to ask about the weird guy in the Captain America suit passing out fliers about Susan Molinari. Should they be concerned? Could he be some kind of dangerous nut? No, I thought. He was the only nut around me who was not dangerous.

Sunday morning was my chance at the podium for a run-through. The convention managers seemed ridiculously nervous when that rehearsal turned into an impromptu media event. No matter what I did, I seemed unable to satisfy them. Finally I asked my friend Fred Cerullo to work with me. In what time he could eke out from his job as commissioner of the Department of Finance of New York City, Fred moonlighted as an actor in the soaps. So that afternoon we hid out in a rehearsal trailer in the bowels of the convention center and practiced. Don't talk so fast. Try not to look directly at the TelePrompTer. Don't wave your hands so much that they hide your face.

Tuesday afternoon, just a few hours before my speech, Jim drove me out to Bella Luna, a restaurant not far from the beach, for lunch with Bob Dole and Newt. Never one to lose my appetite to stress, I stuffed myself into a stupor with gnocchi, penne with basil, and a tomato and mozzarella salad while we talked about babies. It was a surreal moment of sanity in week of absurdity.

Bill and I tried to relax in our suite, but that plan was, of course, a fantasy. I donned my new outfit, dressed Susan Ruby in her best denim overalls, and we headed over to the convention center with my dad. Bill had everything timed and planned to the minute. He would feed Sue and change her diaper just before the lights went on. Then, when I hit the word *Pittsburgh* in my speech, he'd hand the baby over to my father and walk up to join me on the podium. We even had a baby-sitter standing by in case Susan Ruby refused to cooperate and began to wail. I prayed she'd stay quiet. Call it mother's vanity or feminist pride, but I wanted her to grow up knowing that she'd been there when her mother delivered that speech. Or maybe her being there kept my life in perspective so that I could be more focused.

Looking back, I can't quite believe I maintained control that night, because everything possible went wrong. Christie Whitman was scheduled to introduce me with a flowery speech complete with video. But John Kasich ran late, so she winged it and simply presented me to the audience. Someone forgot to adjust the dais to my height, so I could barely see the TelePrompTer. That made little difference, since the machine malfunctioned and showed me just one line at a time. My normal response would have been to stop the proceedings and say, "Hey, you guys down there in the control room, we've got a problem." But I couldn't. The networks had warned us that they would cut away precisely at eleven P.M., and it was already ten forty-five. As I rose to speak, a group of pro-lifers from the Louisiana delegation began to chant. Although Pat Buchanan had quelled the idea of a mass walkout, a handful of delegates got up and left.

I froze for a moment. How could I be standing on the po-dium at the Republican National Convention, speaking to an audi-ence of millions of my countrymen? Then I looked down at the VIP section before me. My husband sat next to Elizabeth Dole with my beautiful daughter in his arms. My father, proudly at his side, was wearing a Molinari 2000 button. I'd watched him swell with pride at each of his own victory parties, but I knew that night was the triumphant moment of his life.

I sighed, and smiled. There was no way I could blow it.

Chapter Eight

....

Newtonian Politics

If the 1994 elections had been about gaining ground, the 1996 elections were about staving off erosion, and that battle had left all of us Republicans bruised and battered. We went into the campaign season with a presidential candidate deemed too moderate by our deepest base of support. While coattails aren't what they were before political cynicism infected the nation and C-Span gave voters direct access to the political process, we had not been naive. Our majority was already slim, which meant that on every controversial piece of legislation we needed to struggle to maintain our unity. Just a few seats lost to the Democrats could spell disaster, and the Democrats were turning the tables on us.

In 1994 we had run our candidates against an unpopular president. In 1996 they ran theirs against our unpopular Speaker, whose approval ratings hovered around thirty percent. Our candidates were forced to defend their relationships with him, and many asked him not to go into their districts for fear of the pickets the labor movement sent to follow him wherever he went. Given that scenario, no national strategy of the type we had used successfully in 1994 was possible. Candidates in hard-core conservative districts worked to distance themselves from our presidential candidate, while those in more mainstream areas fought to distance themselves from our Speaker. It was every candidate for his, or her, self.

Meanwhile, as incumbents, we needed a strategy for how to legislate during the remainder of the session. Some of Bob Dole's supporters urged us not to pass legislation in order to avoid handing the president bills he could sign, and thus claim as his own. But we worried that that tactic would give Democratic House candidates ammunition to portray us as do-nothings, further jeopardizing our majority.

During the convention, Bill predicted that we would pick up twenty new seats, but by the early fall, our pollsters were warning that we'd be lucky to gain five. Newt, on the other hand, riding a high that bathed him in an aura of invincibility, was declaring that victory was ours. "We can relax and smile every day," he'd declared during the convention, "because we're the folks who are going to do it with you, not the folks who are going to do it to you." Nice sentiment. Wrong election.

The NRCC strong-armed incumbents for contributions at what Bill called "prayer meetings." Everyone knew that retaining the majority would give us the first Republican congress reelected in sixty-eight years, and we were not about to become losers again. We poured $8 million into television advertising in districts in danger and cut loose races where our members had utterly safe seats. Mine was one of them. I had a ton of cash in my campaign coffers—almost half a million dollars by late September—and my opponent, Tyrone Butler, had raised only $30,000. So I gave money away right and left, and even took off to Georgia to campaign for Newt, to Ohio to help out Deb Pryce, to Kansas and Iowa.

I spent election night at home in Staten Island with hardly a care in the world on my own account. Bill, however, was hunkered down at the NRCC offices on the second floor of the Republican National Committee headquarters in Washington to sweat out 230 races. He worried about Nancy Johnson, whose position as head of the Ethics Committee, which was working on charges against Newt, had run her into trouble with both pro- and anti-Gingrich forces. He feared the loss of Gary Franks, a black Republican from Connecticut, who'd been battered by Newt haters. In 1994, Bill was breathing easy by seven P.M. Two years later he spent the whole night on the phone with field representatives. Only early Wednesday morning did the results become clear. We'd held on, but by the skin of our teeth. We'd retained our majority by nine votes. Nine votes made us into chairmen and arbiters of what bills would and would not see the light of day. Just nine votes. The new session promised to be a nightmare.

◆

As members geared up for the session due to begin in January 1997, Newt Gingrich's house was not a happy home, and everyone knew it. The long investigation of the Ethics Committee into his use of tax-exempt contributions for activities that seemed like party building had taken its toll on both members and voter confidence in the Speaker. The Democrats were hyping the charges not only for political advantage, but as payback for Newt's treatment of former Speaker Jim Wright, whom Gingrich had literally hounded out of office with a concerted campaign of exposing his every possible misdeed. Suddenly old rumors about the Speaker were being pumped up by the press, and his perceived defeat in the budget battle of 1996 demoralized his troops. The brutal election cycle of 1996, during which unions ran 100,000 ads nationwide attacking him, had already taken a terrible toll on him. By Christmas 1996 he was under self-imposed House arrest.

The election of the Speaker was scheduled for the first week in January, and Bill spent Christmas and New Year's pulling out all the stops to save Newt. He flew to Buffalo, to his parents' house, for Christmas Day, but it made no difference where he was; he was always on the phone pulling together support for Newt. At a time when they should have been planning for the new session and setting a new agenda, he and the other members of the Speaker's inner circle—majority leader Dick Armey, majority whip Tom DeLay, and Republican conference chairman John Boehner—were working the phones to calm members, spinning stories to the press, and designing responses to the dozen possible outcomes of the ethics investigations.

The week before Christmas, Newt's attorneys negotiated a settlement with the Ethics Committee in which the Speaker admitted to having used nonprofit contributions for a college course taught in order to build up the party, and to misleading the Ethics Committee. He agreed to accept a $300,000 fine that was widely billed as a reimbursement to the committee for its expenses. That settlement was made public just as Americans were caught up in their final frenzy of Christmas shopping, so the announcement made a remarkably light impression on voters. Among Republican members, however, the news of Newt's admission and fine was explosive. They'd just been through grueling reelection campaigns during which they'd been flailed with the faults of the Speaker.

Could they afford to put their reputations at further risk by voting him back into office in January? Should they? No one had any room to maneuver because the final ethics report would not be issued until the day after the reelection vote on January 7.

Members were furiously, privately, discussing what to do, when Mike Forbes, another New Yorker and a Newt supporter, publicly called on the Speaker to step down. He also informed the press that at least two dozen other members agreed with his plea. That number was chilling. Given the election results and our slim majority, Newt couldn't afford to lose even twenty votes. Forbes's declaration sent shock waves through the party. The Hill was rife with rumors that Newt would not win the speakership, with discussions about why he should not win the speakership. Prominent conservatives like William Safire and Robert Bork weighed in with their opinion that Newt should step aside for the good of the party.

Bill and I both thought they were wrong. Too much of the unity of the House Republican Caucus depended on Newt. We feared that a shake-up in the leadership, a shake-up that might engender a battle for the speakership, would wound us fatally at the start of a new session. Better Newt than chaos, he said. Let's just get through the ethics investigation and move on.

Newt, however, had trouble doing so. Late one evening he called Bill and told him that he thought the battle might be lost. It would be best for the party if he left the political scene, Newt said. His plan was for Dick Armey to become Speaker and Bill the majority leader. Bill tried to pull Newt out of his funk, and finally goaded him into calling House Republicans to pitch his case. At the same time, Bill, Armey, DeLay, and Boehner linked scores of members together in conference calls to remind them of Newt's prodigious fund-raising ability, his genius for team building, and the clarity of his vision. It was a tape of a related call, limited to the

Republican leadership, to which Boehner connected by cell phone, that was leaked to the press by Jim McDermott, a Democrat from Washington.

The Democrats believed that the release of that tape was a direct hit on the Speaker. But the minute we heard of that development—the night before the story ran—I knew we'd reached a turning point. For weeks we'd been insisting that the ethics scandal was politically motivated, that the Democrats were using it to whip up sentiment against us. Finally we had a concrete example of what they were willing to do—the lengths they were willing to go to—to bring Newt Gingrich down. The willingness of a respected Democrat to make public the tape of a private conversation was our window of opportunity to shift the momentum in our direction and save the Speaker.

Newt was reelected, but that was the only positive note in a continuing symphony of discord. When the Ethics Committee issued its report, Tom DeLay tried to organize a movement against both the recommended reprimand and the $300,000 fine. It was a politically dumb idea. The Ethics Committee deserved the benefit of the doubt, so I refused to join DeLay's band of twenty-nine who voted against the committee's final report.

Once we moved past that vote, we got caught up in the controversy over how Newt would pay his fine. John Kasich publicly demanded that the Speaker use his own personal funds, but everyone suspected he might tap into his campaign coffers, which I thought would have looked awful and been even worse. The matter lingered until Bob Dole bailed him out, a generous offer from a man whom Newt had hardly supported wholeheartedly.

Even after the ethics issues were resolved, the strife continued. We fumbled through the opening weeks of the session, and our poll numbers kept getting worse. Newt insisted that there was no cause for concern. He pointed to what had happened to governors like John Engler of Michigan after they'd forced their states into hard, unpopular budget cuts. "His numbers went down, but they went right back up," Newt counseled us repeatedly. But his analysis was flawed. Engler was the chief executive of the state, who could thus drive the debate. We, as members of Congress, had no such power. Bill Clinton did. While our poll numbers plummeted, his rose just as quickly. Yet we did nothing because Newt refused to worry.

The bottom line was that we had no plan, no coherent legislative agenda, no coherence whatsoever. All the energy that should have gone into planning had been devoted to Newt. During a meeting months earlier, he actually asked Bill to take charge of long-range planning, which we certainly needed. But Bill knew that Newt would never let anyone else do that job, that he thought of planning as his personal project. But Newt insisted. Bill began the work, convening a group of members to work with him. Then Newt turned around and undercut them by announcing his own long-term plans without any consultation. In fact, he made a different announcement almost every week, with a different vision. We were adrift as a conference, and our captain seemed unable to find a direction.

Our leadership structure became diffuse, and members became mired in confusion, unsure who was in charge and what plan we were following. One day Newt would agree to the request of one faction of the conference, then turn around and accede to the contradictory request of another, leaving Armey, DeLay, and Bill to sort out the mess and soothe the ruffled feathers. Just when we most needed a unifying program and a strong leader to help us fight an increasingly popular president, Newt disappeared as a force for cohesion.

Even his most loyal supporters in the conservative wing of the party began to distance themselves from the Speaker. After he invited Jesse Jackson to sit in his box at the State of the Union address and, later, after he visited China, they derided him as a moderate wanna-be. They punished him by helping the Democrats stonewall a routine bill to finance House operations. Newt fought back by calling them unruly children, which certainly didn't improve matters.

By Easter we were in free fall, and Newt fell into an even deeper funk. Moody and irritable, he seemed totally uninterested in the moment, in the immediate problems confronting us. He'd call Bill and other members of leadership and weep openly while talking about resigning because saving the world was simply too heavy a burden for him to manage. We thought he should step out of daily administrative activity, leaving the members of his inner circle—Armey, DeLay, Bill, and Boehner—run the daily operations. But even though Newt liked to talk about team building and quality management, the theory he really subscribed to was management by chaos. He loved chaos, and even when he didn't create it knowingly and intentionally, he managed to leave it in his wake after every meeting, after every press conference, after every phone call.

Then he began talking about what America would be like in 2017 after two two-term Republican presidents would have completed their work in the White House. In leadership meetings we listened politely, but we were growing impatient. We needed the Speaker to focus on our legislative agenda today, not the election of 2016. "Interesting, interesting," someone would interrupt. "Now let's get back to the budget deal." But Newt, who always urged us to think "outside the nine dots," outside the accepted parameters, was off and running on some other track. He would not be deterred.

Newt had always been that way to a certain extent. He would read some new book or article about a perfect system, and suddenly we'd have to throw out everything we'd developed and try something new. One week it would be a system for training and coaching members, the next week a system for long-term planning or responding to members' complaints. It was impossible to say no and stay on the team, so everyone hesitated to demand that he stop, that he focus and follow the plan. And everything was so Newt-centric that we became paralyzed by what Bill began to call Newt's "adhocracy."

In April, when Newt struck an agreement with Bill Clinton to cut taxes and spend less than many conservatives had hoped, Dick Armey began swiping at him for being a turncoat. In June, when Clinton vetoed the disaster relief bill for victims of the floods in the Midwest, Newt agreed unilaterally to take out the riders that had offended the president. Conservative members were furious. Things had been going straight downhill since the government shutdown, and there seemed no promise of relief on the horizon.

The drumbeat grew louder by the day. The conservative press questioned Newt's ability to fulfill the agenda. He'd become a distraction, they declared. He needed to go. Some members went public, calling Newt "political roadkill" and asked him to do the right thing and step aside. Others seethed quietly and echoed those same sentiments in their offices and the back rooms of the Capitol. Even among Newt's most loyal followers, speculation began to mount about who would succeed Newt Gingrich if he was forced to step down immediately. The names that kept cropping up as replacements were Dick Armey and Bill Paxon.

Our supporters across the nation waited for Newt to take on Clinton, to show his old fire. Instead, there was silence. Conservatives within the Beltway were angry, and the conservative press had become hostile. The other members of the leadership knew what had to be done; we needed a clear line of authority and an even clearer legislative agenda. But we could not budge Newt and his closest advisers.

The problem was that we had spent all of 1995 in an incredible state of hubris. A photographer followed Newt around twenty-four hours a day, and the Speaker rode high "at the center of the worldwide revolution," as he was fond of saying. We all got caught

223

up in Newt's vision of himself as a "transformational" leader, as Napoleon or FDR during the New Deal. Then came the budget shutdowns and the 1996 elections, the ethics investigation and Newt's increasing unpopularity with the voters. By the time we reached summer 1997, a crash was almost inevitable. People bailed out of Newt World, as the Speaker's staff called it, at a record rate. They admired him and were grateful for what he had accomplished, but they wanted a conference that worked, that had form and direction. Instead, they had a demoralized Speaker who was still trying to micromanage even the minutiae of House life, and who wouldn't let go. The curtain had been pulled back on the Wizard of Oz.

Once I was on a plane trip with Newt, and I asked him how he got through all the stress—the attacks, the controversy, the distortions. "Focus," he said. "When I leave my house in the morning, I focus myself and remember that we're trying to change the course of civilization." But Newt had lost his focus, and his obsession with changing the course of civilization—his constant preoccupation—was getting in the way of mundane matters like the U.S. budget for 1997 and disaster relief.

◆

Newt Gingrich is one of the most complicated public figures of our day. Incredibly smart and pragmatic, he is at his best when he is building a team. He is at his worst and most self-destructive when he swells with his own sense of invulnerability and moves to the front and center. He never gives a speech or has a conversation; he delivers lectures filled with references to his tome of the month, to military strategy and, always, to his mission as the leader of a worldwide revolution.

After he came back from China, Newt talked incessantly about a Mongolian man he'd met who said that he was following everything Newt was doing. That was his ultimate fantasy: the attention of the universe, the adulation of the planet. There's something admirable in the fact that Newt was never thinking just about what we were doing in the House, that he was always thinking bigger. But in his quest to become the leader of the cosmos, mundane tasks like the schedule for the new session or an organizational chart for members got left behind.

Furthermore, Newt drew few people to him who could challenge him effectively. His upbringing created a tension in him that made him hungry for the approval of the very people who were meanest to him, as if he were reenacting, again and again, his relationship with his stepfather, a stern, tyrannical military man, a father of the old school. So he surrounded himself with people like Bill, who he knew admired and supported him, and then used them as whipping boys, yelling and screaming at them rather than heeding their counsel. However, when confronted with someone like Linda Smith, a member from Washington who told him off within months of her arrival on Capitol Hill, he would turn charming and accommodating. Those tendencies did not invite productive criticism.

When he is high, Newt can whip up even the feistiest troops, unify even the most unwilling team members. He has an extraordinary talent for sitting people down and walking them through issues without browbeating them. He can inspire like few other people I've met. He feels, even seems, invincible. But, inevitably, he swings in the other direction and falls into sullenness and self-pity. Bill and I had watched those drastic swings for years, but they never were as clear as they became when Newt visited us on Staten Island in December 1996. That fall, the Atlanta Braves had battled the New York Yankees at the World Series, and Georgia and New York politicians—George Pataki and the governor of Georgia, Rudy Giuliani and the mayor of Atlanta—paired up to bet on the games. Newt and I joined them, wagering one hundred dinners from our favorite hometown restaurants to be served to the homeless in the other's district. Newt lost when the Yankees won, which meant that he owed the residents of Staten Island's Project Hospitality, a shelter for homeless men and abused women, barbecue from Williamson Bros. in Marietta, Georgia.

Newt planned to fly into town shortly before Christmas and serve the food himself, but I warned him off when a collection of union thugs abruptly announced they would picket the event. I was unwilling to put the Speaker in that kind of hostile situation and more than a little peeved that Newt haters insisted on politicizing that event. But after we'd informed the press that Newt wasn't coming, he decided to slip in anyway. On December 15, Williamson's chefs arrived from Georgia, set up outdoor grills, and served up ribs, chicken, beans, and slaw. While Newt met with Project Hospitality's director, staff, and selected clients, Marianne Gingrich went by to mingle with the residents. It was a relaxed afternoon, and Newt was at his best explaining his approach to welfare reform, his models for helping the poor and disabled.

That night Bill and I invited Newt and Marianne to dinner at Tosca Ristorante, one of our favorite restaurants on Staten Island. We packed the room with friends and members of our staffs. Newt was in an expansive mood as he went through course after course of lobster rustica, linguine in balsamic vinegar sauce, calamari, ravioli, grilled chicken, and gnocchi al pesto with vodka. But in the midst of the drinking and eating and picture taking, Newt repeatedly raced to the office upstairs to talk to his attorneys by phone. They were in the final throes of negotiations with the Ethics Committee, and Newt needed to be in almost constant contact.

After one such conversation with his lawyers, Newt came down, huddled over with Bill and me, and announced that everything was a go for his run for the presidency in the year 2000. We were speechless. The ethics decisions were serious matters, members were grumbling openly, Newt's approval ratings were below thirty percent, his speakership was in jeopardy—and he was planning his run for the presidency. He insisted that even though things might be messy for a while, he thought all signs were positive for his becoming the leader of the next stage of the revolution. He was on a high, and there was no stopping him.

Bill and I recognized the phase he was in, one of those moments when he thinks of himself as Winston Churchill, so adversity means nothing to him. One more near death experience means only that he'll emerge even stronger. The martyrdom of Churchill, who was exiled by his party and unappreciated by his countrymen after World War II, was a constant theme to which Newt returned again and again over the years. The run for the presidency, however, was something neither Bill nor I had ever heard Newt mention directly until then. Certainly it had been a matter of speculation. He'd played with it before the 1994 election, especially when he flew off to New Hampshire to see moose at what seemed a curious moment. And in late 1997, Washington was abuzz with rumors about his intentions.

After years of using his signature and time to help the NRCC, by then he began signing fund-raising letters for the Republican National Committee, and receiving names for his personal political mailing list in exchange. Political operatives and consultants, the kind of people who run political campaigns, were seen coming and going from his office.

I assumed he was running not because of that activity, but because the notion of a Gingrich run for the presidency makes sense in the context of who Newt is and where he has been. It is not just that he sees himself as bigger than the job he is in. It's also that once you've been Speaker for a few years—and he has said repeatedly that he won't remain Speaker beyond 2002—and you're not very old, what do you do for an encore? Newt has never, and never will be, satisfied with being a great Republican first, a great Speaker of the House. He's got to do something intergalactic.

Furthermore, some of his political advisers argue that he has the biggest political mailing list in the country, is a fierce fund-raiser, and has a tremendous base of support, all of which adds up to a real shot at the nomination. Even if he doesn't win, by running he would gain a new forum for framing the national debate between now and the year 2000. Even if he loses, he can leave public service with dignity. The most gracious way for him to get out of Congress, then, is to run for the presidency. And the most gracious way for others to get him out is to support his doing so.

◆

By the early summer, Bill and I were worried that the discontent with Newt, the speculation over his resignation, and the pressure for his resignation had already divided the House. Members looked over their shoulders rather than ahead to the final balanced budget and tax cut negotiations that were just coming to a crest. What would happen to this historic legislation and the GOP Congress in the 1998 elections if Newt were suddenly pushed out and a brutal, party-splintering battle for the speakership ensued? Time and again Newt Gingrich had survived against all odds, and I believed he would again. But even a cat has nine lives.

On one of those particularly dark days, during a private meeting in Dick Armey's lofty Capitol office, Bill made the one gesture he believed might help prevent total disaster. He informed the majority leader that he would support him for the speakership should Newt leave office unexpectedly. Armey seemed stunned. While he had long coveted the job, he had always been a loner in the House. Bill, however, saw no alternative. Conference morale was already low, and our agenda, and future control over the House, in jeopardy. He wasn't looking to push Newt out of office, but he wanted to make sure that if he left, the order of succession would be clear. Better Armey, despite his well-reported shortcomings, than the intraparty bloodbath that any challenge to his ambitions would pose.

Bill's other goal with Armey, however, was to enlist him in a plan to confront Newt and convince him to take the problems in the conference more seriously. We had talked repeatedly about those problems and hoped that if Armey, DeLay, and Boehner joined Bill in pressuring Newt to allow them control over the daily functioning of the House, we might be able to regain our steam.

At Bill's suggestion, the four of them met in Boehner's Capitol office, and the long-simmering frustrations about the Speaker's management style exploded. The chain-smoking majority leader fumed that he was tired of carrying the burden of covering for Newt and was no longer willing to fix the situation. "Let him fall," he said succinctly.

Bill, Boehner, and DeLay, however, had an alternate plan. DeLay had drawn up a list of demands he thought they should present to Newt: regular leadership meetings; a new system for communications with members and the public; more active involvement of committee chairmen; formal leadership and decision-making structures. He proposed a meeting that would be an "intervention" with Newt, a political version of those done with drug or alcohol abusers. "We can't leave the meeting with Newt until we get closure," he said. They all agreed to give it a go.

Newt had arranged a dinner for the group in the Texas Room in the Capitol for the next night, and the men decided to turn it into DeLay's intervention. The dinner took on a surreal quality when the five of them wandered into the room where Speaker Sam Rayburn had gathered his troops every afternoon at five P.M. back in the fifties and sixties for bourbon and water to sort out the problems on both sides of the aisle—girlfriends out of control, alcohol abuse, whatever. As Newt and his team ate beneath ceiling murals of the Texas desert, Newt was upbeat. "It's amazing how well things are going," he said.

Bill interrupted and countered with a full report on the problems plaguing the conference. Then DeLay pulled out his list of solutions. Back and forth they went, around the table, trying to back Newt into a corner. The choreographed political drama was punctuated by Armey's continuous need to use the telephone. His daughter-in-law was in labor, and he kept calling the hospital. After each call he'd rush back to the table and add his weight to the push against Newt. Finally, Newt's face began to quiver. "It's hard," he said. "It's so hard being at the center of a worldwide movement. There's so much to do. It's so hard."

They'd all heard it before—his tale about the burdens he felt because Mongolians in yurts were waving copies of the Contract with America; the story about the father who had abandoned him and agreed to allow his stepfather to adopt him in exchange for a reduction in child support; the difficulties of being the planet's leading revolutionary. The others fumed. Armey, DeLay, and Boehner had seen their share of life's adversities, and dealt with them. Yet, again and again, they had to listen silently to Newt rehashing his own tribulations.

"We don't want to hear how hard it is, Newt," Bill said. "You make it hard. The House has worked for two hundred years. It's an assembly line. You put stuff in one end and it comes out the other. But you're throwing sand in the gears. We can run the House, but not if you insist on micromanaging everything. If you stick to what you are good at, we can make Rolls Royces instead of Yugos."

Newt blew his top and followed the script the four men had heard thirty times before. "It isn't just a matter of bills. People all over the world are listening to us, watching what we are doing. I'm at the center of a worldwide revolution. You will never understand that, Bill." DeLay started pounding the table, insisting that Newt change the way he operated. Meanwhile Armey was running to the phone to check on his daughter-in-law, and the buzzer kept sounding, forcing them to interrupt the meeting to go upstairs to vote.

Finally, on their way back to the Texas Room after yet another vote, the three leaders agreed to make one final attempt at "closure," at getting Newt to agree to DeLay's list of demands. Instead of closure, however, they got a lecture from Newt that stunned even those four veteran politicos. "You don't understand how I operate and never will," Newt said, turning to Bill, who was seated at his right. "I get up every morning and say to myself, 'this is the day I shall die.'"

There was silence in that history-filled room. They had all heard Newt compare himself to Napoleon, FDR, Churchill, and Eisenhower—hugely important figures who had led great peoples in times of deep crisis. Yet there was Newt Gingrich, leading the House of Representatives during a time of peace and relative economic security, still waking up daily thinking of himself as Napoleon in the saddle at Waterloo, or Churchill in a bunker below London with Nazi bombs raining overhead.

That night Newt managed to slip away again. Armey reached his son and announced that he had become a grandfather. The meeting dissolved in the emotion of the moment, without the resolution our party needed.

By early July, however, things became even more demoralizing, if that was possible. Conference elections to replace me as vice chair were scheduled for the middle of the month, and Jim Nussle of Iowa was trying to turn the election into a referendum on Newt. Nussle had been one of Newt's favorite members. Suddenly he was complaining about "mountaintop decision-making, where the tablets are brought down and the masses are told, 'This is where we're going.'"

Nussle's campaign increased the stakes, so tension was high when Bill, Armey, DeLay, and Boehner gathered again on July 9, this time in DeLay's office in the Capitol. Armey walked in wearing his signature armadillo-skin cowboy boots. The air soon became thick from Boehner's chain-smoking. This time there was no talk of how to deal with Newt. A new disaster was pending. Boehner had discovered that a group of dissident members had asked California Congressman Tom Campbell to prepare a resolution calling for Newt's ouster. Boehner had met with the dissidents and was convinced that the rebellion was already under way. Each of the members of Newt's inner circle had heard intimations of rebellion before. Several disgruntled representatives had called Bill at home just a few nights earlier. But pockets of rebellion exist in any political organization at almost any time, so Bill hadn't taken the complaints very seriously. Boehner, however, believed that the pockets had begun to coalesce, and that there was no time to lose.

The men made a list of the known, or most likely, dissidents. When they reached fifteen or twenty, they realized that the question was no longer whether a coup was afoot, but whether it had reached critical mass. Given our slim majority, all they needed was a handful of Republicans voting to remove the Speaker for Newt to fall. Armey walked over to the copy of the Ten Commandments DeLay kept on a table and pointed to the relevant text: "Thou shalt not covet . . ." and "Thou shalt not bear false witness. . . ."

"I do not covet the speakership," he said, but added that he would do nothing to save Newt Gingrich. Furthermore, Armey said that if something happened to Newt, he would ask Henry Hyde to nominate him as Speaker and Bill to second the nomination. Bill was dumbstruck. Bill knew Armey was counting on his promise to support him. DeLay, stunned, announced that he had no interest in running for Speaker. Boehner added that he had no idea what he would do. Bill was silent. He knew that Armey's simple declaration had just dissolved half the threads that held together their tiny band.

The next day, Thursday, July 10, while Newt was immersed in the battle over funding for the National Endowment for the Arts, Armey, DeLay, Boehner, and Bill moved throughout the Capitol and the House office buildings trying to gauge the depth of the rebellion. About seven P.M. Bill walked onto the floor, where I noticed that he was cornered by Chris Shays and Mike Parker.

Shays, a Connecticut moderate, was distrusted within Newt World because he had repeatedly spoken in the press about Newt's ethics problems and, on more than one occasion, threatened not to back his reelection as Speaker. Just after Newt's reelection in January, Parker, a backslapping former undertaker and Democrat turned Republican, had arranged to meet with Bill in private. Predicting that Newt wouldn't last long, he asked, "Are you ready to take over, Bill?" he asked. Bill leaned forward and responded, "Come on, Newt's just been reelected and you know that I support him. Things are going to work out. Don't worry." Parker refused to take Bill's reaction seriously. "Just keep saying that, but consider me your double agent. At the right moment I'll let you know when to move." Parker had never mentioned the strange conversation again.

That history was racing through Bill's head when Shays and Parker pulled him off the House floor and onto a balcony looking down the mall toward the floodlit Washington Monument. Shays told Bill that he'd just been approached by Steve Largent of Oklahoma, an NFL Hall of Famer and one of the most forthright renegades, seeking his support in an attempt to replace Newt. Parker and Shays wanted to know if Bill had any idea about what was going on.

The last thing Bill wanted was to fan the flames of rebellion against Newt, someone he'd worked so hard to elect and reelect. And, given their histories, he also wasn't entirely sure of the motivations of Parker and Shays. So he demurred and raced back to the floor to report to me this most recent bizarre twist in an already bizarre week. Then he headed back to his Capitol office to meet Armey and DeLay for the planned update on their assessments of the rebellion brewing in Newt's ranks.

What Bill didn't know, however, was that Shays and Parker had sought out Bill at Newt's request, having gone to the Speaker immediately after Largent's approach. It was Newt who had sent them to Bill and, only in retrospect, and with that knowledge, did we realize that Bill's equivocation sounded to Shays and Parker— and to Newt, to whom they reported the conversation just moments later—like the silence of a conspirator.

Meanwhile, in Bill's office, the trio of Bill, DeLay, and Armey became a quartet when they asked Dennis Hastert of Illinois, one of the most respected members of the House, to offer some clear thinking. The four agreed they needed more information before they could safely approach the Speaker. So they dispatched DeLay to a midnight meeting with the rebels to check on reports that the members already had a petition to remove Newt, signed by more than thirty Republicans. They needed to know the truth fast in order to defuse the crisis. If it was unstoppable, they needed a plan for saving the party and our agenda.

When DeLay reappeared in Bill's office after one A.M., he looked as grim as the news he delivered. The seventeen rebels he'd met with were drawn from all factions of the party and seemed to be gaining strength. Some seemed ready to try to force Newt out immediately; others wanted his pledge not to seek reelection to the House so that he would not be a political drag to the party in the 1998 election. As the men drooped from weariness, DeLay turned to Armey and dropped the final bomb. "Dick, they won't accept you. They want Bill as Speaker." Bill left his office just after two A.M. that night. He knew that the time had come to talk to Newt.

First he had to talk to me. Not about becoming Speaker. That was the last thing on Bill's mind. But Armey was another matter, although we didn't know at the time just how serious a one. We were not privy to what he was doing that night. But we were not naive about his ambition.

Friday the eleventh was one of those steaming Washington summer days when the temperature hits one hundred degrees and you can't stay dry. Perfect weather for a denouement. The phone rang early with a call from Tom DeLay. Armey was on the other line. Bill instantly knew that something had changed. Armey's voice was icy and distant as he scheduled an appointment for the group to meet with Newt. As Bill got ready to leave for his office, all I could say was Watch your back. Don't trust Armey. Don't trust anyone. Take care of yourself.

At ten A.M. Bill, DeLay, and Armey convened with Newt, Boehner, and staff members in Newt's office. Bill didn't know that Armey had already briefed the Speaker with his own version of the events, but Newt was remarkably calm, trying to pass the problems off as the "usual chaos." Bill and DeLay interrupted. "No," they both said, "it's not the usual chaos." DeLay explained precisely what had happened, who the renegades were, and what they were planning.

Staff members had just begun to offer suggestions on how to defuse the tension, when Newt exploded. "Call a conference right now," he said to John Boehner, the conference chair. "A mandatory conference. I'm going to stand up and I want them to vote me out. Make Steve Largent the Speaker and I will become the leader of the opposition. We will go to the polls next November and I will get Gingrich candidates in every district and we will win back the majority."

Bill interrupted. "We can't do that. We have a budget vote in two weeks, the most important vote of this session of Congress." Newt snapped back. "I've said it before, you and I will never understand each other. I get up every morning, look in the mirror, and say, 'this is the day I shall die.' I have nothing to lose. I will leave Congress. I'll go to teach." He continued with a rant about Churchill in exile.

After everyone calmed down, the dissidents were summoned for a dressing-down in Armey's conference room. They were speechless as Armey berated them for their irresponsible, immoral behavior. Just the night before, they'd been led to believe that Armey was with them. What had happened in the interim? According to accounts he later gave the press, Armey had been praying in the interim, which he offered as the explanation for his change of heart, rather than admit that he'd been chastened by DeLay's report that the rebels would not accept him as Speaker.

Newt had scheduled one of the periodic dinners he holds with his closest advisers for the following Tuesday. The usual group of five was expanded that night and included people like John Kasich and other important members. As they entered the Speaker's dining room, Newt seemed angry and upset. But the dinner conversation quickly turned to the concrete steps leaders needed to take to regain control over the situation. Bill and DeLay, hopeful, pulled out the original list they'd generated for the long-forgotten "intervention."

Midway through the meeting, Armey abruptly stood up and left. The rest of the men stayed to work. Newt asked Bill to run all leadership-related meetings, which quelled any apprehension he'd had that the Speaker had marked him as a traitor. They talked about setting aside both time and a system for members to complain, about how to maximize communications and minimize mistrust, and even about appointing a new communications director— everything Bill, DeLay, Armey, and Boehner had been advocating for months. That night Bill and I slept soundly for the first time in a week. It was the last time we did so.

Wednesday morning the story of the attempted coup appeared in *The Hill,* an inside-the-Beltway weekly. Before Bill and I could even make it through our office doors, members were quizzing us. Had there really been an attempted coup? Who was behind it?

Was Bill involved? Was it my parting gesture? So the air was thick with tension and confusion as we walked into the Cannon Conference Room for the meeting of all 228 House Republicans, where my successor would be elected.

Newt tried to keep conversation about the newspaper report light, joking about the movie *Men in Black,* in which he'd been compared to a space alien. But some members refused to be pacified. "If the leadership was involved in this, they owe us and the Speaker an apology," said Jim Walsh of New York. Armey responded by denying that the leaders had been involved in any attempt to oust Newt. Rebel leader Lindsay Graham, enraged at what he saw as a lie, leapt from his seat so quickly that he knocked over chairs in his lunge for the microphone to dispute Armey. We were saved from an explosion by the members who restrained him.

Jim Nussle was defeated solidly by Jennifer Dunn. And Newt ended the meeting by passing off the events of the previous weeks as childish and self-destructive. He delivered a firm reminder that our focus needed to be on the budget legislation that was pending. Bill and I traded glances. He sounded almost like my husband.

But the air did not clear. Newt's supporters paced the Capitol, looking for blood. Armey's allies spread the word that he had been Newt's only defender, attending meetings only as a spy. Bill wasn't naive. We began to put together a team, members who would support Bill and the best communications people we knew to counter Armey's new version of what had happened.

Late that afternoon, news of the alleged coup broke on the wire of the Associated Press, which ran a quote from Armey painting himself as the single loyal member of the leadership team. Bill exploded. He was not willing to let Armey rewrite history. He and DeLay needed to confront Armey and Newt, and Bill wasn't about to wait. He had a staffer deliver a note to the Speaker's chief of staff, Arne Christensen, requesting an immediate meeting with

Newt. The note was returned with No scrawled across it. When Bill called upstairs to press the issue, he was told that the Speaker had left for the evening.

Bill grabbed DeLay and Hastert from their Capitol offices and headed upstairs to the Speaker's elegant suite. He cornered Newt and Armey just as they were leaving by the back stairs and insisted they meet then and there. When the five senior House leaders moved into Christensen's small office, Bill shoved the AP report into Armey's face and demanded to know why Armey was trying to implicate him and DeLay in a plot in which they were not involved. Bill understood that his position was tenuous. The other members of leadership had been elected by the conference; he alone had been appointed by Newt.

"I'm not reading anything, I'm not saying anything," Armey said, brushing the paper aside. "I'm going home to my wife." He stormed out. The others remained and Bill recounted the events to Newt as he understood it. "You should have come to me," Newt responded. Bill explained that he and the others had been trying to work as a team to resolve the situation calmly. Armey suddenly reappeared and started screaming. Then, just as abruptly, he said, "I'm not going to talk about this anymore," and stormed out again. When he reappeared a second time, Bill insisted that he set the record straight rather than single himself out as the only loyal member of the leadership team. By then, however, Armey was too entrenched in his own spin. Or perhaps DeLay's announcement that the rebels preferred Bill as Speaker was still ringing in his ears.

Bill, sensing that Newt had lost confidence in his team, stood up and said, "Maybe I should resign." Before Newt could open his mouth, Armey snapped, "I accept." Bill wasn't having it. "You don't have that power," he replied.

Bill came home that night with a simple announcement, "It's time to move on." We knew what Bill had been doing over those previous weeks, but we could think of no way around the lies that had been spun. Bill planned to formalize his resignation in the morning. I kept thanking CBS for landing at my door. How would I have survived in the House leadership after Bill's ouster? How would I have survived in the House without being in the leadership? How could I work for "the good of the order" with people who found it convenient to shove my husband out of the picture? How could I respect people who were so wrong?

As we drank our coffee in the morning and played with our daughter, Bill sat in the dining room dreading the prospect of seeing our colleagues. "I've got a case of political leprosy," he said. We both knew that Congress maintains no colonies for the afflicted. When Bill got to work, he asked a member of his staff to prepare his letter of resignation from leadership. Just then, Arne Christensen appeared in his office with the news that the Speaker had accepted his resignation. Arne seemed surprised when Bill replied that the letter would be ready momentarily. "Newt wants you to know that he feels bad, that after a little time has passed, you can come back into leadership," he added. Bill was too wounded to be patronized. "I don't need to be redeemed," he replied.

That night our basement was like a bunker. Bill and I hunkered down with members of his staff and friends. His communications director called every reporter he knew to offer Bill's side of the story. Susan Ruby was racing around with a bottle of detergent, which seemed a perfect comment on the state of affairs. Our friend Julie Wadler stopped by bearing an ice cream cake which we added to the cookies and pies that had already piled up in the kitchen. It was as if we were sitting shivah, the Jewish mourning ritual.

For the following week, Bill tormented himself with the thought that he would have to resign from Congress. I was convinced he needed to wait and watch the fallout. Everywhere I went in the Capitol, all I heard was "Tell Bill . . ." None of the sentiments was hostile.

Finally, Newt's allies forced a late-night meeting of the entire conference to clear the air. Some were looking for blood. The new leadership team suggested that Bill be the first speaker, followed by Armey, DeLay, and Boehner. Bill declined. After all, he was no longer a member of leadership. If he had anything to say, he would raise his hand like any other rank-and-file member.

We gritted our teeth for what everyone expected would be an explosive session and took seats away from the leadership team for the first time in three years. But no rockets were fired. John Boehner spoke quietly about what had happened, then got so choked up that he cut himself off and sat down. DeLay apologized for any encouragement he'd unwittingly given the rebels. Armey offered his side of the story which, surprisingly, at least to us, was greeted with only modest applause. Then Jennifer Dunn looked at Bill, who delivered the speech we had worked so hard to perfect. Bill did not try to defend himself or take Armey on directly. He spoke quietly and concluded, "If you want a head, you've got mine."

By the time he finished, we both were crying so hard that we didn't realize for an instant that our colleagues had risen to their feet in a collective ovation. The only person in the room who remained seated was Dick Armey. Members who still wanted blood were drowned out by others pleading for peace. The planned bloodletting turned into an encounter group. Terry Everett offered Baptist wisdom about healing. Sonny Callahan rose, as a good Catholic, to add his suggestion. "Let's say six rosaries, ten Our Fathers, and a novena, and forget about it." Then Sonny Bono took the microphone and added a homily about letting go. "After *The Sonny and Cher Show* ended, I couldn't let go of Hollywood," he said. "I stuck around and couldn't find any decent work at all. After my fourth spot on *Fantasy Island,* I was down to one line. 'Look, Pontoon, there's the plane.' Only the name was Tattoo, not Pontoon, of course. I had three gold records, a long-running show, and I couldn't let go, so I wound up with some little guy kicking me in the shins because I got his name wrong. That's when I knew it was time to move on. And I tell you, now is the time to move on."

Three hours later the meeting broke up. As we moved toward the back of the room, dozens of members stopped to hug us. When we finally reached the door, Bill turned to me. "Should I go to Newt and say something?" he asked. I looked at the Speaker, who was still at the front of the room, obviously waiting for Bill. I looked at Bill, who had stood by Newt and spent hundreds of hours defending him.

"Don't you dare," I replied. I grabbed his arm, and we departed.

◆

I admit that I tell this story with hesitation because I dread the prospect that readers will assume that I'm just defending my husband, that I'm out to "get" Newt. In fact, my feelings for Newt Gingrich are racked by ambivalence. Despite all rumors to the contrary, Newt didn't help catapult me into leadership. I got there on my own. But from the moment I landed in that position, he was extremely supportive of me. All through the most important battles of our first years in the majority, he trusted me enough to do heavy lifting, especially with the press, heavy lifting that earned me prominence across the country. He appointed me to lead the House delegation to Bosnia. And time and again he supported me and the issues I cared about.

When other members of leadership scoffed at my suggestion that we, as a party, take a leading role in increasing funding for programs to protect women from violence, Newt threw his support to me. He consistently reminded male members that they could not win their next elections without the votes of women, and urged them to organize teams of women to teach them to reach out to female voters. When other members rolled their eyes at my suggestions for new women's initiatives, as if to say, "Do we have to deal with the women again?" Newt would cut off their protests so I could make my full pitch.

Were those positions sincere? Did the Speaker truly care about the health and welfare and future of American womanhood, or was his support a cynical ploy to gain converts to the Republican revolution? Sorry, I can offer no insight into to his private thoughts. All I know is that he supported a significant body of legislation that has helped American women, and a significant number of women—like me.

More than what he offered me directly, Newt served as a kind of mentor to me. In many ways he taught me to be tough, to be a survivor. The biggest and the best have tried to take him down, and he has always come back. I've watched him on television and at lectures and admired the way he consistently mentions other people, empowering them by highlighting their accomplishments. I am exceedingly grateful for the number of times he told me, directly or indirectly, "Just go out there and do it."

But I cannot forget that Newt is also the man who changed the course of the legislative careers of the two most important men in my life, or stop wondering what that says about his character. By ousting my father from the chairmanship of his subcommittee, he pushed an effective Republican out of the House of Representatives. The fact that the effective Republican in question was my dad hung heavily over my relationship with Newt from the day I entered Congress. I can remember mentioning it to Newt only once. Early in my tenure, after an NRCC dinner, he asked me to support his election as Speaker. "You've been really good to me," I said, "but my dad . . ." He had no response.

After twenty years in politics, nothing much surprises me. At my first meeting of the New York City Council, I watched Bob Dryfoos, who had promised publicly to support Sam Horowitz, switch his vote to Vallone in what seemed to be a secret deal. When

Bill was running, unopposed, for the chairmanship of the National Republican Congressional Committee, I heard dozens of members refuse to commit themselves lest they be left without maneuvering room. That's human nature, and politics plays to all of its weaknesses.

But I admit that Bill's being transmogrified into a scapegoat for the seething discontent that racked our party caucus in the House surprised me. Bill's an easygoing guy. Even moderates who don't agree with his conservative politics are comfortable with him because he is tolerant and always willing to listen. In the days and weeks after his resignation, members sent him fruit baskets and notes reexpressing their gratitude for the help he'd provided in their elections, and congratulating him for his candor. He emerged in the press with his future and reputation intact. During fall 1997, over forty incumbents and candidates invited him to their districts to campaign for them.

No one believed that Bill Paxon had plotted a coup against Newt Gingrich, least of all Newt Gingrich. So I was surprised at the disloyalty and dishonesty. But I'm not sure what role loyalty and honesty play in the worldwide revolution.

◆

On the afternoon of December 31, 1997, just a few hours before the new year would begin, Bill and I were relaxing in the kitchen of my parents' condominium in Sarasota, Florida, not even thinking about politics. The phone rang, and I watched Bill's face morph from a mask of puzzlement to one of utter disbelief. As he listened, silently, he signaled to me that the caller was Newt. I moved closer to the phone so that I could hear every word.

A full year had passed since that dark time when the Speaker had been trapped between the ethics charges and the growing restlessness of his troops, since that Christmas holiday which Bill devoted to trying to save Newt from political disaster. Gingrich was calling, he said, because he was preoccupied with those same thoughts. "A year ago I was done," he told Bill, "and it was because of the work that you and Susan did that I was saved. I just wanted to say thank you. I'll never forget that."

Chapter Nine

....

A Fork in the Road

A few days before Clinton's inauguration in 1997, my receptionist buzzed my office and informed me that Andrew Heyward was on the line asking to make an appointment with me.
"What could the president of CBS News want with me?" I wondered. I'd met Andrew at a dinner during the convention and, as I
always did when I was in proximity to senior network officials, I'd
made a pitch about my fantasy of working in television news.

That pitch was something of a tradition for me, dating from the days when I was just out of college and stumped as to how to get my foot in the door of television news.

I know it sounds odd: Sue Molinari knew how to get to Congress but couldn't figure out how to find a TV job. But remember, Congress was my family business. I not only knew how to get there, I'd watched my father do it. Given my bloodlines, it was the path of least resistance. Television, however, was where I'd always wanted to be, although I've never been able to provide a satisfactory answer as to why. The best I can muster is that I grew up with television as my connection to the outside world. It's where I met my first heroes and antiheroes. It was where I hid when I was tired and lonely and fed up. Not a good enough explanation? Probably not. But the dreams of childhood are strongly rooted, and I'm too stubborn to let even old fantasies die.

My problem was that television seemed like some exotic world, and entry into it a mysteriously uncharted path. When I was right out of college and hanging around trying to figure out what to do with myself, I tried everything, and everyone, I could think of to break into TV journalism. I was so desperate that one afternoon, when walked into my father's Staten Island congressional office just as a local television mogul was leaving, I grabbed my dad and complained, "Gee, couldn't you have asked him to talk to me about how to get a job?" I demanded. Dad did his best, calling the man back into his office to meet me. But to no avail.

Once I entered Congress, the television news fantasy still simmered in the back of my mind, and experience did nothing to diminish its power. I spent hours in studios every month—debating moderate Republicanism on *Crossfire,* filming a C-Span special about a day in my life, filling in for Mary Matalin on *Equal Time,* battling it out on *Capital Gang.* For a while I debated Bob Beckel weekly on *Off the Record,* a sort of yuppie version of *The McLaugh-*

lin Group that Fox created. And Chuck Schumer, a New York Democrat, and I did a regular Chuck and Sue show, reporting somewhat irreverently from Washington for Channel 2 in New York.

I had a ball, and—excuse the immodesty—the reviews were great. When I first started appearing on television, Bill Moyers declared that if I ever decided to leave politics, I'd have a great future in TV. In 1995, the Washington bureau columnist for the my hometown paper, the *Staten Island Advance,* devoted a full column to my TV appearances, suggesting that if I ever got tired of chasing voters, I could fall back on a career in racking up TV ratings. He had no idea how close to the mark he had hit.

But no one seemed to take either his suggestion, or my pitches, seriously. By then, of course, I could have approached dozens of people I knew in the news media to express serious interest in a career change, but I was oddly, perhaps, too shy. I didn't really believe that anyone would take such a proposal seriously, so I confined my approaches to off-the-cuff quips and jokes. One afternoon when I was pregnant, I ran into Rupert Murdoch, the media mogul, and Peter Lund, who was then the president of CBS News, in Bill's office. I was just breezing in to give Bill a message, but I stopped long enough to kid them about offering me a job. When I found myself sitting next to Andrew Heyward at a dinner during the convention, I couldn't resist trying again. After all, he was a captive audience at a political dinner, so he could hardly laugh in my face. I never expected that my remark would bear any greater fruit than the fifty-seven earlier pitches I had made.

What I didn't know was that since he'd take over as president in January 1996, Andrew was doing his best to change CBS News's image. He'd hired Bill Bradley, the former Democratic member from New Jersey, to do on-air essays, and Laura Ingraham, Washington's favorite conservative babe, to present commentaries. He'd brought Alison Stewart over from MTV, wooed Bryant Gumbel from NBC, and convinced CNN to share Christiane Amanpour with *60 Minutes.*

Andrew billed his appointment as a "courtesy call." Once he arrived in my office, however, he made it clear that he had stopped by to try to add me to the list as the anchor of a new Saturday morning news show. The timing, and the offer, couldn't have been better.

I'd been a professional funk since the Republican convention. For weeks after my speech, I'd ridden a roller coaster of public reaction, pumped up by the dozens of women who'd stop me in the supermarket or the mall to tell me how much my remarks had meant to them, how clearly I had expressed their fears and frustrations, then plunged into the depths by reviews suggesting that I'd offered precisely the kind of empty platitudes expected from a lightweight.

I had become something of a political rock star, but Andy Warhol would have been the only person able to appreciate how long my fifteen minutes extended. The weekend after the convention, I spent Saturday night on *Capital Gang* and Sunday morning on *This Week with David Brinkley.* I did *Good Morning America,* the *MacNeil-Lehrer NewsHour, Equal Time, Crossfire,* and *Crossfire Sunday.* I was named one of *Glamour* magazine's Women of the Year, along with Rosie, Shannon Lucid, Maureen Dowd, Terry McMillan, and the entire Olympic women's basketball team.

But the celebrity proved remarkably empty. It was worse than postpartum depression. I was still hurting from the marijuana episode. Few things that had happened to me up until that point in my political life had wounded me so deeply. All I wanted to do was to stay home with my husband and daughter.

The results of the election made things look even bleaker. I believed in Bob Dole, believed that he was an honorable man who had served his country well and would have been a first-rate president. His defeat hardly surprised me, but it hurt. And while I again sailed through my own reelection campaign, our loss of seats in the House gave us a tenuous hold on the majority that meant that any dissident group could hijack the entire effort. Bill, Mr. Optimistic, was planning to drive up to the Capitol for the opening of the new session in a 1928 Ford, a Ford from the last year that a Republican House had won reelection. But I couldn't muster that kind of bravado.

The show that Andrew was offering me, at least as described, sounded like precisely my cup of tea, since my TV fantasy had always been about the morning news. Maybe I understood that without experience in journalism, that slot would be more appropriate for me. Maybe it was that I found the format more appealing than hard news since you could also let your personality come through. Or maybe it was just that broadcasting at seven A.M. seemed a less intimidating goal than being the anchor at six or eleven P.M.

Anyway, in the most serious and professional manner that I could muster at a moment when I was ready to jump out of my enormous executive leather chair, I told Andrew that I was ready to consider his offer. Then I ran into Bill's office unsure whether to be elated or terrified. I was a member of Congress at the pinnacle of my career and someone had offered me the job I'd been dreaming about for twenty years! Bill doesn't get caught up in my chaos, so his reaction was serious and direct: If you want the job, you need an agent. And so it began. I never stopped for a serious consideration of the pros and cons, or the long-term implications. It wasn't that I was desperate to leave Congress—I'd gotten, and ignored, plenty of feelers about the kind of jobs members are routinely offered. I was just following my heart.

The negotiations were endless and complicated since CBS wanted the new show to begin in September and I had just been reelected to Congress. How would I handle broadcasting from

New York when I lived in Washington? What would I do if Bill landed at the center of a news storm? As we waded through these questions and neared an agreement, I met with members of the Ethics Committee of the House to make sure that I wasn't crossing any legal or ethical lines. Then Bill, my father, and I sat down to chart how the announcement would be made and when my resignation would become official.

We were preempted from such careful considerations when someone called from the *Hollywood Reporter* tracking a rumor that I was negotiating a contract with CBS. Suddenly there was no time. CBS called a press conference for ten A.M. Wednesday, May 28, to make the announcement. I scrawled a quick list of the people I felt should hear the news from the horse's mouth, and began calling: Newt, Rudy Giuliani, Al D'Amato, and Governor George Pataki. Then I gathered my Staten Island staff in our office there and linked up by phone with the folks in Washington to break the news. Finally I called the *Staten Island Advance,* the local newspaper that had been so supportive of me over the years, and offered them an exclusive.

The next morning I rode over to the press conference at CBS headquarters on West 57th Street with my dad and my friend Julie. I was feeling great and bopped into the half-empty studio they'd set aside for the event, plopped myself into a high-backed chair, and was promptly ambushed by Penny Crone from Fox. "How can you make Susan Molinari a, quote-unquote, CBS anchorperson, when in fact she hasn't put any time into the news business, when she's absolutely an amateur?" she asked. It was the first question of the day, the first question of my new career. Welcome to reality

I could hear the contempt, but I was in too good a mood to be fazed, at least at the beginning. "Hey, hey, hey, hey," I chided her, smiling. Come on, lighten up, I was thinking. Andrew, who was sitting next to me, intervened. It made no difference. "Are you hiring her because she's a Katie Couric look-alike?" Crone persisted, spitting contempt. Dripping with the kind of righteous indignation that might have been appropriate to a White House correspondent who'd been lied to by the president, she declared my hiring an affront to journalistic professionalism and objectivity. She later announced, summarily, that I wasn't up to the job, thus demonstrating the standards of professionalism and objectivity to which she personally adhered.

I expected the press to be doubting Thomases, even naysayers. I'd expected to be criticized for leaving the seat I'd just won, for my lack of experience, for mixing journalism with politics. But I was used to doubts and naysaying. They were the story of my career. What I hadn't expected was the vitriol. It was Carol Greitzer and the Democrats on the City Council when I demanded the perks of minority leader all over again. "Really, who the hell does she think she is?" It was the Democrats on Staten Island when I announced I was running for Congress, "She's only a kid, who the hell does she think she is?" It was the haters when I ran for leadership in the Republican conference and scores of pundits when I was tapped to deliver the keynote. It did not get easier over time.

Andrew and I described the new program as *60 Minutes* meets Rosie, a program that would move seamlessly from what is too often viewed as "real news," which is politics, to the "soft news" that is the stuff of life for most Americans. Everyone found the thought of Susan Molinari handling cooking segments to be vaguely amusing. So did I, since I'm hardly famous for my culinary prowess.

But it was, of course, the "real news" that provoked the controversy. How could I report on politics objectively? How could CBS hire someone with such obvious bias? Those were fair questions, and Andrew and I both thought we had the answers. "I'll deal with it much the same way every journalist in this country does," I explained. "I give the American viewer a lot more credit than maybe some of you in this audience do. They know who I am." Andrew went further: "It's not as though we're pulling a fast one on anybody. Her background, her beliefs, are out there for all to see. And I think the real issue is your relationship with the viewer. And I think our relationship with the viewer is, we're bringing somebody with expertise in an area who's also going to be looking at a lot of other things."

The reporters seemed particularly disconcerted because I refused to state categorically that I would never return to politics. After all, that's how Tim Russert appeased them when he left his job with Mario Cuomo to go on the air. I had, and have, no intention of turning around and going back in the other direction. But I could not make that promise. The Molinari family motto is "Never say never," and I wasn't about to close off any options before I'd even turned forty.

I left CBS news after the press conference, exhausted, returned to Washington, pulled off my suit, changed into sweats, and had a nervous breakdown. Act I was over. I had no idea whether Act II would propel me toward a rousing finish or close the whole show.

Given the tenor of the press conference, I should have been prepared for the storm that erupted over my announcement. I wasn't. It had never occurred to me that anyone other than my constituents and some political insiders would care what I did with my life. I wasn't the president of the United States or the head of the Joint Chiefs of Staff. Members of the House are a dime a dozen, and dozens of them had been quitting politics. Five months into the session, four sitting members of the House, along with three senators, had announced their retirements. They were the tip of the iceberg. I could feel the discontent between the lines of the reaction of dozens of members: God, you're so lucky. I wish someone would offer me a great job so I could get out of here.

But my decision struck too many chords in too many people

to be buried on page 64. For the people, of course, it was the breach I represented in the wall they believed should exist between journalism and politics. But their horror was a tad overwrought. They seized on my announcement to warn of the dangers of a trend that was, by then, too established to be worth that much noise. Journalists like Strobe Talbott, who'd left *Newsweek* for a senior position at the State Department, and Victor Zonona, who'd quit the *Los Angeles Times* for a position with Donna Shalala at HHS, were joining politics at a record clip, and the list of politicians moving in the other direction—including Diane Sawyer, George Stephanopoulos, Bill Bradley, and Geraldine Ferraro—was so long that the movement had become old news.

People who wanted to score political points against the Republican party used my decision to promote their version of the truth. Ross Baker, a political science professor at Rutgers University in New Jersey, explained that I'd had no choice but to leave because the party was simply too inhospitable a place for me. "She found herself all dressed up and nowhere to go," he said. "It is the Christine Todd Whitman effect: Where does a liberal Republican woman from the Northeast go in the Republican party today?" There was a grain of truth to his pronouncement, as I'll explain in a minute. But I found it puzzling that Dr. Baker seemed oblivious to the fact that Christie and I both managed to go quite far, and quite well, in our party, and that few if any women have found the Democratic party even that hospitable.

The loudest cries about my career change, however, came neither from journalists worried about the razor's edge between news and politics, nor from political types advancing their own causes. They came from women who were horrified, or impressed, by the implications of what I was doing. Some hailed my decision as a victory for family values. Others denounced it as sending a dangerous message to American women that good mothers stay home with their children and that decent wives back off to promote their husbands' careers. Those were strange morals to draw from my actions, since I wasn't quitting Congress to become a stay-at-home mom.

And the notion that I was getting out of Bill's way actually provoked open laughter among my friends. Bill had been pushing me forward, and offering to get out of my way, for years. He was the guy who always joked that he'd spend his days as First Gentleman riding the Toro across the White House lawn—and he meant it.

I finally concluded that much of the feminist reaction was not really about the implications of my decision, since everyone seemed to have a different take on what they were. It was about the notion that I was giving up power. The subtext of their criticism was "How dare a woman give up power when so few of us have any!" Frankly, I'd never thought of what I had in the House as power. Sure, I could help shape the budget for the Department of Commerce, but is that power? I could try to reframe the debate over U.S. foreign policy toward Bosnia, but not as effectively as Ted Koppel. I could fight to protect my district from budget cuts, but since I was one of 535 members of the U.S. Congress all trying to do the same thing, I hardly felt powerful.

Power, real power, doesn't reside in the electronic voting card members are issued when they are sworn in. Real power is the ability to keep people safe, to make life, to banish injustice. Would that I had had those abilities, that power.

Even if I had, furthermore, did that mean that I, as a woman, should be shackled to it indefinitely? To paraphrase what Daniel Patrick Moynihan said so concisely at the time, Should I have been condemned to Congress for the rest of my life just because I'm female? Women as some abstract collective might have lost some power, or at least influence, when I left the House. I, on the other hand, took back my power in the process. Ain't I a woman?

◆

From my first minute in politics, I managed to tick someone off almost every day because I had no aptitude for playing the game, at least not by anyone else's rules. My clothes were wrong. I changed my hair color too frequently. I snapped my gum, wore sneakers, looked too young, was not easy to pigeonhole, supported a woman's right to abortion, liked Bob Dole and George Bush and sat at Newt Gingrich's right hand. So it's hardly surprising that I created a minor storm by leaving, by committing the cardinal sin of walking away in my own good time, and for my own good reasons.

So, let me try to lay those reasons out as clearly and honestly as possible, to strip away all the rationales and rumors and get down to the heart of the matter. First, what I wasn't doing: I wasn't advancing any political agenda in preparation for a run for national office. (And if that is your goal, trust me, anchoring a morning television news show isn't the way to do it.) I wasn't fleeing the Republican party. And I wasn't getting out of Bill's way. What I was doing was what millions of American women do every week: making choices, choices about how to balance my professional and family lives, about how much shit I was willing to take, how much control I needed over my life, and how much influence I wanted to exert.

Maybe people who are puzzled by my decision have some romantic vision of what life in Congress is really like, so let me disabuse them. The job can be incredibly rewarding. You get the intrinsic satisfaction of being a social worker because you can help people in dozens of ways—from building child advocacy centers to arranging the funding of programs, by making phone calls to the Social Security Administration to help break their checks loose from the bureaucracy and drumming up contributions to a homeless shelter. But you get paid a hell of a lot more and also get invited to the White House. In a certain sense, then, it is an ideal combination of a job you can feel good about, with comfort and a dash of glamour thrown into the mix.

But being in Congress is also a job and, like most jobs, has plenty of downsides. The hours are horrendous. Most days I started out with a breakfast meeting at an hour when any reasonable person would still be home drinking coffee, and was chained to my office until the day's last vote, which often meant that I missed the eleven P.M. news.

I spent half my working hours fending off special interest groups of one sort or another. Those groups serve a valuable purpose by bringing together citizens who care deeply about given issues. But the problem is that although they have a mission, in the end, like any other corporation, they exist to make money. They do so not by selling a product, but by creating conflict. If an environmental group, for example, wants to raise money or recruit members, it's not going to produce a carefully balanced and nuanced report written in measured prose. That might be accurate and responsible, but it would hardly whip up a membership drive. So they ratchet up the decibel level of the discourse by sending out a mailing reading, "Contribute now or these guys will ruin the air forever." I don't mean to pick on the environmental groups. They're just an example. The same thing is equally true of the AARP, the Family Research Council, and NARAL. As a member, then, you spend a substantial amount of time trying to sort through the rhetoric, and responding to constituents who do not.

But that's a digression. When you serve in the House, you are never more than two years away from losing your job, so you are forced to devote enormous time and energy not only to pleasing your constituents, but to raising money and fending off the political parries of your opponent. That means smiling and eating endless rubber chickens with people you don't like very much, or begging people you do like to give you the $1,000 they had planned on using for a great vacation so that you can buy television time. It means being smeared by your opponent, and even smearing him back, because no matter how disgusted Americans say they are with negative campaigns, the truth is they work, so candidates feel forced to resort to them.

You get a free parking spot at National Airport about ten feet closer to the gate than the public lot. But that's because every Thursday or Friday you have to fly home to your district, which wasn't so bad in my case, but think about poor Senator Ted Stevens flying home to Alaska every weekend. Your plane is always late, which means that you don't make it to the annual Boy Scout dinner on time. And those Boy Scouts don't want to hear about late votes, hectic schedules, and the airlines. They want their member, and they want her there before their event begins.

Contrary to conventional wisdom, you do not get a better table in restaurants, except perhaps in your own district, because maître d's in cities like New York and Washington, D.C., don't care if you're a member of Congress. In fact, they seem to revel in exiling you to the table by the bathroom. But if you're out to dinner and the food is terrible, the waiter unbearably rude, or the bill filled with overcharges, you can't haul off and make a public scene like a normal person. You have to take it because you're a member of Congress and live in mortal terror that someone will think that you're taking advantage of your lofty position.

You and every member of your family live under a microscope, constantly examined and second-guessed by the press, and don't think that's a problem only if you're a crook or a philanderer. A few years ago, the father of my friend Fred Cerullo, who was then the commissioner of finance of New York City, was diagnosed with colon cancer. It was a terrible time because he was sick from chemotherapy and in and out of the hospital. During that period he got a ticket for leaving his trash out. Then he didn't pay the ticket because he was in the hospital. The *New York Post* picked up the story and, despite Fred's explanation to the reporter, printed a piece about how the father of Fred Cerullo, public official, was evading his civic responsibilities. Fred's dad read the paper in his hospital bed and called him crying because he had hurt his son. Worse yet, his grandparents, who lived in Florida and knew nothing about their son's cancer, read the news in that story.

Reporters and politicians usually have a pretty friendly rivalry that is contained by a clear set of rules. Media folk aren't suppose to lie—or cheat by printing off-the-record quotes—and most don't. Politicians are supposed to lie only by omission. They are not supposed to pretend in retrospect that they were speaking off the record when they had never mentioned it, and to cooperate fully with their hometown papers and the *New York Times*—and most don't. Believe it or not, the system works pretty well most of the time. The only problem is that if a politician doesn't play by the rules of the game, the reporter can attack him with a vengeance. But when the situation is reversed—when a member of the press is dishonest or unprofessional—there's almost no way to fight back without looking like you're wiping your feet on the First Amendment.

A case in point: When I was on the City Council, I briefly dated a New York political reporter. Our relationship ended one Christmas when he pulled out an engagement ring and asked me to marry him. I said no. He'd always been a great booster of the Molinari family, but he started ripping into me and my dad in the next paper he went to work for. Talk about bias and lack of professionalism. But I shut up, until now, because I didn't want to be accused of sour grapes.

Journalists aren't the only people who invade your privacy. Your constituents feel that they own you, so they don't hesitate to stop you when you're sitting with your father in the doctor's office waiting to hear whether he has cancer. Or they catch you in the supermarket at midnight, wearing a pair of ragged old sweats and a T-shirt because you ran out of diapers, or milk, or beer. Don't get me wrong. I loved my constituents. They treated me like a part of the family instead of some distant "representative." They always asked about my daughter or my dog, Bill or my dad. They—not the Capitol, the trips, or the "power"—are what I will miss. They're the really great part of the job, especially when you're from my district. But there were still times when every fiber of my being screamed "What's the matter with you, can't you see that I need to be alone here with my father?" or "Excuse me, it's midnight, do we really have to discuss the privatization of social security this very minute?"

Despite all this, many members serve contentedly, even happily, for decades. Some of them like the often tedious process of dealing day to day with the administration of the nation. Others might not enjoy the actual work, but they don't have much imagination or ambition, so are unlikely to leave their comfortable niches unless someone takes a bulldozer and shoves them aside. Still others would never leave because they are too caught up in the rough-and-tumble, too ambitious—for committee chairmanships, for leadership positions, for the hope of a vice presidential nod or the possibility of a presidential race.

Most remain, I think, because they crave acceptance, and politics meets that need. I know that sounds odd. Why would a person who craves acceptance want to put him or herself in a position to get the shit knocked out of him by the press and his opponents, day after day? But when you run for office, your job is to seek acceptance, and receiving a vote, especially receiving a lot of votes, provides you with intense validation. So you wind up with some pretty emotionally needy people in elective office. Think about the leaders of our country today: Bill Clinton, the child of an alcoholic, or Newt Gingrich, the child of a father who was sort of absent.

I was none of these people. After Susan's birth, the fire had gone out in my stomach for a statewide run. And the Rutgers professor who said I had no place to go in the Republican party wasn't entirely wrong. I'd hit a wall in the House of Representatives, and that wall sealed me off from much of the challenge I'd had during the first five or six years. I'd become the vice chair of the Republican conference, which was quite an accomplishment. But that was as far as a moderate female from the Northeast could go in the Republican conference. While my input was accepted, and sometimes even acted upon, I could never feel like a real player. I was a member of leadership, but I was not, for example, a member of Newt's inner circle, the speaker's advisory group, which is where ninety-nine percent of the decisions that were supposed to be made in leadership meetings are actually formulated.

Lest you use this to conclude that the Republicans are uniquely evil, I should note that Democratic women haven't fared all that much better in their conference. In fact, they've probably fared worse. Under Democratic leadership, no woman ever chaired a committee of the Senate, and, from 1976 until they lost the majority, no woman ran a committee in the House. Think about that: Pat Schroeder, for example, spent twenty-seven years serving in a Democratically controlled Congress without ever being asked to chair a committee.

Once I hit that woman wall, then, how much more could I really have accomplished? I was getting ahead, but I still hadn't been offered a place on any of the really important committees. The Republican conference didn't care much about urban issues, so I couldn't accomplish as much as I would have liked for my district. The conservatives would never embrace me since I was immovable in my abortion position and bucked the party line too frequently on the social policy issues they consider the sine qua non of true-blue conservatives. The liberals wouldn't call me one of their own because I believed fervently that the federal government was too big and too unwieldy to right the wrongs of modern-day America.

Maybe I would have held on anyway, which is what I planned to do for one more term, if not for the birth of Susan Ruby. But once she was born, everything changed. The most obvious reason is one every mother can identify with: time. Between votes and commutes, political fund-raisers and leadership breakfast strategy sessions, I wasn't getting enough of her. That reality hit me during Thanksgiving weekend 1996, when Susan Ruby was just over six months old. Bill and I were due to leave for China just after the holiday, on a trip with a group of other members. Susan Ruby had just gotten to the point where she was really interacting, where she was more than a gorgeous lump of flesh who slept and ate. I couldn't face leaving her, no matter how much I trusted the friends who had promised to care for her. Bill offered to stay home so that I could go. But that wasn't the point. It wasn't about what Susan Ruby needed; it was about what I needed.

Bill and I did everything possible to maximize our time with Susan Ruby. Instead of keeping her home with a nanny, we took her with us to our offices and traded her back in forth during the day. But that still wasn't very satisfying. I didn't want to be on the floor debating when she took her first step, or wrangling over the budget when she said her first word. I'm not making a statement about what young children, or their mothers, need. I'm talking about what I personally—Susan Molinari—needed and wanted. And that was a job that would give me more regular hours, and a greater promise of time with my daughter.

There is another aspect of becoming a mother that made politics seems lethal, and it is one of the only motivations for my decision that no pundit or reporter ever put forth. In the weeks before the convention, when the entire world seemed to be talking about me and marijuana, I looked at Susan Ruby and thought, thank God she's only three months old. I swore to myself at that point that by the time she was in school, I would be out of politics entirely because it just isn't fair to kids. Think about what Chelsea Clinton has had to live with as all kinds of ugly rumors swirled around about her mother and father. Childhood and adolescence are hard enough without your friends and classmates whispering in the corner about your parents' sex lives or financial misdeeds.

I have no solution to the underlying problem. Should we muzzle the press? Impossible and undesirable. Should we condemn ourselves to having presidents who are childless, or old enough that their kids can't be hurt by the publicity? I don't think so. Should we bar anyone who has ever made a mistake from the presidency? Even if that were possible, it would be a disaster. We need someone in the White House who has made mistakes, who has failings, who can look at people and not be immediately judgmental, who understands how complicated and complex life is.

Since I had no solution to the deeper problem, the best I could do was to solve the narrower one, which was protecting Susan Ruby. After all, I was the once who decided to have her. She shouldn't have to pay for my ambition.

If I had added it all up on a piece of paper, then, I had plenty of reason to leave. But I didn't make my decision arithmetically. The reasons to leave might have been compelling, but they would never have pulled me out of my comfortable office in the Rayburn Building, and away from a staff of people who were my family, if the incentive on the other end hadn't been so powerful. But they were. After twelve years in public service, I was restless. I needed a new challenge. Growing old in Congress, being one of those wizened veterans who practically dies on the House floor, would never have fit my temperament. I'm a baby boomer raised on television. My attention span simply isn't that long. I might not have smoked pot in more than twenty years, but I still craved the wonderful, entirely legal adrenaline high of taking a risk.

Dozens of possibilities had been paraded before me in the years before I received the CBS offer: running for governor of New York or mayor of New York City, or even Al D'Amato's seat when he retired from the Senate. But I loathe administration, which is what being a governor or a mayor is about. And while I loved the idea of serving in the Senate, the reality of the fund-raising that would be necessary, followed by the endless weekends flying not to my house in my district, but around the entire state, was simply repulsive once Susan Ruby was born.

So by 1997 I was stuck. I knew it was time to go, but I still had no destination. Then Andrew walked into my office and offered me my dream. Destinations don't get better than that.

◆

Leaving—actually saying good-bye—was tough, the hardest thing I'd ever done. Congress wasn't just where I worked. It was the place where my dad had worked. It was where I grew up and met my husband and introduced my daughter to the outside world. The Capitol statuary hall was where Bill and I went late at night to listen to the promise of America. Every nook and cranny of the warrens of offices and basements and sub-basements carried a memory.

For weeks before my departure on August 1, I put off cleaning out my office, even while my staff scurried to find other jobs. My CBS office in New York was still a construction site. My CBS office in Washington was a closet without a single window. I'd wander the halls there without being able to put a name to any face. The security guards didn't come up behind me and grab me. There were no elevator operators to sneak into my office and snatch my daughter for a quick game of hide-and-seek.

Meanwhile, across town, the retirement parties were beginning. The greatest affair was a gathering of the Republican female members of the House and the Senate at the home of Kay Bailey Hutchinson, a senator from Texas. Nothing fancy or formal, just a group of congresswomen gathering between votes to honor one of their own. The high point was the gift-giving, a roast in disguise. Jennifer Dunn presented me with a tape recorder, a special memento since a full tape of one of our more contentious conference meetings had just been leaked to the press. Kay Bailey pulled out a pad of stickers for my new desk that read SO MANY MEN, SO LITTLE BRAINS.

But the prize for boldness and badness went to my friend Ileana Ros-Lehtinen of Florida, who presented me with a calendar Hallmark would never peddle, The Hunks of the House. Between late-night votes, Ileana and I had often passed the endless hours evaluating the physical attributes of our male colleagues. I'd poke her in the ribs and say, "Hey, look at that Scott Klug, he'd make a perfect January." Or, "Don't you think that Kasich deserves a month of his own?"

So Ileana asked each of the most-often-mentioned men for a photograph, not just any photograph, and certainly not a campaign shot. Many passed on the invitation, to their shame. Scott Klug, who's from Wisconsin, sent in his contribution, but not without noting that he preferred to be known for his mind, not his legs. (And it's a good thing too.) Kasich had been married only a few months and insisted that Ileana call his wife for her approval.

Steve Largent of Oklahoma lent the calendar a hint of sassiness with well-gelled hair and his hands behind his head, while Gary Condit of California, one of the two Dems who got in on the fun, looked like a model in blue jeans and a polo shirt. John Thune shocked even Ileana with his offering, an old photo from his college days: John bare-chested flexing his arm muscles. Bill Paxon, my Bill, with whom Ileana had conferred regularly to avoid any possibility of jealousy, contributed the most provocative image: a snapshot of him kissing a sexy little blonde who happened to be his wife.

The finale was staged on Thursday afternoon, July 31. It was the last day of the session before the August recess, and we all felt triumphant at the passage of the Taxpayer Relief Act of 1997. In a bipartisan accord in striking contrast to the budget battle of 1995, we had forged a compromise that left no one entirely thrilled but gave American parents a $500 per child tax credit, some help with college tuition, and even a meaningful cut in inheritance and capital gains taxes. We voted electronically, 388 yeas, 44 nays, and only three members not voting.

Then, as the members began to pack up their briefcases to head for their planes, Jack Quinn, a friend and member from New York, rose and asked permission to speak. "I would like to ask the members on both sides of the aisle to join me in saying farewell and good luck to one of ours as she leaves the House of Representatives today," he said before yielding to Newt. "We will not promise to watch every Saturday," the Speaker said, "but we will watch carefully." Then the floor was handed over to Bill. "I really thought I would never get to the point in my life where I would say this, that I love a member of the press." By the time they got to Ileana, who wished me well by calling me "Mama Sue," I had lost control. And still they continued, Republican and Democrat, floating over memories political and personal.

"When Sue and Bill said they were getting married, I wondered if it was the moon over Kosovo that brought them together," said Elliot Engel, reminding us of our journey to the Balkans, "or the time we were in that hotel and there was no heat or hot water. We figured that might have had something to do with bringing the two of them together."

Deb Pryce, my friend and colleague in the Short Blond Caucus, closed the debate, a privileged position in that austerely tradition-filled body, with a teary "Godspeed."

I requested and, for the last time, was given permission to address the House for one minute.

"It has been seventeen years since my dad took his oath of office. . . . In my family, as in many of your families, this is a place of honor, a place where we are reminded every day that people trust us to make some of the most important decisions of their lives. It is an honor to walk in and out those doors every day and every night.

"To all of you and to those of you in the press gallery, let me admit it and get it out there. I will have a bias in my reporting career. But it is this: When I report, it will be with the full knowledge and understanding in my heart and soul that the men and women on both sides of the aisle that serve in this institution are some of the most honorable members that have ever served this nation."

At the door of the chamber I dissolved into Bill's arms and held Susan Ruby close. I turned and looked back toward the podium, toward so many memories. Newt was still standing there, surrounded by his inner circle. I gritted my teeth, started humming the Marine Corps hymn, and never looked back.

Chapter Ten

Dolls and Guys

My father and I began jogging together on a family vacation to Florida just after I graduated from college. When we returned to Washington, we continued the runs, using the time to catch up, to trade the kind of caustic barbs about politicians that we generally tried to contain in public, to become buddies. Just father and daughter running along the Potomac or around the Capitol. It was heaven for a young woman who idolized a dad who always made her feel that she was loved without condition, and that she could conquer the world.

At the end of the run, when he'd hit the dirt hard on a sprint, I could rarely keep up. I'd never been a jock, and my dad is a former marine who still loves to rough it up on the handball court. As I loped along far behind, he'd look back and throw me a visual taunt. Someday I'll catch him, I thought to myself silently. Someday I'll even beat him. I knew that was a prospect that would both thrill and horrify Guy Molinari.

Almost two decades later, we still run together whenever we find ourselves in the same city, which isn't that frequent anymore. My father still beats me on the sprint because he has the discipline I lack to really push himself. But I can finally go the distance. By the mid-1990s we had fallen into a comfortable routine: For the first couple of miles, we'd pace each other, chatting idly or mixing it up politically. Then, without warning, he'd blow it out and leave me in the dust. After a mile or so, however, he'd fall back while I kept on until I reached my full five.

But one icy cold afternoon, when the wind was so fierce that it fought you all the way, we went jogging in Great Kill Park on Staten Island. It was our typical run, along the road out to the water. I paced myself, running slow and steady. My dad would stop every once in a while, then sprint to catch up again. But I still managed to stay at least a couple of steps ahead of him. I admit that I was struggling by the time he dropped back entirely, but I pushed on. Then, the next thing I knew, he was coming up toward me off another path through a wooded area I always avoided. "How the hell did he do that?" I wondered. But I kept moving, assuming he'd found a real shortcut.

A few minutes later he dropped back again, and I lost sight of him. By that time I was aching. My lungs were bursting. Suddenly, out of nowhere, he came up behind me and blew me away without missing a beat. This is my father, I thought. He's thirty years older than I am. I'm in good shape. I've been practicing. I'm such a wimp. I'm not going to let him do this.

I literally hurt myself trying to beat him. When I stumbled to the end of the trail, I was dying, trying to catch my breath. My dad took one look at me and cracked up. Then he fessed up: He'd conned me. A friend in a car had picked him up and driven him around me. I couldn't decide whether to kill him or celebrate. My dad had cheated. But I'd finally gotten to the point that he had to cheat in order to beat me.

I'm not sure what the story sounds like to outsiders, especially to women with fathers who didn't raise them to win. But make no mistake about it, from the inside it felt like love and respect and just enough prodding to remind me that I could be invincible. My father raised me to be tough in a world where people believe that women can't handle power. He taught me to take risks and be prepared to fail. Failure is no loss of dignity, he'd say. Not trying is.

No matter the circumstance, he refused to let me wallow in self-pity. Whether I blew an exam, or a speech on the stump, he'd pat me on the back, then tell me to brush myself off and snap out of it. He loved me enough to make sure that I never, not for one minute, thought of myself as a powerless victim. He respected me enough to make sure that I developed the stamina to go the distance. He trusted me enough to make sure that I knew never, ever to try to be anyone but myself.

There were times I wanted to kill him, of course, when I longed for a Robert Young who would hold me in his arms and comfort me when I lost. But those times were few and far between. And for those times, I had, and have, my mother. If Bill and I get into a fight, it's not my father I call. He'd want to solve the problem in a sentence and move on to Fresh Kills or Rudy Giuliani's latest sin. My mother, however, will talk to me for hours, stroking and comforting me, and she always calls me back to make sure everything is okay. When I'd call home from someplace like Sarajevo, my father would want to talk about the players and the negotiations. It was my mother who'd say, "I saw you on CNN. You looked thin. Are you eating enough?"

The day after I gave birth—when I was recovering from twelve hours in labor and anesthesia that had me out of it for two days—my hospital room was like Grand Central Station, with my father and the mayor, security guards and members of the press passing Susan Ruby back and forth. I was in pain from the cesarean, and I'd been throwing up all morning. My mother came in, kissed the baby, then sat by me. "The baby's beautiful," she said. "Now, what's happening with *my* baby?"

Yet it's hard for me to imagine who I would have become had I been only my mother's baby. Where my mother tried to protect me, my father taught me never to run from controversy and to always stand my ground. While my mother comforted me when I was attacked, my father taught me to turn those attacks to my advantage. So I find it odd that female writers and women's magazines have spent years obsessed exclusively with mothers and daughters, with the ways in which our mothers are our succor and solace, our guides to our futures as women, our fantasy reflection and projection of ourselves. Our fathers are also our role models. It was my father who served as guide to my potential. He mentored me and encouraged me and pushed me until I knew that the woman I could be was far more—more accomplished, more tenacious, more self-assured, more successful—than most of my friends ever dreamed they could be. He cocooned me in the kind of unconditional love that made me feel safe enough to take chances. And I suspect that I'm not the only woman in America who has had this experience.

My father insists that he saw no sign of my mettle until years after I graduated from college. He says I was a sweet and well-behaved child, which is not a compliment. I realized that only when he began to crow about Susan Ruby's being like a longshore-man. He brags that when my mom bought her a wheeled toy and warned her that it was very heavy, Susan refused to roll it around the room. She picked it up and carried it.

He loves to talk about how my daughter stood her ground when he tried to keep her away from the blinds in his living room, afraid that she might hurt herself. He warned her. She looked at him quizzically, then returned to the blinds. He yelled at her. She looked at him seriously, then returned to the blinds. He slapped her on the hand. She looked at him defiantly, and went right back to her play.

I was not, in fact, that tough. It wasn't just that I wasn't tough enough for politics. I wasn't tough enough for life. When my parents disciplined me, I melted from mortification. If my father looked at me with disapproval, I burst into tears. When my parents sent me to day camp at the Staten Island Academy, I was lost. All the other girls knew each other, and they singled me out for the kind of miserable bullying only kids can devise. I had no idea how to fight back or stand my ground.

So when I told my dad that I was thinking about running for City Council, he raised his eyebrows. New York's a rough town. If your opponent doesn't get you, the tabloids will. Could I really cope? I tossed back a positive response with more confidence than I felt. I had arrived at the point in my life where I needed to learn to take myself seriously. I'd chosen to do so by seeing whether anyone else would.

If that first election was my political boot camp, my dad was first sergeant. Every time my handlers tried to remake me, my dad would take me aside and tell me to ignore them. "Be yourself. Don't try to be what anyone things the public wants you to be. You've got to be good enough to be who you are." When the press mocked me as Guy's Doll, whose campaign was being engineered from his office, he offered no sympathy. "It'll only make you stronger. The challenge is to grow strong enough so you can stand up and tell them to go to hell."

I was more afraid that I wouldn't make my father proud of me than I was that I would lose that election, which guaranteed me victory, of course. I still remember asking him before almost every presentation, "Dad, if I throw up on the stage, how are you going to handle that?" I knew the answer: I was not going to throw up. I was not going to let them see me cry. No matter how often they derided me as a gum-chewing political brat, chided me for worshipping both Ronald Reagan and Bruce Springsteen, or needled me for being Guy Molinari's kid, I refused to back off from the fight. Through the course of the campaign, I began to grow into a woman to deal with.

For those of you who aren't New Yorkers, I should note that my dad and I evolved into a kind of mini-political dynasty in the state of New York. We struck out at bureaucrats and politicians we deemed unfair to Staten Island in coordinated attacks from City Hall and Borough Hall and the halls of the United States Congress. When a company wanted to build an oil pipeline across the island, we asked them to make their presentation to the two of us together in my dad's office just across from the Staten Island ferry. I, the young, cheerful congresswoman, asked polite if probing questions about the project. My father sat glowering in the corner. When the company officials concluded, he looked pointedly at me. I shook my head no. "It's not going to happen," my dad said. "If you try to pull this off, we'll tie you up in court. We'll tie you up with the federal government. If necessary, we'll meet you at the bridge and fight you off." We escorted the men to the door, and never heard from them again.

On a dozen Staten Island issues, we forged family loyalty into political teamwork, backing each other up, watching each other's back, and threatening to sic the other one on our opponents. It was father-daughter fun with a vengeance, and extremely successful. The battle to close the Fresh Kills dump was a classic Molinari family victory. My father needed leverage both with the city and the state, and turned to me to provide it. I twisted a few arms at the Environmental Protection Agency to launch a study of the facility. My dad then took that ammunition to the courts. Fresh Kills, which has been open since the 1940s, will be closed by 2001.

The home port was our greatest victory, and our ultimate failure. My dad was instrumental in getting the navy to award Staten Island the base in the first place, and he fended off repeated challenges to it before he left Washington. Before I was even un-packed in my office, he passed me the ball. I, too, succeeded in keeping the project alive, at least until the base closure commission made a final decision. Before each vote, during each major battle, he'd come to Washington so we could huddle and lay out our strategy. He'd call his guys while I called mine, and we traded each other's chits.

It wasn't all serious, of course. My father is the guy who sings "Pennies from Heaven" at Republican Christmas parties, plays Santa at nursing homes, and organizes Blues Brothers skits for Halloween. During my campaigns, he loved to play practical jokes on me, calling my headquarters pretending to be a reporter from the Associated Press with a hot, and damaging, tip. When we went to official functions, we'd sit in the audience making faces at each other to see who could get whom to crack up first. Once when I was hosting a national talk radio show, he called in and, in an incredibly serious tone, asked the congresswoman when she was planning to give her father a granddaughter.

I gave almost as well as I took. When I was first running for Congress, a reporter asked me how I'd do in a debate against my dad. "He'd kill me," I responded. But I didn't stop there. "But that's not a forecast forever," I added.

It wasn't always easy, of course. First we had to learn to

disagree respectfully on things we both feel incredibly strongly about, like abortion. What made it harder was that my dad isn't known for biting his tongue, and every time he said something controversial, every paper in the country would call me for comment. "Do you agree with your father?" "Do you think he should have said that?" "Did you know he was going to say that?"

The first big storm of that kind hit in October 1994, when Karen Burstein, a Democrat, was running against Dennis Vacco for attorney general of New York State. My dad made a statement about Karen's being a lesbian. He was hardly outing her; she had used her sexual orientation to whip up interest in her campaign. But the press went crazy because Guy Molinari raised the issue of her sexual orientation. He didn't back down. He simply released a statement explaining that she was the one who had raised the issue of her sexual orientation, so that it had become a legitimate topic of discussion. But my phone started ringing off the hook.

No matter how we dealt with things privately, or what I said to him when we were alone, once people from the outside entered the fray, everything changed because people were trying to pit us against each other. We both had same reaction: We became incredibly protective of each other. No matter how important an issue was, we weren't willing to say anything that would hurt the other person. It just wasn't worth it.

The same thing happens with all families that are in the public eye. Think about the Kennedys, with Joe serving from Massachusetts and Patrick from Rhode Island, Kathleen as lieutenant governor of Maryland and John running a magazine. The minute one member of the family got in trouble or did something that hit the news, everybody gets called for comment and, at least until recently, everybody circled the wagons. I think that's a natural reaction.

So when my father blasted Karen Burstein, I reserved my right to disagree with the reasons he'd given for opposing her, although I also noted that I agreed with his opposition to her candidacy. And when my father said that we should suck out the brains of doctors who perform partial birth abortions, I wasn't going to tell every reporter who called that I thought that was an incredibly insensitive comment about an incredibly complex issue, even though that was what I believed. I just sent out a dry press release saying that my father had spoken what was on his mind. I didn't agree with his assessment, although I agreed with his right to say whatever he thought.

It was harder when what he said and did became a liability for me in a political sense, which, fortunately, wasn't all that often. But imagine what it felt like in 1992 when I wasn't invited to speak at the Republican convention, and I knew that part of the reason was that my father had told reporters that Dan Quayle was a liability to George Bush's chances for reelection. I couldn't, and wouldn't, disavow my father, especially because I agreed with him and had made that agreement public. But I resented like hell being blamed for what he'd said.

It happened all the time. In 1990, in the middle of my campaign for my first full term in Congress, I was hoping to get the backing of the state AFL-CIO. My dad had run into trouble with the group when he took on the transit workers union over whether they would allow more private van and bus companies to operate on Staten Island, but I never imagined that would have anything to do with me. The group had given me high ratings and the Executive Council recommended my endorsement. But that recommendation was voted down on the convention floor. When Ed Cleary, the president, was asked what had happened, he wasn't shy about telling the truth. "People just had it in for her father."

Usually my problems were the result of my father's loyalty and overprotectiveness, so it was even harder to get upset. During the fight in Congress over the crime bill, Rudy Giuliani, whom my father had helped launch as mayor, campaigned with Bill Clinton for its passage and openly criticized those of us who had blocked consideration of the Democrats' initial version. That was it. My father, who loves huge public political brawls, kicked Giuliani out of our political family and declared war on the mayor, a war that became headlines all over the city. It was the clash of the Titans, and all I could do was stay quiet and pray that the storm would blow over.

I figured out pretty quickly how to deal with the political conflicts, but the personal ones were more sticky. I wanted my dad's approval, and he rarely gave it to me in the direct way that I thought he should. When I was young, we got into it all the time. I wanted more than anything to be rewarded when I got good grades on tests or all A's on my report cards. He refused. He just told me he'd love me no matter my grades and left it at that.

The day I received my acceptance into the graduate program at SUNY-Albany, along with notification that I'd been awarded a teaching assistantship, I handed the letters to my father and waited for some major show of congratulations. He muttered a perfunctory congrats, then turned back to whatever he'd been thinking about.

Once I became more independent, I began to realize that he was showing his pride in a dozen ways I hadn't been able to see when I was younger. When I got into Congress, for example, other members began coming up to me and telling me how much they knew about me because my dad talked about me all the time. At first I was shocked. Then I realized that just because my dad didn't say "Oh, hey, you did a great job" didn't mean he wasn't proud of me, that he wasn't bragging about me constantly. That was that wonderful point in my life when I recognized that my parents were human beings, and I could cut them a break.

Ironically, but typically, once I stopped needing overt expressions of pride, my father started giving them to me. After the near debacle at my debate with Sal Albanese during my 1992 reelection campaign, my father presented me with a plaque for my wall, a personal medal he'd designed: FOR EXEMPLARY SERVICE AS A MARINE IN TIME OF WAR, it reads. SEMPER FI. And he turned to marine symbolism again, on Mother's Day, two days after the birth of Susan Ruby. He walked into my hospital room and handed me his Marine Corps pin. That might not sound like much to other people. It might even sound stupid to some. But I'd learned how to read my father, and I'd received a Medal of Honor.

◆

Few people ever understood our relationship. For years many people in New York sincerely believed I was his pawn. It was an appallingly patronizing belief. They obviously didn't know either of us very well. If they'd known my father, they would have known that he would never have put up with a child willing to be anyone's pawn, even his. If they'd known me, they would have understood that I was too much my father's daughter to be so easily moved around the political chessboard.

But even people relatively close to us have trouble grasping our competitiveness, which is notorious in some circles. It's not just about jogging. If I came up with a good line about an issue, he'd steal it and make it his own. If we were working together on an issue like Fresh Kills or the home port and won a victory, we'd race to see who could get the press release out first. Or we'd agree not to tell reporters something and, suddenly, the information would appear in the *New York Post*. I'd call my father, who would insist that he hadn't mentioned the item to the reporter more than once or twice. Later I'd find out that he had actually sent out a press release.

People around us found the behavior odd, or inappropriate, or even mean. They were wrong. Every time my dad stole a line from me, he was acknowledging how clever I was. Every time he beat me to the punch with the media, he taught me to move quicker. Our rivalry was a game of pride, our private game, an affirmation of love and respect that only a daughter who goes into the family business can enjoy.

Few women ever have that opportunity, and I can't imagine the loss. Fathers and daughters who don't have it miss the chance to know each other as peers as opposed to parent and kid. You wind up with a level of respect you simply can't develop in any other context. And you get to turn the tables, to move from child to adult, from disciple to peer, which is the greatest thrill of all.

When I first entered politics, I felt totally dependent. I turned to my father for help finding a campaign team. I used his connections to raise money. I counted on his active support so that I could win my elections. I called him a dozen times a day for suggestions on how to push through my bills or word my amendments. Pundits disparaged me, but I was acting like any kid who enters the family business or follows her dad into his profession.

Gradually, after I'd been in Congress a year or two, things tilted into a more equal balance. My phone would ring with calls from my dad looking for advice, for contacts, for suggestions. He'd turn to me for support during his campaigns. He began treating me as an asset. I delighted in doing for my dad everything I hated to do on my own behalf—working a room, hitting people up for campaign contribution. And he responded in kind. Suddenly my father, the big macho guy, turned his attention to issues affecting women and children, to issues he discovered through me. He started attending seminars on problems like spousal abuse or breast cancer and worked with me on the creation of a child advocacy center on Staten Island.

None of this has been easy for my mother, since she hates politics with a passion. For her, politics means watching her husband and daughter get battered in the press and brutalized by their opponents. It means canceled vacations and family dinners and endless conversations about people who interest her not at all.

Yet I should add for the record—and this is, I believe, the record—that despite the fact that I am publicly Guy's Doll, and he the Doll's Guy, my mother deserves much credit for my political success. She was the one who instilled in me a passion for the feminist issues that guided so much of my work. And if my father bequeathed to me a set of traditional "male" political skills—fearlessness in the face of confrontation, delight in the rough-and-tumble—I inherited from my mother a softer but no less lethal arsenal. Women of the generations before mine were shy about using traditional "female" skills in the political arena. They hesitated to solicit votes by appealing to male honor. They eschewed encouraging older male colleagues to think of them as daughters. In the process, they lost half their weapons.

As a woman who grew up taking for granted the social changes achieved by feminism, I comfortably wield all the ammunition available to me, male and female, polite and down-and-dirty. And, in the end, it was my mother—the same mother who filled my bedroom with ruffles—who showed me just how dangerous that combination of perkiness and tough can be.

One evening during a family vacation in Florida, I went out to dinner with my parents. While we were in the parking lot waiting for our car, some young guy walked by with his girlfriend, checked me out, and muttered, "Nice ass." My father did a double take. He has no truck with men who are disrespectful to women. "Hey, buddy, get over here," he yelled, seemingly intent on picking a fight.

The kid walked tentatively toward my dad, who, after a moment of indecision, actually raised his fists. The young man froze; his girlfriend did not. "What the hell are you doing, old man?" she screamed. "Get away from him, you stupid old man." My mother's eyes lit up with fire that illuminated her careful makeup and perfectly coiffed hair. "Don't you call my husband an old man, you bitch. I'll scratch your eyes out."

I looked at my parents and saw Bonnie and Clyde on Staten Island. I could almost imagine the leather jackets. I laughed and tucked away that memory. Male and female, perky and tough. What a lethal force.

Chapter Eleven

Back to the Future

One day I was a competent grown-up debating the federal budget, giving interviews with the press, and negotiating with labor unions and railroad executives. The next I was an awkward adolescent who didn't know what she was doing.

Three days after the press conference at which I announced my resignation from Congress, I flew to California for a meeting of the CBS affiliates. Those local stations are the lifeblood of a network, and their support—their enthusiastic support—was essential to my success and the success of *CBS Saturday Morning*. An enormous stage had been built that swirled around the front of the largest auditorium I'd ever seen, almost an enclosed football field. Lighting designers had softened the already elegant dimensions of the room. Leslie Stahl, Ed Bradley, and Don Hewitt wandered around casually.

Just before Andrew Heyward was scheduled to present the two new shows that the news division would offer in the fall, I was herded into the holding room so that I'd be ready to be introduced to my new constituency. I paced back and forth, terrified and unable to contain my excitement. I looked around for someone to share it with and lit on the star of the other new show, who looked a lot more relaxed than I did. I sidled over to him and asked, "Aren't you incredibly nervous?" He looked at me with total disbelief. My mind changed gear into my new reality. That star was Bryant Gumbel.

I was Alice again, but this was a new Wonderland.

Throughout August I worried about the dozens of things I simply didn't do right. My cadence and diction fit New York, but my audience was suddenly national. I was clumsy reading a TelePrompTer. I knew I tilted my chin up too far and knitted my brow when I was thinking. That made no difference in face-to-face meetings, but those quirks looked odd on television. I talked too fast, used my hands too much, crossed my legs at the knee, and occasionally spit in the middle of a sentence—none of which worked on the air.

I had to unlearn a dozen habits. Television isn't as easy as it looks.

We spent hours figuring out the opening sequence. Hal wanted to see what it would look like to open the program with Russ Mitchell, my co-anchor, and me walking onto the set. "Hands in pockets?" I asked as we were about to start the first run-through. "Great," Hal responded. Hold on, hold on. You're walking too fast. No, that's better, but don't forget not to tilt your chin up so much. Try it again a little quicker, a little slower. See what happens if you're chatting. No, that doesn't work.

You get the picture. Only on the eleventh try did we actually get to speak.

I missed the comfort and security of my old office and job, of doing work I knew I was good at, of familiarity. I kept screwing up my voice mail. I still couldn't figure out how to use my beeper.

Connie Chung sent me a note of encouragement, just as Barbara Walters had done with her. Hang in there, she wrote. Hang in there, I told myself. You got through kindergarten; you can get through this.

The night before the first show I worked late, but I was still on the set the next morning before dawn. Suddenly I was on the air reporting on Mother Teresa's funeral. Three minutes later I was sampling fruit smoothees. Then a break to commercial, and I was reporting that showers were going to be moving into the Northwest. I was relieved when Russ got to the news, reporting on the army's proposal to tighten fitness standards for women. Okay, I thought. This is okay. We're supposed to do some chitchat about the news, and women in the military is something I can talk about knowledgeably.

"Maybe those standards should be reevaluated, Russ, but women deserve the right to serve in the artillery and infantry, which they're not allowed to do now." I was so intent on what I was saying that I didn't notice Hal cringing in the corner. "We've got to go a long way until there's some fairness. I certainly hope that if we are going to look for some level of fairness with standards and training, that we at least investigate this and give women a chance to prove themselves in defending their country if they wish to, so that we can truly be equal."

Oops . . . I guess I went to far. This is television, not Congress. I regained my mission. "Tummies are out and abs are in," I said.

The minute we were done, I was ready to try it again. I was over that insanely terrifying hump of doing something hard for the first time. Then I read the reviews, which were a form of Chinese water torture. The show looked like amateur hour. A television star is not born. Our ratings were behind ABC's cartoon marathon. What a crock, I thought. How can you compare the ratings of a show on day one to those of shows that had been running for years? Did they think that news anchors emerge from the womb looking cool and confident and knowing how to read a Tele-PrompTer?

I gave myself yet another firm lecture, probably the thousandth of the month: You're in a transition, Susan, and transitions are hard. This is what you've always wanted. It will get better. Things will be fine. You're a former member of Congress, keynote speaker, mother, wife—honorary marine! You can do it. You can beat them all. Don't look back.

◆

I can't help it, of course. Looking back is what human beings do. And, at least in my case, looking back makes it less scary to move forward. When I'm totally stressed out, I drive past the White House and the Capitol and look up at those buildings and think, hey, I worked there. I know that in some quarters people think it is passé to talk about patriotism and the flag and service to your country. But there's no way you can work in those buildings without feeling a connection to the Big Idea that's America. You walk through the halls, especially at night, and wonder what Thomas Jefferson was worried about when he passed that statue, or if Jeanette Rankin, the first female member, ever even fantasized about the day when there would be enough women in Congress to form their own caucus.

No matter where I wind up professionally three decades from now, I can sit back and say to myself that there are an unknown number of women in the United States who will have easier access to health care because of what I did, or that some terrified women will find safe refuge when they're being battered because I muscled the Republican leadership into increasing funds for shelters. Pretty soon, I, as all Americans, will be able to go to my local post office and buy a breast cancer stamp. It will be a slightly more expensive way to pay my bills or write to my friends. But the extra money might help save women like my Mama Sue, and, if it does, I'll be able to take a tiny bit of the credit for it.

I hate the thought that some readers will see all this, scrunch up their noses, and dismiss me as a braggart. That's a terrible tendency we've adopted in America, a tendency to question the motivations of even the sincerest acts, to disparage every advance as insufficient, to refuse to give people in government what they crave the most—some recognition that they are doing good.

I am not, by character and temperament, a grenade thrower like Newt, or an expert at the artillery of bombast like Maxine Waters. I've never been one to win my issues by threatening to impale myself on a sword. Some people consider that a deficiency. "Oh, Susan Molinari plays the game," they say.

They sorely misunderstand the nature of the political process. In American politics, your greatest strength is your ability to get along with your colleagues and to forge compromises. That's not weakness or lack of principle. It's reality. Scarlett was right. Tomorrow is another day, and if you throw yourself on your principles on Tuesday, you're out of the loop by Wednesday. I would have loved to scorn the people who voted against me in my leadership race, but a year later I needed them on the Bob Dole campaign or for a critical vote.

I was a politician. That was my *job,* which means that I bit my tongue when it seemed wise, even if it bled. And I slept soundly at night knowing that I had cut the best deal I possibly could for my constituents, and that I pushed the nation forward, even if only an inch, on the issues I believed were making America less than it could be.

I'm clear on that, but I'm not sure of all that much else. I always thought that by the time I reached forty, a kind of magic age of adulthood, I would have it all together. I'd be cool and competent, smooth, self-assured, and certain. Fat chance. No matter how I look from the outside, the reality is ambivalence—constant, gnawing ambivalence. Some days I feel ready to conquer the world. The next I'm convinced that I'll be happiest curled up on a couch in my sweats eating Chinese food with Susan Ruby and George.

In the weeks before I went on the air, CBS sent me around the country to make presentations to local affiliates. One morning I had to fly to St. Louis. I was harried by the time I got on the plane because I'd played too long with Susan Ruby and then gotten caught in traffic. When I settled in my seat, I realized I had nothing to read but the shopping catalogue in the seat back. I began browsing through it, and when I got to the section of success posters, I honed in on one that had a golf ball and read YOU'LL MISS 100% OF THE SHOTS YOU DON'T TAKE. I started to shake my head, another one of those nasty TV sins. Absolutely, I thought. That's why I'm doing this.

I flipped the page and came to a poster with a little kid looking off across a field. It read A HUNDRED YEARS FROM NOW IT WILL NOT MATTER WHAT MY BANK ACCOUNT WAS, THE SORT OF HOUSE I LIVED IN, OR THE KIND OF CAR I DROVE. . . . BUT THE WORLD MAY BE DIFFERENT BECAUSE I WAS IMPORTANT IN THE LIFE OF A CHILD. It hit me in the gut. Just what I needed at ten thousand feet, poster guilt.

During the whole trip, my mind was like a Ping-Pong ball. Gotta take chances, gotta take shots! Where's your child? You gotta be somebody. I'm a working mom. I'm a working mother. I love my kid. I'm trying to make a difference. All this makes a difference. But where's your real job? I'm sorry, I can do both. But I can't pretend that I'm doing both well.

I was scheduled to spend the following week in New York City for daily rehearsals. That was fine, because Congress was in recess, so Bill, the baby, and the dog all were with me on Staten Island. I'd get up with Susan, change her diaper, and play in bed with her for a while. After her bottle, I'd pack her in the stroller, and she, George, and I would walk for a mile and a half. Then I'd get her dressed for the day, walk out the door, and be back in time for dinner. It was heaven.

But three nights before the first show, she started waking up at three A.M. yelling, "Mommy, mommy." I'd bring her into bed with us, but she refused to sleep. I'd take her into her room and read from her favorite book, but the minute I tried to put her in her crib, she started screaming again. Bill kept insisting, "You have to let her scream," but I couldn't. And no matter what I did, she just wouldn't go back to sleep. I was exhausted and worried about getting up and going to work. But I also kept thinking that if I were home all day to make sure that she napped and was fed appropriately, maybe she would sleep. And I knew that was stupid because my friends Mama Rose, Maria, and Barbara were taking care of her during the day and they are better mothers than I am. But the guilt was washing over me and I couldn't stop sobbing.

Bill was due to leave for Washington, and I couldn't imagine how I would cope with the job and Susan Ruby and everything else you have to do just to make sure you eat and are healthy and get your bills paid. I kept going over and over in my mind how I would take care of everything. I have to go to the dentist, and it's okay because my parents can watch the baby. But what will I do if they can't? Round and round, writing and rewriting scenarios, until I couldn't think straight. I was so stressed that I was screwing up, saying stupid things. And I kept telling myself, It's okay, Susan. You're making a personal transition. It will be all right. The lecture had no impact.

Finally Bill suggested that he take Susan Ruby and the dog back to Washington so I could concentrate. I balked. I didn't want to spend that much time away from my daughter, and it didn't seem fair to saddle him with the full burden, when he had plenty of stress of his own walking back into the storm that is the reopening of Congress after summer break. But he insisted. "Susan, this is the job you've always waited for, and for a couple of weeks it has to come first. Your daughter won't even remember, and you're buying yourself the flexibility to do the things you want to do for her. Make the sacrifice for two weeks." All I could think was, God bless Bill.

The first day they were gone, I went for a jog with some friends. They were dying after a couple of miles, but there was nothing that could stop me. I didn't have to race home. I didn't have to worry. I had time. I got up the next morning and drank a full cup of coffee. Then I took a shower and blew my hair dry. Such a simple pleasure. But the day before I hadn't had that luxury because Susan Ruby had gotten into my lipstick when I was getting dressed. She was so cute that we couldn't resist getting out the video camera. I wouldn't trade that moment for anything in the world, but it meant that I ran out of the house with my hair half wet, yet again.

Suddenly I could actually blow-dry my hair. I could make sure I didn't wind up wearing one pearl earring and one diamond stud without even noticing, which was precisely the kind of thing I'd been doing. Then I thought about Bill and Susan. I saw them taking a walk or playing on the bed. I couldn't let go of the image of Susan. I started thinking about her, about her hair. I could almost smell her. I didn't care about sleep. I didn't care if my hair was wet and my earrings mismatched. I wanted to be with my daughter.

Does this sound familiar? Probably so if you're a woman with kids. If women's magazines are right, we're traumatized by guilt twenty-four hours as day. Everything we say, everything we do, everywhere we look. Guilt. I worry that the makeup woman and the hairdresser at the show, people who work hard to make sure I look good, don't feel taken advantage of. If I have a toothache and am a little cranky, I feel a need to apologize to everyone. I want to succeed in television—really, really succeed—but I can't bear the thought of missing my daughter's laughter.

◆

But I also can't bear the thought that she won't grow up stronger and feistier than I am. I need to know that the soil that nourishes her—not just Bill and me, but our friends and families, her teachers, television role models, and political leaders—will make it easier her for than it was for me to be able to stand up for herself. I need to know that she will never be afraid to say "Hey, that's not fair" or "Stop it, I won't be treated that way." If she turns out, like her mother, to be a member of what Deb Pryce and I call the Short Blond Caucus, I need to know that she won't spend a lifetime battling to be taken seriously, and that if anyone ever pushes her, she won't hesitate to push back.

I can imagine people reading this and saying, "Oh, come on, you've done pretty well for yourself," and they certainly are right. But don't be fooled by the facade. Even the most successful American women are still racked by self-doubt, by guilt, by a need to be nice. I want Susan Ruby to be nice. I don't want her to be cocky. But I want her to feel good about herself when being something less than nice is appropriate, and I want all her doubts to be justified. I've learned to brazen it out like a good marine, but gritting your teeth for years on end is hard on the enamel, both emotional and physical.

I've met too many young girls, and even older women, who have never learned to dream. They're convinced they're not pretty enough or not smart enough. They're so focused on what they are not that they never get around to working on what they can be. I like to think that in my own small way I encourage those girls. I need to know that in my not so small way I can make sure that Susan Ruby doesn't become one of them.

These are modest goals, I think, at least compared to hoping that she will grow up in a world without child abuse, hunger, or homelessness. They are the goals of a representative mom of the nineties who's a work in progress herself. I'm still racing to take my chance, and wondering whether my dreams are better dreamed than pursued. Not going for it means never knowing what you can really achieve. Taking your best shot not only means learning how badly you can fail, but risking even your oldest illusions. Dreams are as much opportunities for regret as for success, after all.

Ten weeks into the first season of *CBS Saturday Morning,* ratings were beginning to show a little improvement and I was beginning to relax and have fun. I'd spent an afternoon on a clown care unit at a hospital. I'd discussed teen pregnancy with Jane Fonda and dieting with Suzanne Somers. I'd weathered the predictable disasters and could almost—not quite, but almost—laugh about the day when a dog on a segment about overweight pets refused to follow the script, leaving me on the floor practically begging him to eat a dog biscuit.

My confidence was rising, and, with it, the attention my producers paid to my opinion. Not bad, I thought most Saturday mornings. Sticking your finger into ten different pots each week was proving to be fun.

When I was alone on an airplane, or on those nights when

Bill was away and I was curled up on the couch with Susan Ruby and George, I still wasn't sure, as if sure were some unattainable state. I let down all the defenses, the toughness bred into me by my father, and every doubt and fear came home to roost. The skepticism of scores of reporters and politicians rang in my ears. "Who does she think she is anyway?"

She's still not sure. Check back in another decade.